CRIMINAL DEFENCE

The Good Practice Guide

ROGER EDE

Solicitor, Secretary of the Law Society's
Criminal Law Committee

and

ANTHONY EDWARDS

Solicitor, Senior partner at
TV Edwards Solicitors

law society publishing

ISBN 1 85328 611 7

Published by the Law Society
113 Chancery Lane, London WC2A 1PL

Typeset by J&L Composition Ltd, Filey, North Yorkshire
Printed and bound in Great Britain by
TJ International Ltd, Padstow, Cornwall

Contents

APPENDICES

Preface

This guide is a dynamic text. It does not merely describe the process. It outlines the actions you should take so that the defence case is fully prepared at the earliest possible time, and the issues that you should consider to ensure that your client receives a fair trial.

You can no longer merely react to what the police and prosecution do. Your role involves not only the traditional skills of a lawyer but the ability and willingness to investigate the prosecution and defence case. You should view the preparation of the case as a whole: something to press ahead with from start to finish, rather than waiting for court hearings and other procedural stages to spur you on to further work.

Acknowledgements

We are indebted to David Roberts and Mike Fitton much of whose text, notwithstanding changing times, survived into this edition.

We are grateful to our editorial board for their helpful advice:

Michael Caplan of Kingsley Napley;

Robin Irvine of Chivers Walsh Smith;

Steven Wedd of Wedd Daniels; and

Ed Cape of the University of the West of England.

We would also like to thank the following for their comments on the text:

Martin Iller;

Paul Bacon of Bryan & Armstrong;

Superintendent Bob Golding of the Trial Issues Group;

Kevin McCormack, the Justices Chief Executive of West Sussex;

Joyce Plotnikoff and Richard Woolfson;

David Kyle of the Criminal Cases Review Commission;

Ian Chisholm and Chris Potter of the Home Office Procedure and Victims Unit;

Sally Cole of the CPS;

Mary McKinney and Samantha Toyn of the LCD;

James Riches-Walker of NACRO's National Race Issues Advisory Committee;

David Hartley, Penny Letts, Gail Hardcastle and Nicola Taylor at the Law Society.

Responsibility for the final text is, however, ours alone.

Table of cases

Table of statutes

Table of statutory instruments

List of abbreviations

ABH	Actual bodily harm
ABWOR	Assistance by way of representation
ACPO	Association of Chief Police Officers
ASBO	Anti-social behaviour order
ASU	Administrative support unit
CCRC	Criminal Cases Review Commission
CDA	Crime and Disorder Act
CJA	Criminal Justice Act
CJCC	Criminal Justice Consultative Council
CJPOA	Criminal Justice and Public Order Act
CJS	Criminal justice system
CPD	Continuing professional development
CPIA	Criminal Procedure and Investigations Act
CPS	Crown Prosecution Service
CRO	Criminal Records Office
CTM	Contact trace material
DCW	Designated caseworker
DPP	Director of Public Prosecutions
DVLC	Drivers and Vehicles Licensing Centre
EAH	Early administrative hearing
ECHR	European Convention on Human Rights
EFH	Early first hearing

GBH	Grievous bodily harm
LAB	Legal Aid Board
LAFQAS	Legal Aid Franchise Quality Assurance Standard
LCD	Lord Chancellor's Department
MCA	Magistrates' Courts Act
MHA	Mental Health Act
OAP	Offences Against the Person Act
OSS	Office for the Supervision of Solicitors
PACE	Police and Criminal Evidence Act
PDH	Plea and directions hearing
PMS	Practice Management Standards
POA	Prosecution of Offences Act
PSR	Pre-sentence report
PTI	Pre-trial issues
PTR	Pre-trial review
ROTI	Record of taped interview
SDN	Short descriptive note
SOCO	Scene of Crime Officer
TIC	Taken into consideration
TIG	Trials Issues Group

CHAPTER 1

The defence solicitor

THE DEFENCE SOLICITOR'S ROLE

As a defence solicitor you have a vital and challenging role. You must believe in the adversarial process and the need for the prosecution to prove its case; you must actively investigate and prepare the case for the defence, systematically examining the prosecution case and taking nothing at face value. That process begins with your obtaining details of the prosecution case, advising on the law and allowing your client to give an account of what happened in your client's own words, with the minimum of interruptions. Even if your client admits guilt, you must enquire further and make sure that your client is actually guilty in law and that there is sufficient prosecution evidence to convict him. If your client contests the allegations, you must piece together your client's defence. Having drawn up a case plan, this may involve investigating and recording the scene of the crime, analysing the prosecution witness testimony, tracing and interviewing witnesses, and challenging prosecution forensic evidence by engaging an expert. You must do much more than just speak for your client.

Your responsibility as the defence solicitor is to do what is best for your client, consistent with his instructions, rather than bend to pressure to oil the wheels of the criminal justice system. You must be prepared to challenge the police if necessary, and not mind being considered 'difficult' by police officers when that is unavoidable. Defence solicitors make themselves available to help the client whenever that is necessary: at night in the police station; at court during the day; in prison if the client is in custody.

Criminal law and procedure has been in a process of continuous change for some years. The battleground in a contested case has to some extent moved from the trial hearing to the police station where the work has become much more complex and demanding.

The law on defence and prosecution disclosure may now penalise the client

1

who has failed to give a written statement of the defence and make a focused and specific request for unused material which assists the defence case. This, and the change in the law relating to silence, demand particular skills from the solicitor and a more thoughtful and planned approach to the preparation of the client's case pre-trial.

Criminal defence is skilled work, and for a solicitor's firm to succeed it must include solicitors who are skilled managers, able to supervise and motivate professional staff and paralegals to whom part of the preparation work may be delegated. The firm must also plan strategically for the major changes which block contracts will introduce. The requirements of the *Legal Aid Board's Franchise Quality Assurance Standard* (3rd edition, December 1998) (LAFQAS) are designed to ensure that the firm is successfully run and that it provides a quality service for the firm's clients. You should incorporate them into your management systems and approach them in a positive way.

It is important that senior and experienced solicitors continue to be involved in the preparation of criminal defence work within the solicitor's firm, and are able to play a significant part in the advice given to the client in the investigation of the defence case before trial; in the training of those who prepare the case; and in file review. This preparation, and the commitment which goes into ensuring that no stone is left unturned, are the most significant factors in the proper presentation of the case for the client. A case may be fought in the courtroom, but the success or failure of the defence will depend largely upon the work which is done in the police station and on the investigations and preparation undertaken before the trial.

As a defence criminal lawyer you will be an all-rounder:

- a legal technician well versed in the relevant law – an advocate for your client's interests;

- socially skilled – able to enjoy a working relationship with people who may be difficult and demanding;

- assertive – able to stand up for your client;

- a negotiator – able to persuade others to see your client's point of view;

- an investigator – questioning, challenging and analysing the prosecution and defence case.

THE SOLICITOR WORKING WITHIN THE CRIMINAL JUSTICE SYSTEM

Criminal justice system strategic plan

The Government's expectations from the criminal justice system (CJS) are set out in the strategic and business plans for the criminal justice system.[1] One of the two overarching aims is 'to dispense justice fairly and efficiently and to promote confidence in the rule of the law'. An objective for this aim, shared by the different agencies, is 'to respect the rights of defendants and to treat them fairly'. Other objectives within that aim include 'to meet the needs of victims, witnesses and jurors within the system' and 'to promote confidence in the criminal justice system'.

Whilst rigorously undertaking your role you will work constructively with other agencies as part of the whole criminal justice system.

Part of the new approach to a 'whole' criminal justice system involves agencies working more closely together. The geographical boundaries of the different agencies and services in the CJS are being aligned to 42 CJS areas in England and Wales so that agencies can work together more effectively at local level.

Criminal Justice Consultative Council (CJCC)

This national forum for consultation within the criminal justice system was established following Lord Justice Woolf's report into prison disturbances in 1990. It meets quarterly. The Council was established to promote better understanding, co-operation and co-ordination within the CJS. It recommends issues for discussion by the Area Criminal Justice Strategy Committees. Chaired by a senior judge, currently Lord Justice Rose, members are:

- Permanent Secretaries from the Home Office, Lord Chancellor's Department and the Department of Health;
- the DPP;
- a Chief Constable;
- a Director of Social Services;
- a solicitor;
- a magistrate;
- a justices' clerk or chief executive;

- the Director General of the Prison Service;
- representatives from the Bar and Probation Service.

Area Criminal Justice Strategy Committees (ACJSC)

By October 2000 there will be 42 committees, which work at a local level, supporting the work of the CJCC by reviewing the operation of the criminal justice system in their areas and working to make improvements. Each committee has either one or two solicitor members who are usually appointed following their recommendation to the committee chairman by the local Law Society. Other members of the committee are the senior representatives of the criminal justice agencies in the area.

Trials Issues Group (TIG)

This began as the Pre-Trials Issues Steering Group in 1990. Its membership includes not only the police, the prison service, probation service and main departments responsible for the CJS – the Home Office, Lord Chancellor's Department and the CPS – but also the Magistrates' Association, the Justices' Clerks' Society, the Law Society, the Bar and the Association of Justices' Chief Executives. It focuses on operational issues and seeks to achieve a consensus between the wide range of criminal justice interests represented.

The Manual of Guidance

The *Manual of Guidance for the Preparation, Processing and Submission of Files* by the police to the CPS was first produced in 1990, following a major report by the Pre-Trials Issues Steering Group which recommended national file standards and preparation submission times. It is produced by an editorial board which is a sub-group of TIG and is regularly updated.

Local TIGs

There is a local TIG for each of the 42 CJ system areas. Membership is similar to TIG, and includes a defence solicitor. Their prime purpose is to assist the CJS in their area to achieve the objectives set out in the CJS Strategic Plan. They identify and share best practice and are responsible for piloting and implementing new initiatives referred by TIG or agreed locally. They keep TIG and the Area Criminal Justice Strategy Committees informed of their work.

THE CHANGING LEGISLATIVE SCENE

Crime and Disorder Act 1998

This is being introduced in stages. The full implementation of the pro-visions in relation to indictable-only crime will be brought into force in mid-2000 and the relevant parts of this text are italicised to indicate that they are not yet in force nationally.

Human Rights Act 1998

The Human Rights Act will be implemented on 2 October 2000. The Act incorporates rights and freedoms guaranteed by the European Convention on Human Rights (ECHR) into UK law. The Human Rights Act will:

- make it unlawful for a public authority to act incompatibly with the Convention rights;

- allow for a case to be brought in a UK court or tribunal against the authority where it does so (however, a public authority will not have acted unlawfully under the Act if, as the result of a provision of primary legislation, it could not have acted differently);

- require that all legislation be interpreted and given effect as far as possible compatibly with the Convention rights.

The Act will fundamentally alter the way in which the courts approach the interpretation of the law. The courts will have to find a meaning which is compatible with the Convention rights. The fact that a court may have interpreted a law in a certain way before the Human Rights Act comes into force does not mean that it will interpret the provision in that same way afterwards.

The Act will have a significant impact on criminal cases and the Conven-tion rights are an important resource for criminal defence lawyers. There are increasing instances of the courts already taking Convention points in domestic proceedings in advance of implementation.

There is a hierarchy of Convention rights: some are absolute, some can be limited and some are qualified. Absolute rights cannot be derogated from. They are:

- the right to life;

- the right to protection from torture, inhuman and degrading treatment and punishment;

5

- the prohibition on slavery and enforced labour;
- protection from retrospective criminal penalties.

Other rights, such as the right to liberty and right to a fair trial, can be limited under finite, explicit or implied circumstances defined in the Convention itself. Qualified rights include the right to respect for private and family life, the right to freedom of expression, religion and association, the right to the peaceful enjoyment of property and to some extent the right to education. Interference with these rights is permissible subject to various qualifications. These include the qualification that any restriction must have its basis in law, be necessary in a democratic society and be related to the permissible aim set out in the relevant Article (e.g. the prevention of crime or the protection of public order or health). Convention rights must be balanced, one against another.

Although the courts will be required to take into account Strasbourg case law, the interpretation of the Convention rights here is likely to develop its own momentum quickly. Moreover, the Convention is a living instrument whose interpretation changes over time to reflect different social attitudes. This means that the outcome of previous Strasbourg cases is not an infallible guide to what might happen under the Human Rights Act.

If a victim does not find a remedy on a Convention point in the UK then he may still make an application to the Strasbourg Court. Given that the Human Rights Act provides a system of remedies for a breach of the Convention rights, the admissibility provisions of the Convention may require people to seek those remedies in the domestic courts before going to Strasbourg.

You should always be alert to ECHR issues which can be raised on behalf of your clients. The existence of a Convention argument may justify the granting of legal aid for an alleged offence, the nature of which would not normally attract legal aid.

Relevant articles from the ECHR are set out in Appendix 1.

Access to Justice Act 1999

During 2000 the Access to Justice Act 1999 will replace the Legal Aid Board with a Legal Services Commission and a Criminal Defence Service. For convenience, this text continues to refer to the Legal Aid Board. The current legal aid regulations will be rewritten and eventually replaced by contracts.

Youth Justice and Criminal Evidence Act 1999

This Act introduces new provisions for the protection of vulnerable and intimidated witnesses. It also brings in Youth Offender Panels to sentence first-time young offenders who plead guilty to non-serious offences. These panels will be piloted before national introduction.

THIS GUIDE

You should aim to progress cases speedily, but this must not be at the expense of following proper procedures. Many factors in the criminal justice system can unavoidably contribute to defence delay. It may be necessary to request further disclosure from the prosecutor before advising on plea. It may be difficult to obtain an appointment to take instructions in person from a client in custody. An adjournment to allow time for discussions with the prosecution to take place may lead to a case being discontinued or a lesser charge being substituted.

You will constantly have in mind the best interests of your client. An essential element of good preparation is effective case management from the outset:

- taking proper control of the case;
- taking responsibility for the decisions which need to be made and actively planning;
- thinking ahead so that the defence is able at the earliest opportunity to make enquiries;
- raising proper issues and reacting to developments in a case.

The purpose of this guide is to provide a practical model which will help you to prepare cases efficiently and effectively to the necessary standard. It does not cover advocacy skills. This guide takes account of the many recent changes for criminal practitioners and brings together essential information from a range of criminal justice agencies. It incorporates the Legal Aid Board's Crime Transaction Criteria (3 March 1998 issue) to which the numbers in square brackets refer.

It emphasises that you and your staff must maintain full records, at all stages, of all steps taken, of advice given and reasons for that advice, both for evidential purposes and to ensure that you work to acceptable quality standards. You should keep your clients informed of what is happening at all stages of the case.

No guide can seek to deal with every circumstance, and this does not. It is intended to describe preferred practice and to offer general advice. It is not a substitute for the exercise by you of your professional judgement. Where imperatives are used, they are used for emphasis and should not be taken to imply the existence of a duty.

Ethical problems

A solicitor with a question about an ethical issue may contact a guidance officer in the Professional Ethics Department of the Law Society's Policy Directorate (tel: 0870 606 2577).

Practice Advice Service

Other enquiries should be made to the Practice Advice Service at the Law Society (tel: 0870 606 2522).

Complementary books

The Law Society publications which complement this guide are:

- for police station advice: *Police Station Skills for Legal Advisers: A Pocket Reference*; *Police Station Skills for Legal Advisers* – the training kit;

- for investigation of the prosecution case; disclosure; defence statements; and defence investigations: *Active Defence: A Lawyer's Guide to Police and Defence Investigation and Prosecution and Defence Disclosure in Criminal Cases*;

- for sentencing: *The Advocate's Sentencing Guide*.

These can be purchased from Marston Books Services, DX 130431 Didcot 2, PO Box 312, Abingdon, Oxon OX14 4YH. Tel: 01235 465 656. Fax: 01235 465 660.

Criminal Practitioners' Newsletter

Criminal practitioners are kept up to date by the *Criminal Practitioners Newsletter*, issued free, quarterly, by the Policy Directorate, the Law

Society, 113 Chancery Lane, London WC2A 1PL; DX: 56 London/ Chancery Lane (tel: 020 7316 5525). You will also find it on the Law Society's internet site (see details below).

Internet

The Law Society's internet site is at http://www.lawsociety.org.uk. You can use it to obtain Legal Aid Board forms or find out about the Police Station Accreditation Scheme. It will also help you to keep up to date with legal aid matters, and guidance and responses by the Criminal Law Committee on criminal law reform and policy issues. It also has a searchable directory of solicitors.

End note

1 *Criminal Justice System Strategic Plan 1999–2002* and *Business Plan 1999–2000*, published by the Home Office, March 1999.

CHAPTER 2

Legal and professional duties

Your duty to obtain the best result for each client has to be exercised in the context of the criminal law (legal duties) and the professional codes of conduct (professional duties). In general terms you must keep information about your clients' affairs confidential unless, by doing so, you would commit a criminal offence.

Perverting the course of justice

Perverting the course of justice is a criminal offence. Be aware that it may be committed in these circumstances:

- manufacturing and helping to manufacture false evidence;
- destroying or concealing potential evidence;
- interfering with potential witnesses to persuade them not to give evidence or to give false evidence (see also CJPOA 1994, s.51);
- knowingly acting for a defendant who has assumed a false name or other false details with intent to deceive the court or police (e.g. that the defendant has no previous convictions);
- deliberately assisting your client to evade arrest;
- assisting offenders (note CJA 1967, s.4).

Dealing with potential prosecution evidence

It may happen that a client approaches you with a request that you keep an item for him, and you either know or suspect that the item is of an incriminating nature so far as he is concerned. You should refuse to accept the item unless he authorises you to hand it to the police.

You may find that an item has been left in your office by a client or friend of a client. Where it is clear that the item is of value to the prosecution, you should arrange for it to be delivered to the police. You should not offer information to the police of the manner in which it came into your possession or of any other circumstances surrounding the delivering of it. Your client should be informed of your action and the question of conflict of interest with your client should be considered.

When, in the course of investigating your client's defence, you come across evidence which is clearly material to the prosecution case, you should not interfere with it in any way but should make a record of it. You are under no duty to disclose it to the police or the prosecution.

Interviewing prosecution witnesses

There is no property in a prosecution witness. The Law Society advises that: 'It is permissible for a solicitor acting for any party to interview and take statements from any witness or prospective witness at any stage in the proceedings, whether or not that witness has been interviewed or called as a witness by another party.'[1]

Traditionally, English defence solicitors have had a distinct disinclination to interview prosecution witnesses. Clearly there are risks:

- rehearsing the witness for cross-examination. There is the risk of warning the witness in advance of the defence case that will later be put to the witness, so that you inadvertently rehearse him for cross-examination at trial. If a witness is not telling the truth the jury should be able to see the witness respond to a challenging question for the first time;

- legal risks. If you interview a prosecution witness and subsequently the evidence is inconsistent with an earlier account, which the witness gave to the police, you could find yourself accused of interfering with a witness and/or perverting the course of justice.

The Law Society advises:

> A solicitor should be aware that, in seeking to exercise the right to interview a witness who . . . is likely to be called by the other side . . . the solicitor may well be exposed to the suggestion that he or she has improperly tampered with the evidence. This may be so particularly where the witness subsequently changes his or her evidence.

> In order to avoid allegations of tampering with evidence, it is wise for a solicitor to offer to interview the witness in the presence of a representative of the other side. If this is not possible a solicitor may record the

interview, ask the witness to bring a representative and ask the witness to sign an additional statement to the effect that the witness has freely attended the interview, and has not been coerced into giving the statement or changing his or her evidence.[2]

There are persuasive arguments for interviewing prosecution witnesses despite the risks. With the abolition of live evidence ending the opportunity to cross-examine prosecution witnesses at committal and the clear research evidence of how police officers may shape witness testimony,[3] the need to interview certain types of prosecution witnesses becomes more pressing. The witness may have information which you cannot afford to leave until cross-examination at trial to obtain. It may by then be too late to follow up a lead which the witness provides.

Where appropriate, you must interview prosecution witnesses, having weighed up the factors for and against and arrived at a reasoned decision for doing so – particularly one founded upon shortcomings you, and experts, have identified in the witness's statement.

You should interview the witness in a way which demonstrates best practice. You should employ appropriate procedures to ensure the treatment of the witness is beyond reproach and ensure there is a recording of this, or an independent third party or representative of the other side is present.

You should keep a full attendance note of any contact with a potential prosecution witness.[4]

In *Active Defence: A Lawyer's Guide to Police and Defence Investigation and Prosecution and Defence Disclosure in Criminal Cases*, published by the Law Society, full advice is given on:

- identifying witnesses;

- weighing up factors for and against interviewing;

- shortcomings in the way in which the police interview witnesses;

- approaching a witness (including a specimen letter to a witness);

- the extent to which you should keep the prosecutor in the picture;

- who should conduct the interview;

- who else should attend;

- where the interview should be conducted;

- how the interview should be conducted;

- safeguards;
- tape-recording.

Change of instructions

If your client makes inconsistent statements, only where it is clear that your client is attempting to put forward false evidence to the court should you cease to act. Remember that the defendant is entitled to put the prosecution to proof of its case. The client should (except where it amounts to the offence of 'tipping-off') be advised of the reason for any decision not to continue to act, and that he is free to instruct other solicitors.

Your duty to your client

You are your client's adviser and, if appropriate, his advocate.

Your client is the principal and you are his agent. Your duties to your client include:

- giving independent advice;
- not permitting any compromise of your integrity;
- acting in your client's best interest;
- ensuring the confidentiality of information about your client and his affairs;
- using reasonable care and skills, proper diligence and promptness and keeping him properly informed.

Your objectives include:

- seeking relevant information;
- considering relevant facts, law and procedure;
- advising your client;
- preparing your client's case for presentation in court, including as appropriate:
    - interviewing and taking a statement from your client and any potential witnesses;
    - investigating the prosecution and defence case, including the scene of the crime;

- securing documentary evidence;
- seeking expert assistance;
- passing information when appropriate to the court and CPS.

Your duty to the court

Your primary duty is to your client, but you have a concurrent duty to the court and the administration of justice generally. Your duty to the court is to act in good faith. In the context of preparing a case this means:

- never knowingly letting the advocate, your client or his witnesses, by what they say, mislead the court or tell the court facts which you know to be untrue;
- never inventing a defence or assisting your client to invent one.

Identity

If, to your knowledge, your client has adopted a false name or address or date of birth with intent to deceive the court (e.g. by evading identification your client seeks to avoid being linked with his previous convictions or to impede the court's communication with him) you should advise your client of the dangers of failing to identify himself properly and if he refuses, you should withdraw. This does not apply if a change of name was without intent to deceive, or if the address given, although not your client's place of residence, is a genuine point of communication. If in doubt, decline to act.[5]

Refusing instructions

Generally, you are free to decide whether to accept instructions from any particular client, but it is inadvisable to refuse without good reason, examples of which are:

- refusal of legal aid or failure of your client to make adequate financial provision for fees;
- a conflict or potential conflict of interest between you and your client (or prospective client) or between your client (or prospective client) and another.

Any refusal must not be based on the race, colour, ethnic or national origins, sex, creed, disability or sexual orientation of the prospective client.[6]

Confidentiality

Your duty is to keep information about your client and his affairs confidential.[7] The basis of the duty is the public interest in ensuring that persons suspected of crime can communicate privately with their solicitors; that way, there is a much greater prospect that all relevant information will reach you and on which you can base your advice and assist the court. Otherwise, relevant information would be withheld from you, and the administration of justice would suffer.

Scope

The scope of the duty extends to all communications between you and your client. Your professional duty of confidentiality is wider than the concept of privilege in the law of evidence.[8] Clearly all advice you give your client and all instructions you receive from him are confidential, unless the circumstances clearly indicate to the contrary, e.g. it is knowingly given, as may sometimes be the case, in the presence of a police officer.

The duty does not end with:

- the conclusion of your client's case;

- the withdrawal, ending or lapsing of his instructions;

- his death.

It does end:

- with your client's consent, expressed or implied. Where consent is obtained, it is wise to have it in writing, signed and dated;

- by court order. A court may order the disclosure, in defined circumstances, of confidential information. It may not order the disclosure of privileged information unless total privilege has been expressly or impliedly waived by the client;[9]

- when it is reasonably necessary to:

  - defend yourself against a criminal allegation or civil claim;

  - defend yourself when your conduct is under investigation;

  - prevent your client committing a criminal act which you believe on reasonable grounds is likely to result in actual bodily harm;

15

- prevent you being prosecuted under the Drug Trafficking Act 1994 and other money laundering legislation.

If you believe that your duty of confidentiality has come to an end you should keep a detailed note of your reasons.

You must not use confidential information to your client's detriment or to the advantage of others, including yourself.

Confidentiality and privilege distinguished

Legal professional privilege protects communications between a client and solicitor from being disclosed, even in a court. But privilege applies only to communications made for the purpose of seeking and receiving legal advice. It does not protect a record of a client's appointment in a solicitor's appointments diary, or of the time of his attendance in an attendance note or fee charging sheet as these documents record nothing which passed between the solicitor and the client and had nothing to do with obtaining legal advice.[10]

Staff

Ensure that your staff are fully aware that your duty of confidentiality applies to them. When a junior member of staff is faced with a problem of confidentiality, he should consult urgently with a senior member of the practice.

Co-defendants

Where you originally acted for two co-defendants and one, who now has separate representation, decides to run a 'cut-throat' defence or plead guilty and give evidence for the prosecution against the other, problems of confidentiality may become insurmountable and you should consider whether to cease to act for your remaining client.

Where you act for two co-defendants you should not pass confidential information from one to the other, if to do so may assist them to concoct a defence. Otherwise it must be in the interests of both clients and be done with the authority of the client giving the information.

Where you act for one defendant and another solicitor acts for a co-defendant and you propose exchanging confidential information, the same considerations apply.

Conflict of interest

Constantly review your client's instructions and be aware of possible conflict of interest problems. Bear in mind that if your duty of disclosure to one client conflicts with your duty of confidentiality to another you should cease to act for both.

A witness for your client

You must not accept instructions to act as an advocate for your client if it is possible that you or a member of your firm will be called as a witness on behalf of your client unless the evidence is undisputed.

As a consequence of advice given to a client in the police station, you may later advise the client to waive privilege so that the police station adviser can give evidence about that in court.

Alternatively, the police station adviser might have witnessed events whilst advising or assisting your client at the police station. In exercising judgement you should consider the nature of the evidence to be given and its importance to the case overall.[11]

WITNESS CARE

National standards of witness care

The Law Society has formally recognised the various responsibilities which you owe to witnesses in a National Statement which was produced by TIG. Implementation of the statement is co-ordinated by the local TIGs, incorporating the National Standards into Local Service Agreements on Witness Care.

The national standards include some timescales for the defence, during which it is expected that a particular action will be taken. These actions have been carefully phrased so that a solicitor is only asked to do something which it is in his power to do, rather than something for which he depends upon the co-operation of the client or defence witnesses. Likewise, only timescales which are realistic for all solicitors have been adopted.

Local TIGs may choose to set their own timescales. Although TIG accepts that a solicitor who chooses to agree to a shorter timescale does so only on behalf of that solicitor's firm, the Law Society is concerned that this may have the effect of pressurising other firms in the area. The Law Society recommends that solicitors instead concentrate on keeping within the time-scales negotiated for them by the Law Society in the National Standards which, unless varied locally, will automatically become part of any local agreement.

The detailed standards

The National Standards make various demands on the police, CPS, barristers and the courts as well as on defence solicitors. Under the terms of the agreement, you are required to look after your own witnesses.

1. When taking statements, note details of witnesses' availability and record details of any special needs the witnesses have including standby arrangements (e.g. permitting witnesses to wait at known locations near the court where they can be contacted by telephone) for child, expert/professional, intimidated and vulnerable witnesses. Note: this includes those with disabilities who may require communication aids or assistance with access to court facilities. Contact the court customer services officer for assistance for disabled court users.

2. Immediately identify difficulties which witnesses have in expressing themselves through differences in languages, mannerisms or expressions.

3. Where a witness is under a mental disability, consider how their special needs can be addressed, for example by arranging for the attendance and assistance of a key worker or support worker as appropriate.

4. Give the witness a copy of the leaflet entitled *Witness in Court*, deal with any queries and encourage the witness to inform you immediately of any change in his availability for court. Note: you may wish to draw the witness's attention to the availability of the witness service. There is a service in all Crown Courts and some magistrates' courts. All magistrates' courts should be covered by 2002.

5. If children are witnesses in cases involving cruelty, sexual abuse or violence, give them and their parents or carers an information pack called *The Young Witness Pack*.

6. At the time of taking a statement, enquire whether the witness has been or is at risk of being subjected to intimidation and, if so, take necessary steps, for example informing the police and indicating to the court that circumstances make it necessary to prioritise the case. Where intimidation is an issue, the witness at risk should be provided with the name and telephone number of a police contact, additional to the officer in the case, who works during normal office hours.

7. Where interpreters are required for a hearing, establish that they are familiar with the particular dialect or regional variation of the language which the witness uses. Interpreters should be familiar with the terms used in court proceedings. Note: there are also different forms of sign languages for deaf people.

8. Decide the order in which witnesses should be called to give evidence and consider whether it is possible to stagger their attendance so that any inconvenience to them can be minimised. The court's agreement should be obtained to the staggering of witnesses.

9. Within four working days of being informed of a trial date or the appearance of a case in a warned list, the defence should inform a defence witness of this and of the time they are required to attend court.

10. Defence advocates and, when permitted, those from the instructing solicitor's office who attend the Crown Court should meet their witnesses at an agreed time.

11. Unless it is necessary for evidential purposes, witnesses should not be required to disclose their addresses in open court.

12. Deal with any queries about court procedures raised by witnesses. Action should be taken to ensure that witnesses understand the procedure for claiming their expenses.

13. In the event of witnesses having to wait for more than two hours[12] from the time they are required to attend court to the time they are called to give evidence, they should be informed of the reason for the delay and told how long they may have to wait.

If a case is to be adjourned part-heard, the court should provide the defence with sufficient time to ascertain the availability of witnesses so that the case can be adjourned to a date that is, so far as is possible, convenient to the witnesses.

The defence solicitor and the CPS are also required to communicate with each other about the case:

1. When undertaking a review of the full file, the prosecution should decide which statements can appropriately be tendered in evidence under s.9 CJA 1967. Copies of these statements should be served on the defence within seven working days of the review date.

2. Within seven workings days from entering a not guilty plea in the magistrates' court, the defence should serve on the court and the prosecutor copies of the defence statements in their possession which can be appropriately tendered in evidence under s.9 CJA 1967.

3. In cases to be tried in the magistrates' court, any additional witness statements should be served on the other party and the court as quickly as possible and in any event within seven working days of possession.

4. In cases to be tried in the magistrates' court, the defence and prosecution should make admissions of fact in writing within seven working days of knowledge of those facts.

5. If the defence or prosecution advocate has proposed a section 9 statement or section 10 admissions, the defence solicitor or the CPS should inform the other party within four working days.

YOUTH JUSTICE

The Crime and Disorder Act 1998, s.37 sets out a new principal aim for the youth justice system of preventing offending by children and young persons.

It places all those who carry out functions in relation to the youth justice system (including you) under a duty to have regard to that aim in addition to their other duties.

It is accepted that different youth justice agencies have different roles to play and different professional and statutory responsibilities.

The Home Office guidance on section 37 states that: 'each of these (criminal justice) agencies and individuals have a particular contribution to make and a particular role to play. Each has its own traditions and working practices . . . (some) have professional codes of practice'.

The purpose is to encourage practitioners to consider how their actions and decisions, when dealing with young people, can assist in preventing offending. The guidance lists the key contributions that defence practitioners can make:

*   having familiarity with and understanding of the law relating to youth justice;

*   effecting the swift administration of justice so that every young person accused of breaking the law has the matter resolved without delay (defence lawyers acting quickly and efficiently, once instructed by their clients, can help reduce delay, particularly where the young person admits the offence and wants to make an early guilty plea);

*   helping the child or young person to understand what is required when a sentence is imposed;

- ensuring the child or young person can participate in the proceedings (allowing the child or young person to speak for himself and to be addressed directly by the court).

SAFEGUARDING CHILDREN'S VIDEO EVIDENCE

The Home Office and Department of Health's *Memorandum of Good Practice on Video Recorded Interviews for Criminal Proceedings*, published in 1992, sets out guidelines for the conduct of interviews, and the storage, custody and disposal of video tapes. It emphasises the sensitivity of such a tape which 'may well . . . contain intimate personal . . . information and images and, in the child's interests, should be held strictly in confidence . . . It is therefore essential that adequate arrangements are made to store the recording safely and securely and to ensure that access to it, and to copies which are made, is restricted to those who are authorised to view the recording'.

- No one should have custody of a tape unless they are willing to safe-guard it to the standard recommended in the memorandum.

- Any person borrowing a tape should be made aware that the tape is the property of the police and is likely to be used in the course of a criminal trial, and that its misuse or unauthorised retention may cons-titute a contempt of court or other offence.

- Log books should be maintained by anybody authorised to have custody of a copy, and such log books should be subject to periodic inspection by management.

Tapes are at their most vulnerable when in transit, and when passed on to third parties. CPS practice, recommended to practitioners, is to use recorded delivery post where hand delivery is impractical. When delivering tapes, do not leave them unattended in your car, because of the risk of theft. Before handing tapes to third parties, you would be wise to safeguard your position by requesting a written undertaking first.

The memorandum requires you to give a written undertaking to safeguard the recording.

A form of undertaking recommended by the Law Society is set out in Appendix 2.

End notes

1 *The Guide to the Professional Conduct of Solicitors 1999*, Principle 21.10. The Law Society.
2 *Ibid*. Principle 21.10.
3 Shepherd, E and Milne, R 'Full and Faithful: ensuring quality practice and integrity of outcome in witness interviews', *Analysing Witness Testimony*. Blackstone Press.
   McLean, M 'Quality Investigation? Police Interviews of Witnesses', *Medicine, Science and the Law*, 36, 116–122. 1995.
   Shepherd, E 'Representing and Analysing the Interviewee's Account', *Medicine, Science and the Law*, 35, 122–135.
4 It is a contempt of court for the police to interfere with a defence solicitor's attempts to interview prosecution witnesses: *Connolly* v. *Dale* [1996] 1 All ER 224.
5 *The Guide to the Professional Conduct of Solicitors 1999*, Annex 21F. The Law Society.
6 *Ibid*. Principle 12.01. The Law Society.
7 *Ibid*. Principle 16.01. The Law Society.
8 See *Belabel and Another* v. *Air India* [1988] 2 All ER 246, CA.
9 *R.* v. *Derby MC, ex p. B* [1996] 1 AC 487.
10 *R.* v. *Manchester Crown Court, ex p. R.* (Legal Professional Privilege) [1999] Crim LR 748.
11 *The Guide to the Professional Conduct of Solicitors 1999*, Principle 21.12. The Law Society.
12 There is pressure to reduce this to one hour in the magistrates' court.

CHAPTER 3

Practice management

LAW SOCIETY

Practice Management Standards

The Law Society launched the *Practice Management Standards* (PMS) in 1993. They were developed, drawing on other quality systems, to provide a practical and sensible framework for the management of a legal practice.

The PMS was designed for a number of purposes:

- a practical management tool to benefit lawyers and their clients;
- guidelines against which law practices can measure the way they currently manage themselves;
- a checklist for planning improvements and developments.

Purchasers of legal services require them to be backed by a recognised quality assurance system. This is why the Legal Aid Board has introduced its own Legal Aid Franchise Quality Assurance Standard. The Board has reflected the relevant parts of PMS where they are applicable and it is possible to do so.

The Law Society has introduced a certification scheme which enables practices to undergo assessment by an independent assessor who can certify that the practice has complied with the core requirements of PMS. The Board recognises the progress made by the Law Society in the development of this scheme, Lexcel, and will continue to discuss with the Law Society the alignment of PMS, Lexcel and the Franchise Quality Assurance Standard.

The Law Society has produced a *Practice Management Standards* kit which includes the following:

- *The Office Procedures Manual* (book or disk);

- *A Guide to Implementing the Practice Management Standards*;

- *The Assessment Guide* – what a firm must do to achieve Lexcel accreditation;

- *An Introduction to Quality Systems* – a guide to the current range of quality systems available, explaining the advantages and disadvantages of each.

The complete kit or any one of the above publications can be obtained from Marston Book Services (tel: 01235 465 656).

Lexcel

Lexcel is the new quality mark available to law firms and legal departments which meet the Law Society's Practice Management Standards. Assessment is by independent bodies but the Practice Management Unit deals with the policy and administration of the scheme.

The Practice Advice Service at the Law Society deals with the initial enquiries from the profession on the scheme (tel: 0870 606 2522).

Law Management Section

The Law Management Section (LMS) was launched in July 1998. It is the second section to be piloted by the Law Society. The LMS is open to anyone involved in managing a legal practice and is not restricted to solicitors. Some of the services currently available to members include a quarterly newsletter, an annual conference, local management seminars and discounts on management publications. The LMS website includes an on-line directory of members to encourage networking and an on-line database of management information is being developed (http://www.lms.lawsociety.org.uk).

Software Solutions Guide

To assist smaller firms without in-house information technology (IT) expertise and resources, the Practice Management Unit has published the *Software Solutions Guide* which lists five legal software suppliers who meet certain criteria on functionality, customer satisfaction, etc. It also provides advice on how to choose the right practice management system. Copies of the guide are available to the profession from the Practice Advice Service.

The Practice Management Unit is also looking at other initiatives to help solicitors find the right IT solution for them. IT enquiries from the profession should also be referred to the Practice Advice Service.

Client care

Recommended letters and terms and conditions of business to comply with the Solicitors' Costs Information and Client Care Code 1999 are set out in *The Guide to The Professional Conduct of Solicitors 1999* and the [1999] *Gazette,* 21 April, published by The Law Society.

LEGAL AID FRANCHISE QUALITY ASSURANCE STANDARD

The *Legal Aid Franchise Quality Assurance Standard* (3rd edition, December 1998) (LAFQAS) requires management standards which may be successfully incorporated into your firm's practice management systems to ensure that you provide a quality assured service of a universal standard. The standards include:

- a written equal opportunities policy;
- a written business plan, including future business strategy;
- a written description of your management structure;
- written recruitment procedures;
- written procedures to provide induction;
- written performance appraisal procedures;
- a training and development plan;
- written procedures for training and development;
- written arrangements for dealing with complaints;
- an office manual collating information on organisational practice and updated annually;
- a central register of, and written procedures for instructing barristers, business, agents and any other experts used to provide services;
- written arrangements for the periodic review of case files;
- documented and effective supervisory controls;
- written procedures dealing with the conclusion of a case;

- financial information monitoring:
- income;
- expenditure;
- overhead costs;
- average cost per case.

References with letters and numbers in square brackets below are to the relevant section of LAFQAS.

Welfare benefits

LAFQAS requires firms to have at least one employee who either meets the Welfare Benefits Category Supervisor Standards or has attended an accredited welfare benefits needs recognition course and maintains current knowledge through the acquisition of at least two hours' CPD in welfare benefits annually. [B1.1]

All fee-earners must be trained (with annual updates) to recognise the need for welfare benefits advice. [B1.2]

Equal opportunities and non-discrimination

LAFQAS requires firms to have a written equal opportunities policy which is in effective operation, making it clear they will not discriminate on grounds of race, gender, religion, disability or sexual orientation including whether to accept instructions from clients, instructing counsel and other experts, in the provision of services or in the selection, recruitment and treatment of staff. [F1.1]

The Law Society's Solicitors' Anti-Discrimination Rule and Code deal with the selection, treatment and promotion of staff; the acceptance of instructions from a client; and the instruction of counsel.[1] The Rule states that:

- solicitors must not discriminate on grounds of race, sex and sexual orientation, and must not discriminate unfairly or unreasonably on grounds of disability, in their professional dealings with clients, staff, other solicitors, barristers or other persons; and
- principal solicitors in private practice must operate a policy dealing with the avoidance of such discrimination. Those who have not developed and adopted their own policy dealing with the avoidance

of such discrimination will be deemed to have adopted the model anti-discrimination policy for the time being promoted for such purposes by the Law Society and set out in *The Guide to the Professional Conduct of Solicitors 1999*.

Race awareness and equal opportunities

Equal opportunity policy and practice in the context of race awareness does not mean 'we treat people equally'. It means 'we respond appropriately'.

For racial minority groups, equal opportunities programmes have succeeded when inequalities (if any) cease to be ascribed to the skin colour of that minority – directly or indirectly – by anyone.

Being 'race aware' does not mean that people should be apologetic one to another or should think that national identity is at stake. Being 'race aware' does mean that people – white and black – should value cultural diversity, i.e. they should be receptive and sympathetic to differences of response in many social situations.

Cultural diversity/multiculturalism is specifically relevant to members of the legal profession as lawyers and as service providers.

In both roles, lawyers need to become familiar with:

- the importance of names and naming systems;
- religions and religious practices;
- styles and types of (so-called) body language.

In both roles lawyers need to learn to:

- avoid stereotyping and the assumption of superiority;
- apply good practice within and throughout the working environment.

Good practice (for employers) means:

- adopting positive action strategies to promote recruitment, retention and promotion of staff from racial groups other than their own (but only on merit) with the target of producing a balanced work force;
- conducting surveys to tease out prejudiced and discriminatory attitudes;
- establishing a mandatory race awareness training regime for all levels of staff;

27

- monitoring and evaluating, and (most importantly) ensuring that any and all action that is required as a result of this process is implemented.

Good practice (for service providers) means:

- ensuring that the system for service delivery produces equal outcomes regardless of the ethnic origin of the user of that service; and

- monitoring and evaluating all parts of the system to achieve such equality.

Just as there are gender (and generational) differences which evoke an appropriate response, so there are cultural differences. These have to be treated in exactly the same way.

Business planning

LAFQAS requires firms to have a written business plan which is an expression of the firm's business strategy. The plan must be current, give in detail the key objectives for a period of 12 months and in outline for a further two years. The plan must include:

- future business strategy, which must incorporate:
    - a detailed description of services that the organisation wishes to offer;
    - the client groups to be served;
    - how the services are to be provided;
- identification of the resources and skills necessary to deliver the strategy for the future;
- finance plan and budget to support the planned business activities.

The business plan must be reviewed at least six-monthly and the results of the reviews documented. [H1.1]

PMS requires a documented outline strategy to provide a framework within which the practice may review its performance and take decisions about its future. The strategy document should provide a framework for decisions about, for example, purchase of computers, office location, staffing and targeting new business. In setting practices' strategy, regard should be had to setting goals for the practice for the coming three to five years, adopting a 'practice purpose statement' describing the long-term aims of the practice and identifying specific objectives that the practice would like to achieve.

Management structure

LAFQAS requires firms to have a written description of their management structure and designate the responsibilities of individuals within it. They must document the skills, knowledge and experience required by all staff, including partners (this will usually be in job descriptions). [J1.1]

It is important that everyone in the firm knows who takes the decisions in each area of management. All the important responsibilities should be clearly assigned to an individual or individuals.

A job description allows the practice to set the level of skills, knowledge and experience required and enables staff to understand what their responsibilities are. It will set these matters out in detail, together with the tasks which the staff are expected to perform. A job description, describing the role to be performed in the firm, the specification for the job, and characteristics of the person required to carry out the job is an essential reference point at an appraisal as well as the basis for recruiting another person to that post.

PMS also requires firms to have a written description of their management structure so that incoming partners or staff may have this easily explained to them. This will include the name of a supervisor for each area of work and list the designated responsibilities of individuals in the practice including those who may be responsible for adherence to PMS. The reporting structure in the practice should be shown by the use of a 'family tree' so that everyone in the practice is clear about who reports to whom.

Recruitment and induction

LAFQAS requires written recruitment procedures that involve evaluation of the skills, knowledge and experience possessed by applicants for posts in the organisation. LAFQAS also requires written procedures to provide a core induction process for all new post holders. The recruitment procedure should be designed to ensure that:

- recruitment is fair and effective, with no discrimination;
- advertising reflects the job and person description;
- interviewing is conducted consistently;
- documentation is retained to provide feedback to candidates or to the Board. [J1.2] [J1.3]

It is helpful to debrief properly an outgoing member of staff to ensure an understanding of the particular demands of the job to be filled and where improvements to the post can be carried out. It is also worth considering whether the job could be just as well performed by someone with a narrower or different training and skills. The job description should be analysed and rewritten to reflect any developments that have taken place in or changes made to the post.

To ensure that you have a good system of induction in your firm, ask the outgoing person what his replacement will need to know about the practice and how soon they will need that information. It is important that the new recruit knows:

- who is who in the practice;
- who their immediate supervisor is;
- who will monitor their work and how it will be done;
- what their short-term and long-term aims are;
- who they can turn to for advice;
- who they can complain to;
- what training they can expect;
- what resources are available to them;
- what the practice objectives are;
- the administrative procedures; and
- the operational procedures which help to guarantee a constant standard of work.

Appraisal

LAFQAS requires written procedures to:

- appraise the performance of all personnel who are directly or indirectly concerned with the provision of legally aided services, including partners, at least annually against their responsibilities and objectives;
- record in writing and agree with the job holder the performance appraisal.

Firms are also required to:

- identify any deficiencies in performance; and

- monitor and record the corrective action in the period up to the next appraisal or review. [J1.4]

An appraisal should be a constructive dialogue between the people involved. Fee-earners should be appraised by their supervisors. Notes of guidance should set out the process involved and appraisal forms should be used to structure the interview, record the objectives set out and training needs identified and provide continuity.

A first appraisal may be carried out six months after the person commenced employment and then annually with informal reviews at regular intervals in between.

If the person being appraised completes a self-appraisal form beforehand it will help him to identify his own areas of difficulty. It will also help him to prepare by reviewing the period concerned and his performance against the objectives which were set, and consider what is to be achieved in the next period and whether the objectives should be amended or new objectives agreed.

At the appraisal, it is important to agree an acceptable level of performance and let people know:

- what is expected;

- how they are doing;

- whether they have achieved the required results or not.

There should also be agreement about what support is required: coaching, counselling or training.

At the end of the appraisal, you should agree dates for reviewing performance, confirm what disciplinary action will be taken if agreed targets are not met, and make a clear record of what is discussed.

Training and development

LAFQAS requires firms to have written procedures to ensure that:

- training and development needs are assessed for all staff at least annually;

- appropriate written training records are maintained, recording for personnel:

31

- the dates of any external and in-house training attended;
- the course/training titles;
- the names of course providers;
- the number of CPD hours credited. [J1.5]

In addition, there must be a written training and development plan for the firm, reviewed at least annually, supporting the objectives identified in the business plan. [J1.6]

Staff training should be linked to appraisals, where the person's training and development needs are discussed.

Supervision of work

LAFQAS requires a named supervisor who is available personally to the staff or by telephone. The supervisor must have gained experience, knowledge and understanding in the work, and maintain and cascade knowledge of the subject. The supervisor must be able to demonstrate experience of supervision or complete a course in supervision and supervisory skills. [L1.1; L1.2; L2.2; L2.3; L2.4]

PMS suggests the following arrangements that practices may wish to institute to ensure proper supervision of casework:

- checking incoming post;
- outgoing post signed by a supervisor;
- regular review sessions with a supervisor covering:
  - new cases taken on and discussing 'case plans' in complex cases;
  - progress review of current cases;
  - evaluation of outcomes of completed cases;
  - consideration of training needs in relation to legal knowledge skills.

File review

LAFQAS requires written arrangements for the periodic review of case files, covering legal advice and procedural compliance issues and face-to-face supervision by the named supervisor. [M1.1]

PMS requires the practice to have in place arrangements to ensure that the status of the matter and the action taken can be easily checked by other members of the practice. Reviewing files is an important element of the arrangement that must be in place to supervise the conduct of casework. Files should be reviewed periodically on a random basis by a fee-earner who has not been involved in the day-to-day conduct of the matter.

The use of checklists and having a standard format for the presentation of information in a file will make file review easier.

Office manual

LAFQAS requires firms to maintain an office manual collating information about the firm's quality procedures. It must be updated at least annually and each page annotated with dates and/or issue number.

The manual should explain your firm's system of working. It is useful for induction purposes and ensures that everyone works in the same way and to a constant standard. [W1.1; W1.2]

LAFQAS also requires firms to have a central register of, and written procedures for instructing barristers, agents and any other experts used by the firm to provide services, including:

- clear selection criteria;
- evaluation/monitoring of performance (failure to meet standard should be recorded);
- granting, withdrawal or amendment of approved status;
- those not to be used;
- arrangements for payment of fees (bearing in mind that in legally aided cases payment will not normally be made to the expert until payment of disbursements is received from the Board).

In addition:

- where appropriate, the client should be consulted about selection;
- instructions must clearly specify the type and level of service required;
- all opinions and reports received must be checked, if possible by the fee-earner adviser who initiated the instructions. [U1.1; U1.2]

It is a strict requirement of PMS that practices have an office procedures manual which collates together in one place all the information that anyone working in the firm would need to know about office practice.

33

A typical office manual would commence with an introduction describing the history of the firm, and its main objectives as they appear in the business or strategic plan. The introduction may also refer to the standards that all personnel should strive to attain, e.g.

- courtesy – clients must be treated with respect;
- commitment – clients expect the firm to attach urgency to dealing with their instructions;
- knowledge – fee-earners must have the necessary expertise to offer a truly 'professional' service;
- confidentiality – all clients must have confidence that their dealings with the practice will be treated confidentially.

The office manual will describe:

- the organisation's structure;
- the client service standards expected and the way in which the work will be supervised;
- the health and safety provision and office security details;
- personnel forms and procedures;
- the firm's training policy including details of training methods and records;
- the firm's policy on finance and accounting;
- how post and communication is handled;
- how the practice deals with client's files;
- file and case management procedures;
- other miscellaneous office procedures.

Listed below is some information you could use as a basis for your office manual. Personalise it for your firm and the area where you work.

- telephone numbers, fax numbers and addresses of:
  - police stations;
  - courts (including sitting times and how to get there);
  - experts you have used and how to find an expert;
  - CPS;

- – advocates;
- – probation officers;
- – prisons and remand centres (including how to get there);
- – hospitals, psychiatrists;
- – Legal Aid Board area offices;

- standard letters:
  - – clients;
  - – CPS;
  - – courts;
  - – experts;
  - – interpreters;
  - – Legal Aid Board;
  - – police;

- copies of forms commonly used and instructions on completing them (see Appendix 3):
  - – legal aid application;
  - – Legal Aid Board applications for prior authority for expenditure/ review of refusal of legal aid/assignment of counsel/change of solicitors/withdrawal of Legal Aid Order;
  - – financial information form;
  - – notice of applications relating to bail;
  - – notice of application relating to disclosure;
  - – appeal forms;

- how to take instructions:
  - – clients – core information/bail/plea of guilty/trial;
  - – witnesses;
  - – comments on prosecution statements;

- costs:
  - – charges for private work;
  - – use of enhanced rate for legal aid bills;[2]
  - – targets for submitting legal aid bills;[3]
  - – legal aid rates.[4]

35

OFFICE DIARY

Keep a central office diary to keep track of important dates, in which all bail to returns and next hearing dates are recorded as soon as they are known. As soon as you can, make a note, against the hearing, of who the advocate will be. Plot the whereabouts of all fee-earners and other staff members and note how you can locate them urgently if necessary.

TIME: RECORD-KEEPING

Have systems which ensure that all fee-earners record everything that happens: the date and time of every attendance; every telephone call; all the time spent considering the case (including before and after seeing your client); drafting and the reasons why the work was necessary. It is common to underestimate the length of time spent on each aspect.

Ensure that fee-earners record each item of work separately, as they complete it. They should know exactly how long it took them to do it. If something took longer than usual, they should make a note of the reasons why. This written record is the foundation of your claim for costs, or contract negotiations, and supports your time recording system.

You should record all the time spent on dictation and on research or instructing another member of your staff to work on a case and time spent supervising what they are doing.

You should write down everything of importance. You should not keep information in your head as someone else may need to work from it. Files should be interchangeable and the information in the file should be kept in a uniform way so that everyone can have easy access to it.

TIME MANAGEMENT

Encourage your staff not to put off something which is difficult, tedious or will take time.

Help them to plan what needs to be done on a case, prioritise it and work out time targets by which it should be done, allocate time in their diary to do the work and do not let other less important work get in their way.

You should note in your diary (electronic or paper) when you need to have heard from your client or someone else, e.g. the CPS, and when time-limits expire.

BILLING

Your staff should bill immediately at the end of each billing stage. Have time targets for the submission of all bills. Keep records of the dates when a billing date is reached, when the bill is submitted and when it is paid.

End notes

1 *The Guide to the Professional Conduct of Solicitors 1999*, Principles 7.01 (Rule) and 7.02 (Code). The Law Society.
2 Until replaced by the contracting under the Access to Justice Act 1999.
3 *Ibid.*
4 *Ibid.*

CHAPTER 4

Case management

CASE MANAGEMENT SYSTEMS

It is essential to devise workable systems for the processing of criminal case work. They must be used by all fee-earners. Case management systems help to:

- ensure all necessary work is undertaken and in good time;

- prevent repetition;

- make supervision and file review easy and enable fee-earners to understand the state of a case quickly; and

- protect against error and are a defence against wasted costs applications.

Identify the person responsible for the case, having regard to the seriousness of the offence and the nature of the client.

Each firm should aim to produce an office manual containing its procedures and standard documents (see page 33).

Delegation

Subsidiary work should be delegated, if appropriate:

- ensure that the delegate's workload enables the task to be reasonably carried out;

- explain the purpose of the task and the context in which it is to be carried out: the key results to be obtained and the time allowed for it;

- clarify the scope of the authority given and any limitations, for example whether any advice should be given as to the likely length of sentence if the client asks;

- enable competence and confidence with appropriate training;

- remain accountable: delegation is not abrogation and you remain responsible for the task that you have delegated;

- phase the process so that as confidence is gained you progressively hand over control of the task;

- let go! Let them get on with the job and do not make on-the-spot requests for detailed information;

- monitor and supervise without interfering;

- accept that a reasonable number of errors will be made and provide support;

- remain available and interested.

Where the file is transferred to another office, department or fee-earner within the same firm, the client should be given:

- an explanation of the reasons for the transfer; [93.1]

- the name of the person taking over the case; [93.2]

- an opportunity to comment or raise any issues. [93.3]

The file

The information in the file should be kept in a uniform way so that anyone can have easy access to it. A quick look at a file should tell you everything of importance about a case. Key information about a client and his case should be readily available on the front cover of the flap and/or a 'state of case' pro forma in the file together with dates for specific action (see Appendix 4).

General information

The following general information should be kept in the file:

- client's name, name at birth, place of birth, date of birth, address, telephone number, contacts;

- client's national insurance number;

- person responsible for client and conduct of case;

- police/CPS unique case reference number;

39

- police station/officer-in-case; CPS office;

- co-accused and representatives;

- court/next hearing date;

- charge (and date of arrest and charge);

- language needs;

- on bail or in custody. If on bail, conditions including sureties. If in custody, where, and telephone number;

- date advance information given (if relevant);

- date committed/sent/transferred to Crown Court;

- date primary disclosure given;

- date of service of defence statement; [79.1]

- notification of guilty plea;

- stage when guilty plea entered; [85.1]

- advocate instructed;

- brief delivered;

- conference held; [81.1]

- agreement on taped evidence;

- prosecution witnesses required to give oral evidence at trial: s.68 CPIA 1996; PDH – Practice Rule 5;

- date of conviction/sentence (for appeal).

Legal aid

The following legal aid information should be kept in the file:

- police station advice – whether used and detail;

- advice and assistance – whether used and detail;

- Legal Aid Order – date applied for/ date granted/ date bill completed/ date sent/ date paid;

- details of costs estimate and date given;

- details of disbursements incurred/date paid;

- legal aid authorities – date sought/date granted.

Private information

The following, private, firm-related information should be kept in the file:

- fixed price;

- costs estimate (date given and who by);

- revised estimates;

- payment arrangements: instalments;

- money on account;

- dates and amounts of interim bills;

- disbursements.

Progress sheet

Ensure each fee-earner keeps a 'state of case' pro forma sheet at the front of the file (see Appendix 4). This should show at a glance the present stage the case has reached, who requested any previous adjournments and the reasons for them.

Check that fee-earners know what will happen at the next hearing and that this has been agreed with and communicated to the court, the CPS and your client, and that it is necessary for them and their client to attend. Endeavour to adhere to agreed steps in the progress of a case, so that court hearings achieve their purpose.

Case information systems

Have systems for investigating the prosecution evidence and collating, managing and analysing the information which you obtain in a case.

Active Defence (published by the Law Society) advises about significant milestone stages in a case:

- to analyse and take stock of the information obtained so far;

- to consider the implications of this for the prosecution and defence cases;

- to make decisions about the actions to be taken as a consequence, particularly defence investigation.

41

Milestones

1. POLICE STATION

    At the police station:

    - you will need to seek disclosure from the police;

    - you will need to advise on and consider disclosure to be given to the police by your client;

    - you will need to consider obtaining information which was not revealed;

    - you will need to carry out investigations which the police did not undertake;

    - you will need to obtain instructions from your client.

2. TAPE-RECORDINGS OF POLICE INTERVIEWS

    You will need to obtain instructions from your client if you were not present at the interview. The recording is the only authentic and reliable record of the police interview. You will wish to listen to the tape in all cases if only to establish areas of mitigation. If there is to be a trial you must listen even to a no-comment interview to see whether there are possible inferences from silence.

3. BAIL HEARING AT COURT

    The prosecution file can be a valuable source of information.

4. ADVANCE INFORMATION

    For advance information:

    - only witness statements are acceptable;

    - you will need to obtain further instructions from your client;

    - you will consider:
        - whether there is a *prima facie* case;
        - the strength of the prosecution case;
        - the merit of putting the prosecution to proof;

    –   the advantage of claiming a sentence discount for a plea of guilty;

    –   plea;

    –   mode of trial;

    –   type of committal;

    –   the likelihood of obtaining bail.

5.   PROSECUTION WITNESS STATEMENTS IN SUMMARY CASES

These should be available if you make a request to the CPS following a plea of not guilty:

- you will need to obtain further instructions from your client;
- you will consider:

    –   which witnesses need to give oral evidence;

    –   whether expert evidence is required.

6.   COMMITTAL BUNDLE/PROSECUTION EVIDENCE FOLLOWING TRANSFER OR SENDING

At this stage:

- you will need to obtain further instructions from your client;
- you will need to consider:

    –   missing material which you should request from the prosecutor if it is not served as primary disclosure;

    –   which witnesses need to give oral evidence;

    –   whether further investigations or expert evidence is required;

- you will be able to draft the defence statement;
- you will be able to brief the trial advocate and hold a conference with him.

7. PROSECUTION PRIMARY DISCLOSURE: UNUSED UNDERMINING MATERIAL AND SCHEDULE

At this stage:

- you will establish whether there is further unused material which should have been disclosed;

- you will request it by reference to the schedule MG6C and by refining your defence statement.

8. PROSECUTION SECONDARY DISCLOSURE: DISCLOSURE OF MATERIAL WHICH MAY ASSIST THE DEFENCE CASE

At this stage you will establish whether there is further unused material which should be disclosed to you.

Active Defence (published by the Law Society) also recommends systems for managing the information obtained in your client's case:

- organising case files;
- a case chronology;
- an actions management sheet;
- collation methods.

Active Defence explains ways of analysing:

- statements;
- tape-recordings of suspects;
- recordings of witness interviews;
- contemporaneous notes;
- records of tape-recorded interviews;
- the custody record;
- video recordings.

Time guidelines and time-limits

Work out the timetable for the case. Take into account custody time-limits, PTI time guidelines (Appendix 5) and any effective hearing date. For information about time-limits under s.22 POA 1985, as amended by ss.43–44 CDA 1998: see Appendix 6.

Custody time-limits

These are considered more fully on page 110.

The Prosecution of Offences (Custody Time-limits) Regulations 1987 and Amendments Regulations 1991 provide for maximum periods of remand in custody – generally 56 days before summary trial and 70 days before committal proceedings; 112 days following committal (or 182 days where s.51 CDA 1998 applies). The custody time-limit continues until 'start of trial': when the court begins to hear evidence or accept a guilty plea if summary trial; when a jury is sworn or a guilty plea or the start of a preparatory hearing if trial on indictment.

These periods may be extended before expiry on application after notice has been served by the prosecution, at the discretion of the court.

Other time-limits

Be aware of the Working Group on Pre-Trial Issues recommended guide-lines for different stages of the criminal process: see Appendix 5. Diarise these in individual cases as appropriate. They set down timescale targets which can be achieved in most cases by the police and the CPS if the PTI recommendations are implemented. There may be local arrangements with shorter timescales.

Good practice by solicitors will help the CPS attain its targets. Examples of good practice are:

- using common reference numbers;
- applying for legal aid at an early stage;
- advising the CPS of changes of representation with an associated prompt exchange of case materials including advance information;
- the early notification of change of pleas.

CLIENT CARE

Client care letter

At the outset, a 'client care' letter should be sent.

The Solicitors' Practice (Costs Information and Client Care) Amendment Rule 1999 came into force on 3 September 1999 and requires you to give information about the costs and other matters and to operate a complaints handling procedure in accordance with the Solicitors' Costs Information and Client Care Code 1999. The code and recommended letters and terms and conditions of business are set out in *The Guide to The Professional Conduct of Solicitors 1999* and the [1999] *Gazette,* 21 April, published by The Law Society.

LAFQAS requires the following matters to be covered usually in a client care letter:

- the effects of an order for costs, against the client or in the client's favour;
- the client's potential obligation to pay legal aid contributions and the consequences of any failure to do so;[1]
- informing the client about:
    - the name and status of the individual responsible for case conduct;
    - the name of the individual responsible for case supervision;
    - to whom, and how, any complaints should be made. [P1.1]

When writing to clients, it is advisable to:

- use short sentences;
- write in short paragraphs;
- use few long words;
- be logical in the order in which you present things;
- avoid legal jargon.

Dealing with your client: a written record

LAFQAS and PMS requires firms to have written procedures for taking instructions which ensure that fee-earners/advisers agree and record and confirm to the client in writing:

- the requirements or instructions of the client;

- the advice given;

- the action to be taken by the firm;

- key dates in the matter. [P1.1]

The first three items above will usually be recorded on the file on attendance notes with matching sub-headings. It may be necessary to tell the client that it is not possible to give advice until further investigations have been undertaken.

Keeping the client informed

Clients must be kept fully advised in writing as a case proceeds. Use standard letters where possible.

LAFQAS requires a firm to have written procedures which ensure that:

- information on the progress of a case (or reasons for lack of progress) is given to the client at appropriate stages. This is particularly important when new information emerges or there are changes in tactics;

- information about changes in the action planned to be taken in the case is given to client;

- clients are informed of any change in the fee-earner/adviser having conduct of the matter. [S1.1]

Keeping in contact

Keep in regular contact with your client in writing, on the telephone or in person. Further information about letters to a client on remand is given on page 113.

A solicitor's letter should not be opened and read by the prison authorities if it is sent within a double envelope. The outer envelope should be addressed as normal to the prisoner concerned; the inner unstamped envelope should be marked clearly 'Prison Rule 39' (or 'YOI Rule 14' if addressed to a young offender). The inner envelope should also be annotated with the prisoner's name and prison number, if known, address and telephone number of the solicitor's office; a reference number, if possible; and the signature of the solicitor or his clerk.

The interview

Get to know your client during the interview and let your client feel he has your complete attention. Interruptions undermine the relationship; have a system in place to minimise them, e.g. take no telephone calls unless they are very urgent and nobody else can deal with them.

Listening

- Approach things with an open mind.
- Do not interrupt:
  - unless the conversation goes off the topic;
  - unless you need to clarify something.
- Pay attention: to concentrate and comprehend.
- Encourage the person who is talking.
- Do not jump in and answer for the person.
- Summarise the points being made.
- Invite feedback.

Advise your client what is in store for him in terms of the various stages of the court procedures (including whether he will have to give evidence). See your client 'through the system'. Central to your client's concern are the questions 'will I be found guilty?', 'if I am found guilty/plead guilty what will I get?' Always be realistic; that way you will gain your client's confidence which is the essential basis of your relationship.

Talk to your client in a language he understands; avoid legal jargon. Make allowances for your client's nervousness.

Talking

- Be calm.
- Take your time.
- Be logical in the order in which you present things: do not topic hop.
- Use clear understandable language.
- Speak in manageable chunks.
- Tailor what you say to the understanding of the receiver.

- Avoid interruptions, noises, distractions.

- Do not talk over anyone else.

- Summarise the points you are making.

- Invite comment and feedback.

- Check out non-verbal signs.

You are your client's agent, not his tool; act professionally and preserve a distance between you, otherwise your ability to give independent advice will be compromised.

- Be alert to any mental disability and seek medical or specialist assistance when appropriate (see page 54).

- Do not interview your client or take his statement in the presence of any potential witness.

- Explain to your client that his attitude to the conduct of his defence could have cost implications. Tell your client that you will act as his representative, within the constraints of your professional rules, but you need his constant co-operation. At the conclusion of the case, if the court is satisfied costs have been wasted by an unnecessary or improper act or omission by your client or on his behalf he may be liable to pay them.

- Ensure that, to the extent practicable, all significant decisions are taken after consultation between you. Your client will need to ensure you can contact him readily.

- Advise your client to notify you of any change of address.

- Advise your client to notify you of any dates to be avoided or holiday commitments, when he cannot attend court.

- Confirm in writing any decisions which may have professional or cost implications.

Many clients do not appreciate that giving you proper instructions takes time. It is often helpful at the beginning of the interview to explain to your client how long it is likely to take, what you hope to achieve by the end of it; how the statement will be used and who will see it.

- Always write a statement for other people to use.

- Write your client's statement in the first person, as if he is writing it.

- If your client cannot give a satisfactory answer show this in the statement.

- Do not put words into your client's mouth; use his words wherever practicable.

- Do not coach your client – do not suggest what your client might say or help him to invent a story.

- Explain that everything he tells you is 'on the record'.

- It is a matter of professional judgement how much information you should obtain from your client at any particular stage.[2]

- When taking the statement be positive and sympathetic.

- Set out your client's version in chronological order.

- The statement is essentially what your client will say in evidence but is not limited to that; it will include relevant background information which is necessary for a proper understanding of the main events.

- Afterwards send your client a copy of the statement for checking and possible amendment.

- Explain that he should not show the statement to or discuss it with anyone who may give evidence in the case.

- Your client should always sign and date his statement.

- Consider putting the statement in the form of a s.9 statement. Also, obtain the client's signature to the caption as well as to each page and date it.

Set out the information you obtain in a structured way, in blocks with appropriate headings. If you always follow the same pattern this will act as a checklist of the information that you need to obtain and in court the advocate will be able to find what he is looking for quickly.

Child witnesses

Good practice for defence practitioners interviewing child witnesses includes:

- controlling the number of interviews with children;

- having the original interviewer go back to clarify any points with the child;

- not dominating the relationship with the child;

- not driving the conversation with the child through questions inviting the child to confirm what is in the adult's head;

- interview as soon as you can after the event;

- be aware that children become tired and distracted more quickly than adults;

- proceed at the child's speed;

- do not jump in, when the child pauses, and take the talking turn too quickly;

- tell the child that 'I can't remember' or 'I don't know' are perfectly acceptable;

- when asking closed questions to which the child answers 'yes' counter-balance them with questions to which the consistent answer would be 'no'.

Difficulties in communication

If at any time you have difficulty in obtaining instructions you should advise the court of that fact, but your duty of confidentiality otherwise applies.

If a client fails to attend on you to give instructions, write to him saying that if the failure continues you will have to inform the court and get the case listed for hearing. If he still fails to attend on you, write to the court informing it that you are without instructions and asking for the case to be listed without witnesses.

If your client is not fluent in English or has a hearing or speech impairment, arrangements must be made for your instructions to be taken through an interpreter: see page 54 and Appendix 7 on finding an interpreter.

Various organisations are able to provide specialist advice on the needs of clients with physical and learning disabilities. These include the Royal National Institute for the Deaf, the Council for the Advancement and Communication with Deaf People, and MENCAP. In the case of a learning disabled client, the solicitor should consider making an application to the court to order the removal of wigs and gowns and any other measures to assist them to give evidence. The series of 'Books Beyond Words' is produced by the St George's Hospital Medical School and includes picture books which explain procedures relating to arrest, trial and going to court as a witness. Further information can be obtained from the Royal College of Psychiatrists, 17 Belgrave Square, London SW1X 8PG.

INTERPRETERS

Interpretation plays a far greater role in the criminal process than is realised and can potentially make all the difference between a defendant being found guilty or not guilty. An interpreter needs to have linguistic competence, a professional attitude, an understanding of the legal process and of his duties and the need for impartiality and confidentiality. The fact that a person calls himself an interpreter does not necessarily mean that he has these qualities. How often has the interpreter spoken the language recently? Does he understand a particular dialect and slang words?

Organising an interpreter for a defendant

- Establish if a defendant has difficulty understanding English, especially formal, legal registers; or has a hearing or speech impediment.

- In the case of a foreign language speaker, find out the person's preferred language.

- In the case of a deaf person, ascertain the preferred means of communication, e.g. sign language or lip speaker.

- Discuss the person's preferences in the selection of an interpreter: sex; age; religion; ethnic origin; other.

- Select an interpreter with an authentic language match.

Organising an interpreter for court

The Law Society has agreed with the other agencies in the criminal justice system that the following agency is responsible for arranging a foreign language or sign language interpreter for court proceedings:

- the police or other prosecuting agency, for a defendant who is charged with an offence and first appears in court within two working days (not including Saturdays) of charge;

- the court, (magistrates' court, Crown Court or Court of Appeal) for a defendant in all other circumstances;

- the prosecution, for a prosecution witness;

- the defence for a defence witness.

The Criminal Law Committee of the Law Society gives the following guidance.

Helping the court to organise an interpreter for the defendant

The magistrates' court will usually be informed by the police before the first hearing that an interpreter is required for a defendant. If the need for an interpreter only becomes apparent after the defendant has been released from the police station or the case has been committed or transferred or sent for trial, the defence solicitor should inform the magistrates' court or Crown Court of this as early as practicable.

The defence solicitor should be able to help the court to appoint a suitable interpreter. The solicitor should collect relevant information about the defendant and pass this on to the court. The information to be collected is the same information which a solicitor must obtain to organise an interpreter for a defence witness. A form which may be used for this purpose and as a checklist for the solicitor when organising an interpreter for the defendant when taking instructions or for a defence witness is shown in Appendix 8.

That information will have been obtained if the solicitor has already employed an interpreter to enable the solicitor to communicate with the defendant. If the solicitor considers that the same interpreter could be employed to interpret for the defendant in court (providing that the interpreter was not used at the police station), the solicitor should inform the court of the interpreter's details as early as practicable. It is the court's decision whether this or another interpreter is used in court. The court will inform the defence of the name of the person whom they have appointed.

The solicitor should inform the court and the prosecution of the name of the interpreter to be employed to interpret for a defence witness, to avoid duplication.

Terms of engagement

If you require an interpreter for the preparation of a case, use APP7 to obtain authority from the Legal Aid Board to incur this expense.

In legal aid cases, the interpreter's fee for attending at court is assessed and paid by the court out of central funds, and not by the Legal Aid Board. You should make it clear to the interpreter that you are not responsible for the interpreter's fees in these circumstances. The court should agree fees and conditions of appointment with the interpreter before the proceedings and the interpreter should be advised to contact the court for this purpose. Guidance on fees has been issued to courts in the *Guide to Allowances* published by LCD.

Keeping a record of the use of interpreters in a particular case

It is good practice to keep a record on your case file of the details of the client/witness for whom an interpreter is required; a person who is instructed to interpret on the client/witness's behalf; any briefing given to an interpreter about any special terminology or procedure involved in the conduct of the case; and previous hearings when an interpreter has been involved. An example of such a record is in Appendix 8.

Materials to be supplied to the interpreter

The interpreter will be helped by having sight of a copy of the statement made to you by the person whose evidence is to be interpreted, as well as copies of any prosecution witness statements which are likely to be put to the witness in cross-examination.

The following information is set out in Appendix 7:

- Finding an interpreter: The National Register of Public Service Interpreters (the solicitor's preferred choice);

- Registered Qualified and Trainee Sign Language Interpreters.

MENTALLY DISORDERED DEFENDANT

Obtaining instructions

You may find yourself in serious doubt about your client's mental capacity because of your own observations, or those of police or court staff.

You may be unable to obtain any sensible instructions or any communication from your client. It is a matter for your professional judgement whether you consider yourself 'instructed' to act. Explain your difficulty to and try to obtain additional information from the following sources, which may enable you to make an informed decision:

1. Court clerk

If you cannot obtain a signature to the legal aid application, ask the court clerk to consider assigning legal aid to you. He may know of the defendant from previous appearances.

2. Prosecutor

Ask for full access to all case papers. Note in particular any account by witnesses of bizarre behaviour; verbal responses; interview; medical problems; evidence of drugs, etc. Note any previous recorded Mental Health Act orders amongst any previous convictions.

3. Police

If necessary, you may need to contact the police to obtain a copy of the custody record; to trace any relatives who were in contact during your client's detention in the police station; to trace doctors called in to advise during the detention.

4. Probation Service/Social Services Department/local mental health services

They may be aware of your client from previous contact with court including diversion schemes and community mental health teams and may have access to previous relevant reports.

5. Family or relatives

They may be present at court or available by telephone to give history and practical assistance – in particular to offer accommodation.

Mental disorder

Be aware of the breadth of the statutory definition of mental disorder: 'Mental disorder' means mental illness, arrested or incomplete development of mind, psychopathic disorder and any other disorder or disability of mind: s.1 Mental Health Act 1983 (MHA). Enquire if your client has been prescribed tranquillisers or anti-depressants; it may therefore indicate a diagnosed depression.

Psychiatrist's report

Consider the following possible means of access to a psychiatrist at short notice:

1. Court duty scheme

Some courts have psychiatrists available at short notice. Transfers between courts may be desirable to gain access to a scheme.

2. Police referrals

Ascertain from the police details of any doctors or psychiatrists who saw the defendant in police custody.

3. Prison doctors

If the defendant has already spent a period in custody on remand, contact the prison medical staff for an opinion.

4. Private referral

If you seek a psychiatric opinion of your own accord, you will need a psychiatrist who is able to provide prompt assistance. You will wish to find a psychiatrist with relevant expertise and you may require him to provide a bed if hospital treatment is to be considered as an alternative to prison. Make contact first by telephone to explain the position and obtain an estimate of costs. Obtain your client's consent if possible and an extension of the Legal Aid Order to cover costs.

5. Court order

Generally, the court will not be in a position to order reports until after conviction, or hearing evidence sufficient to establish the act or omission charged was done. Note that under s.4 CJA 1991 the court will have an obligation to obtain a medical report if considering a custodial sentence for a defendant who is, or appears to be, mentally disordered.

Suicide risks

If you suspect your client is suicidal by reason of your own observations or those of the police, prosecution or family, consider with your client:

- where your client will be most or least at risk;
- an urgent need for psychiatric referral (you should be aware of the arrangements available at courts in your area);

- an urgent need to warn the police and prison authorities by telephone and in writing of the issue. Request prison medical authorities to consider the use of their suicide risk procedure;

- your ethical position and your relationship of confidentiality with your client.

This is a difficult area of potential conflict of duty. Seek the advice of a professional colleague and/or a psychiatrist in confidence. Keep careful notes.

Subject to the above, beware the 'false alarm' raised on some occasions by the prosecution in a bail application, which is vigorously denied by the defendant and contradicted by others, e.g. family doctor, etc.

WASTED COSTS

Wasted Costs Order against legal representatives: s.19A POA 1985

'Wasted costs' are defined as costs incurred by a party as a result of any improper, unreasonable or negligent act or omission on the part of any representative or employee of a representative or which the court considers it is unreasonable to expect that party to pay in the light of any such act or omission occurring after they were incurred: s.19A(3) POA 1985.

The wasted costs jurisdiction does not affect the duties which you owe to your client. It is a control on the way you carry out those duties.

A court intending to exercise the wasted costs jurisdiction must concisely formulate the complaint and grounds upon which such an order might be sought. It must consider:

- Has there been any improper, unreasonable or negligent act or omission?

- As a result, have any costs been incurred by a party?

- Should the court exercise its discretion to make an order? If so, what specific sum was involved?[3]

Further guidance was given by the Court of Appeal in *Ridehalgh* v. *Horsefield* [1994] 3 All ER 848:

- the key question will usually be whether the lawyer has been guilty of any 'improper or unreasonable or negligent act or omission' under s.51

Supreme Court Act 1981. Improper conduct is not confined to conduct which violates the letter of a professional code of ethics, and negligence is not confined to actionable breaches of the lawyer's duty to his own client;

- although advocates are immune from an action in negligence over the way in which they conduct cases in court, they can still be liable to a Wasted Costs Order. However, the courts should make full allowance for the fact that an advocate in court often has to make decisions quickly and under pressure. It is only when an advocate's conduct of proceedings is quite plainly unjustifiable that it could be appropriate to make a Wasted Costs Order against him;

- legal privilege is the client's, which he alone can waive. This can mean that lawyers are unable to tell the court the whole story. Judges should make full allowance for this. The lawyer is entitled to the benefit of any doubt;

- save in the most obvious cases, the court should be slow to initiate the enquiry whether a Wasted Costs order should be made. Applications for Wasted Costs Orders are generally best left to the end of the trial;

- no order can be made unless costs have actually been wasted as a result of the lawyer's conduct. If conduct was proved but no waste of costs was shown to have resulted, the court could do no more than refer the case to the professional body or the Legal Aid authorities;

- even if the court is satisfied that costs have been wasted as a result of the lawyer's conduct, the court is not bound to make an order. It should give sustainable reasons for its decision either way.

The power is thus to compensate, not punish; costs liable to be awarded are only those caused by the default. The amount of costs must be specified in the order.[4]

The representative must be allowed the opportunity of making representations before any order is made.[5]

The *Practice Direction* of 3 May 1991[6] indicates that hearings should normally take place in chambers. Because this may be difficult to arrange in a magistrates' court, consider requesting that the matter first be examined in writing.

Whilst the court cannot delegate its decision, it may be desirable for the clerk to the justices to make enquiries of the representative and inform the court of the outcome. A simple explanation may put right misunderstandings.

Notwithstanding the words in s.19A, a solicitor's first duty is to his lay client and the propriety or reasonableness of his conduct must be judged in the light of that paramount duty. A solicitor is under a duty to follow his client's lawful instructions.[7]

A legal representative should not be considered to be negligent because he acted for a party who pursued a claim which was bound to fail unless to do so amounted to an abuse of the process of the court. A competent advocate might take a point which is fairly arguable and is under a duty to do so if it is in the interests of his client. Ultimately, the test is whether the point taken is 'fairly arguable'.[8]

Any potential liability for negligent acts applies to the way you carry out your professional duty to promote and protect the best interests of your client. It does not impose any limitation on that duty. These issues must be examined without the benefit of hindsight and not from a prosecution viewpoint.

Your duty to your client to keep information about him confidential prevents you from revealing that information to any third party (including the court and the CPS) except to the extent that it is reasonably necessary where your conduct is under investigation. If your client is at risk, consider whether he should be separately advised and represented because of a possible conflict of interest between you.

A court may, if appropriate, postpone the making of a Wasted Costs Order to the end of a case if it appears more appropriate to do so because the likely amount is not readily calculable or the legal representative concerned is unable to make full representations because of a possible conflict with the duty to his client: *Practice Direction* 3 May 1991, para. 8.4.

These considerations will normally require any consideration of the making of a Wasted Costs Order to take place at the end of a trial (which in the case of a committal or transfer will be at the conclusion of the Crown Court proceedings).

An appeal against a Wasted Costs Order in the magistrates' court must go to the Crown Court within 21 days: reg. 3c.

A common problem is when a client on a serious charge, such as robbery, protests his innocence and instructs you to apply to the magistrates for bail. The client has numerous previous convictions and the court knows that he had absconded whilst on bail in the past. You are not surprised when the magistrates refuse bail.

The client is anxious to try again for bail as soon as possible and instructs you to apply to the Crown Court. You hesitate, you know that your client has a right to apply for bail but consider it a hopeless application. How would the court react? What if the court also regards this application as hopeless? Would you face a Wasted Costs Order for taking up the court's time unnecessarily? Should you consider your own position on receiving those instructions from the client?

The Law Society Criminal Law Committee's advice is that you act correctly by making the Crown Court application. On those clear instructions it is not improper, unreasonable or negligent and should not result in a Wasted Costs Order against you. You are under an obligation to carry our your client's instructions (unless they would involve you in an unlawful act or a breach of the rules of the professional conduct of solicitors) and to represent your client fearlessly. You should ensure that everything the client wishes to say is before the court, regardless of your personal opinion about its lack of merit or chances of success.

End notes

1 This requirement becomes redundant upon the implementation of the Access to Justice Act 1999.
2 In appropriate cases a solicitor may defer taking instructions until the prosecution case is known, but must not encourage a client to procrastinate before saying what his defence is: *R*. v. *McFarlane* (1999) *The Times* 24 March (CA).
3 See *Re A Barrister (Wasted Costs Order) (No. 1 of 1991)* [1992] 3 All ER 429.
4 reg. 3B(1).
5 reg. 3B(2).
6 para. 8.3 Practice Note (Criminal Costs) [1991] 2 All ER 924.
7 'We take the view that notwithstanding the words in s.19, the solicitor's first duty is to his lay client and the propriety or reasonableness of his conduct must be judged in the light of that paramount duty. If he (the solicitor) is instructed to ask for a witness, whether this witness comes from Halifax or abroad, the solicitor is under a duty to act in accordance with his client's interest and he is under a duty to follow his lay client's instructions. At the end of the day the interest of the lay client is paramount and if there is a conflict between the two (the interests of the court and the interests of the client) it seems that in accordance with the best legal tradition, the first duty is to the client and any other duty takes second place: *per* HHJ Atkinson (see Criminal Practitioners Newsletter, July 1992).
8 *Per* Aldous LJ, *Sampson* v. *John Boddy Timber* (1995) *The Independent*, 17 May, CA.

CHAPTER 5

Obtaining core information

In every case which proceeds beyond the police station you must obtain core information about your client. This will inform your decision making and representations and will become particularly significant in the event of a conviction or plea of guilty.

STATEMENT OF PERSONAL HISTORY

File reference number

This should be at the top of the statement. Each case should have a separate file and reference number.

Date

This is the date that you took or updated the statement.

Personal details

1. NAME [1.1]

   Make sure that your client has identified himself correctly. Include the name at birth.

2. ADDRESS [1.2]

   You will need to find out a little about the address: how long has he been living there; who does he live with there; and is he a tenant/licensee/owner/guest or squatter?

3. DETAILS OF BAIL OR CUSTODY AND NEXT COURT HEARING

4. DATE OF BIRTH AND AGE [1.4]; PLACE OF BIRTH

5. MARRIED/COHABITING/SINGLE/SEPARATED OR DIVORCED [1.6]

6. CHILDREN AND OTHER DEPENDANTS, AGES AND RELATIONSHIP TO YOUR CLIENT [1.7]

7. NATIONAL INSURANCE NUMBER [1.5]

8. EDUCATION

   (a) Is your client studying for exams?
   (b) What is his attendance record?
   (c) What are his school reports like?
   (d) What are his career plans?
   (e) Has he changed schools, or left unexpectedly?

9. WORK, TRAINING AND EMPLOYMENT

   (a) Find out what training schemes, apprenticeships or day release courses your client has taken part in.
   (b) Set out the different jobs your client has had in chronological order. Number them, and specify reasons for leaving and periods of unemployment between jobs.
   (c) Give the dates of starting and finishing jobs and when he was promoted.
   (d) If your client is not in permanent employment, how much of the year is he usually working for?
   (e) If your client is unemployed, what are his job prospects?

10. EARNINGS [1.8]

    Find out the family's total weekly income[1] and source of that income, including state benefits, so that this can be compared with weekly outgoings. Does your client require welfare benefits advice? [1.10]

11. EXPENSES

    List these, also on a weekly[2] basis, setting them out one under the other: rent/mortgage; electricity, gas and telephone bills; travel to work and back and meals at work; hire purchase, catalogues, credit card and bank/finance house loan repayments (including how much is still outstanding and what the goods are); council tax; water rates; car running expenses (including petrol, oil, tyres, maintenance, tax and insurance); clothes, food and other household shopping; and if currently paying fines to a court, the amount and frequency of payments and the amount outstanding.

12. SAVINGS AND DEBTS

Take your client's instructions on what weekly^3 rate a fine could be paid at. Advise your client that the offer must be realistic and it should not normally take longer than 12 months to pay. What is the amount of capital owned by your client? [1.9]

13. HEALTH

(a) If your client has a medical condition:
   (i)   what is the nature of it? [36.1] [90.1]
   (ii) what is the effect of it on your client? [36.2] [90.2]

(b) Go into detail if your client has a drink, drugs or psychiatric problem. You will want to know when and in what circumstances the problem started, when it was at its worst, and what it was like then, what stage it is at now, and what your client is doing to cure himself.
   (i)   find out the relationship, if any, between your client's condition and his offending.
   (ii) has your client consulted his GP or a consultant about it? Has your client received any treatment? Is he receiving medication for it?
   (iii) note any details and obtain your client's signed authority to obtain a medical report [67.1] [90.3].
   (iv) record the name and address of your client's doctor and/or consultant [36.4].

14. INTERESTS, ESPECIALLY CHARITABLE WORK

15. FAMILY BACKGROUND

Find out anything in your client's family background which may help you understand why he committed the offence if he pleads guilty or is convicted, e.g. problems with parents; matrimonial difficulties; difficulty in forming relations, etc.

16. PAST RECORD [32.3]

Obtain a copy of his past record from the prosecution. This should always be obtained as the details of dates can be significant. If the record includes prison sentences you may require additional verified information on time of remand or date of release and any time lost or recalled to prison.

Check with your client:

(a) If you obtain the details from your client find out the dates he was sentenced, the courts which sentenced him, the facts of the offences and the sentences and whether your client pleaded guilty or was found guilty.
(b) If your client is in breach of a court order, take instructions in some detail about the circumstances of the offence for which that order was imposed.
(c) Check whether time was spent on remand.
(d) If the present charge is similar to any of your client's previous offences you will need to have sufficient information about them to attempt to distinguish them.

17. OTHER PENDING CHARGES [32.2]

(a) Ask about other courts your client is due to appear in; when; what he is accused of; what his conditions of bail are; what stage the proceedings have reached; and who represents your client.
(b) If your client is represented by other solicitors, ask if he would prefer them to represent him in this case as well, and whether your client would like the cases consolidated if possible.

18. IF YOUR CLIENT IS UNDER 17 OR HAS A MENTAL DISORDER

(a) What is the name and contact details of the appropriate adult? [31.1]
(b) What is the relationship of the adult to your client? [31.2]

19. IF YOUR CLIENT IS INVOLVED WITH A SOCIAL WORKER/PROBATION OFFICER

What is the name and contact details of the social worker/probation officer?

20. PRESENT CHARGE/PLEA

(a) State what each charge is in detail [33.1]. Identify whether it is indictable either-way or summary only.
(b) Summarise the allegation [33.2] and establish any connection between the charges.
(c) Once a decision has been made, say what your client will plead, or that he is unsure.

21. ETHNIC ORIGIN: WHITE/BLACK/ASIAN/OTHER

End notes

1 If it is more convenient for a particular client to express this on a different time basis, e.g. monthly, this should be done, but the same period used consistently for the collection of all information.
2 *Ibid.*
3 *Ibid.*

CHAPTER 6

Shaping the case in the police station

PREPARATION IN THE POLICE STATION

Work done in the police station plays a critical part in the later handling of criminal cases. You should be fully conversant with the Codes of Practice under PACE 1984 and consider the effect of every step taken by you at the police station in the context of its eventual outcome and a possible trial.

Your duty is to obtain the best result for each client and you must balance the risks involved particularly in advising whether or not your client should answer questions in interview:

- you should made a full record of information obtained, advice given, reasons for the advice, and representations;

- you should take a pro-active approach to obtaining information from the police, and considering the legality of the arrest and detention;

- you should advise that your client does not provide evidence which strengthens a prosecution case;

- you should take appropriate steps to avoid inferences from silence and understand the difference between s.34 CJPOA 1994 on the one hand and ss.36 and 37 on the other;

- you should consider the need to give early evidence of matters relevant to the defence:

  - because they weaken or undermine the prosecution case; and may therefore require primary disclosure of unused material;

  - because they make the defence more credible;

  - because they provide grounds (where a case will be proved) to avoid prosecution or to mitigate its effects.

Detailed advice on these issues is contained in *Police Station Skills for Legal Advisers* and *Active Defence* (both published by the Law Society).

Evidential consequences

You should consider the evidential consequences of each step you or your client takes at the police station.

Privilege

When you have been at the police station you are a competent and compellable witness in relation to all that took place. You should maintain good records to assist in recollecting details. However, at trial you may not answer questions about the instructions your client gave you in order to obtain advice, or the advice you give, unless your client waives or has waived privilege. Be aware that serious consequences at trial may follow the giving of reasons for advising silence which arose from a privileged meeting: privilege may be waived[1] and the prosecution able to examine your notes.

Consider ways of overcoming this.

Record-keeping

It is essential to keep proper records: if the suspect remains silent on your recommendation, the court may still infer guilt. Therefore it may be necessary to make sure that the court understands the circumstances which led you to advise the suspect to remain silent. This means you have to keep full, clear contemporaneous timed notes of the prevailing circumstances and the advice which you gave so that you can:

- refer to them;
- produce them in court if necessary and privilege is waived.

Keep careful note of:

- the physical and mental state of the suspect;
- the general conduct of the police and the 'atmosphere' in which the investigation is being conducted;
- representations made by you at all stages and the reasons for them;
- what information is made available by the police to you;

- what requests for information are made of the police by you;

- what information is given to you by the suspect;

- the suspect's apparent understanding of the significance of the allegation, and the significance of his replies or failure to respond;

- the advice given by you to the suspect, and the reasons for that advice;

- what was said at the time of charge/report for summons.

Confidential advice

In order properly to fulfil your role you need access to suitable facilities which recognise the need for both confidentiality and your safety. Home Office Circular 24/98 (see Appendix 9) advises Chief Constables that 'delays in court may be avoided by ensuring that conditions are right for a solicitor to take confidential instructions from a detainee at the police station'.

Interviews

You will advise on one of three ways in which your client should handle any interview with the police. You should take sufficient time to advise your client because of the evidential consequences of each:

- making no comment. This will have evidential consequences when an inference can be drawn under CJPOA 1994;

- preparing a statement with your client. This may be used at the police station, to weaken or negative any inference from silence at charge, or held back to use if required at trial. It is a self-serving statement and so does not at present prove the truth of its contents.[2] It may, however, be used should the prosecution allege a recent fabrication, attack the credibility of the defendant or seek to draw an inference from silence in interview;

- answering proper and relevant questions. Be aware that answering some relevant questions but not others will result in the whole interview being heard by the court. If your client makes some admissions but also makes some denials then the whole statement is evidence of the truth of its contents and later will serve, for instance, to put the prosecution on notice of general defences such as self-defence and duress so that it must disprove them at trial.

REPRESENTATIONS AS TO EVIDENCE

The making of appropriate representations in the police station can play a critical part at trial. In particular they can affect:

- a court's decision whether to draw/allow the jury to draw appropriate inferences;

- a court's decision whether there has been oppression or whether by reason of something said or done, a confession is unreliable;[3]

- the court's decision whether it is unfair in the proceedings to admit evidence.[4]

You will consider representations at least in the following areas.

Disclosure

The prosecution must prove a *prima facie* case and you will need to be persuaded that there will be evidence which is admissible and available at trial to achieve that purpose. You should make representations if you consider that the extent of disclosure makes it impossible for you to give useful advice.[5] No one may be convicted on an inference from silence alone[6] and this enables you to negotiate for greater disclosure.

Suspect's circumstances

Be aware that in deciding whether it is reasonable for a suspect to mention facts before an inference can be drawn under s.34 the court will have regard to the defendant's:

- age;
- experience of the criminal justice process;
- mental capacity;
- state of health;
- sobriety;
- tiredness;
- personality; and
- to the time of day.[7]

Be prepared to raise relevant issues even if a doctor has decided that your client is fit for interview.

Police conduct

This will apply particularly to the legality of the arrest and detention and conduct during interview. Be aware that the court will hear your representations if they are made on tape and they should therefore be put in a professional way.

Searches and samples

If you do not consider that the relevant statutory criteria have been met be prepared to make representations accordingly and where consent is required advise your client on the arguments for and against giving that consent. Where consent is not required you are unlikely to change the view of the relevant police officer but if your representations were correct you may succeed in excluding evidence at trial.

Sufficiency of evidence

Consider making representations that no interview should take place where your client wishes to make no comment and there is sufficient evidence to charge. Particularly where there is direct police evidence that an offence has been committed, it may be unlawful for an interview to take place.[8]

Identity procedures

In appropriate cases and with the client's agreement seek a parade (even if there has been a street identification – a refusal to agree may exclude the street identification at trial if that identification was not full and complete and a parade may serve a useful purpose).[9]

Be prepared to justify a parade ahead of a group identification; a group ahead of a video identification; and any procedure ahead of a confrontation. The identification officer may not be persuaded, but you may have the less good procedure excluded at trial if it produces evidence against your client.

REPRESENTATIONS AS TO OUTCOME

You should address a number of relevant issues whilst at the police station as follows.

No further action

Consider the strength of the evidence and make appropriate representations.

Bail to return

In appropriate cases consider seeking bail for your client whilst enquiries continue. Conditions may not be placed on such bail.

Diversion: those 18 and over [10]

Can you persuade the police to caution rather than charge your client? Approach the issue with care. A caution is for many purposes the equivalent of a conviction. It can result in an entry on the Sex Offenders Register, the making of a Sex Offender Order, and a disclosable record at the National Records Office. Cautions are never spent under the Rehabilitation of Offenders Act 1974.[11] Home Office Circular 18/1994 (Appendix 10) gives advice to Chief Constables. There must be evidence of the offender's guilt sufficient to give a realistic prospect of conviction and the offender must admit the offence. By supplying information to the police about the offence and making representations to reduce its gravity, it may be possible to persuade the custody officer to consider cautioning rather than charging your client.

Guide to case disposal

Consistency of case disposal within and amongst police forces in England and Wales has come a significant step nearer, with the introduction of a nationwide case disposal system.

With the declared aim of being more open internally about how the police assess cases and deal with suspects, a *Guide to Case Disposal* has been developed nationally which advises police officers on the preferred disposal option for particular offences and offenders.

Although content that solicitors could be given the level of information about it contained in this guide, it otherwise remains a confidential document for internal police use.

The scheme is made up of specific gravity factors, which relate to offences, and general gravity factors which relate to offenders and victims. These are then applied to five possible disposal options.

1. Low gravity: formal warning or not proceeded with.

2.   High probability of a caution: the decision maker needs to be able to justify the decision not to caution.

3.   Medium gravity: pivotal – the particular circumstances of offences and the offender, and any aggravating or mitigating factors, will determine whether the disposal moves up or down.

4.   High probability of prosecution: the decision maker needs to be able to justify the decision not to prosecute.

5.   High gravity: in normal circumstances the offender will always be prosecuted (mitigating gravity factors are unlikely to affect the decision to prosecute).

Assaults span the disposal options, ranging from common assault (option 3: pivotal), through ABH, s.20 GBH and assault with intent to resist arrest (option 4: high probability of prosecution) to wounding with intent (option 5: always prosecute in normal circumstances).

Kerb crawling is allotted disposal option number 2: high probability of a caution. Aggravating factors specific to that offence (nuisance or annoyance caused to innocent women/children in the neighbourhood; residential areas affected) and mitigating factors (no innocent people affected) can make the offence more or less serious.

Possession of any class of drug is allotted disposal option number 3: pivotal. Aggravating factors are that the quantity was not small or the offender was involved in other criminal activity to feed his habit.

There are separate sets of specific gravity factors for crime, traffic and licensing offences. Dropping litter is the only criminal offence allotted disposal option 1.

There are separate gravity factors – those common to all offences – for criminal and traffic offences. Criminal offence factors reflect the likely penalty, the impact on the victim; the attitude of the offender; his recent relevant offending history; his state of health; premeditation; whether he was in a position of trust; whether a weapon was used; the prevalence of the offence; provocation; reparation undertaken and so on. An aggravating factor is if an offender of the age of 18 years or over received a caution or warning less than three years ago (less than 12 months ago if the offender is under 18 years).

The presence of these factors must be considered and, if significant, can change the decision that would otherwise have been made, up or down. The guidance stresses that the system is designed for flexibility and allows for discretion at all stages: 'The mechanical adding or subtracting of gravity numbers is not part of the scheme.' The application of gravity factors may mean that the original grading remains the same or moves a lot. Every case disposal decision and the reasons for making it must be recorded.

Diversion: those under 18

Ss.65, 66 Crime and Disorder Act 1998: the final warning scheme

In 2000–2001, the final warning scheme will replace cautions for children and young people. Both informal warnings and formal cautions are abolished but cautions will continue for adults. A scheme is already in force on a pilot basis in some areas.[12]

Cautions will be replaced with a statutory police reprimand and final warning scheme. Once a young offender has received a warning a further offence will usually result in a criminal charge.

You should make representations as to whether formal action is necessary.

One previous caution is equivalent to a reprimand. Two or more previous cautions are equivalent to a warning.

The first step is to decide what offence is supported by the evidence and is likely to be charged unless a reprimand or warning is given.

The decision to issue a reprimand or a warning must be based on that offence, and not on any technically possible offence.

All four of the following criteria must be met before a reprimand or warning can be considered:

- *there is evidence against the young person to give a realistic prospect of conviction if he is prosecuted;*

- *the young person admits the offence. The Crime and Disorder Act has abolished the presumption that a child is 'doli incapax'. In cases where an offence is committed by a juvenile under the age of 14, it is therefore no longer necessary to establish that the young person knew what he did was seriously wrong;*

- *the young person has not previously been convicted of an offence (remember that a conditional or absolute discharge is not a conviction, and to keep confidential convictions of which the police are unaware);*[13] *and*

- *it is not in the public interest for the young person to be prosecuted.*

Once the officer dealing with the case believes that all the above criteria are satisfied, a decision can be taken as to whether a reprimand, warning or charge is the most appropriate disposal, taking into account the following:

- *first-time offenders should normally receive a reprimand for a less serious offence;*

- *first-time offenders should normally receive a warning for a more serious offence;*

- *second-time offenders who have been reprimanded previously cannot be given a further reprimand – they should normally receive a warning;*

- *second-time offenders who have received a warning should not receive a further warning and should be charged. The only exception is where the new offence is committed more than two years after the date of the previous warning and the offence is not so serious as to require a charge to be brought, having regard to the circumstances;*

- *those offending for the fourth time, or more, cannot receive a reprimand or warning in any circumstances. They must be charged.*

The key factors, which will be relevant in deciding whether to charge, warn or reprimand a young offender for an offence, are:

- *the seriousness of the offence; and*

- *the young offender's offending history.*

The seriousness of the offence relates to both the nature of the offence and to the circumstances which surround it.

The seriousness of an offence is crucial to decisions as to whether:

- *a first offence warrants a warning rather than a reprimand;*

- *a second or third offence which is committed more than two years after the issue of a final warning warrants charging.*

The police officer will have regard to gravity factors developed by ACPO to assist him to assess the seriousness of the offence.[14]

There is no precise definition of seriousness, as each case must be considered on its individual facts, taking into account the circumstances of the offender, including any aggravating or mitigating factors relating to the offence.

The age and maturity of the offender will be of relevance in most cases, and other general factors, which can affect the decision on how to proceed, may include the following.

74

Mitigating factors:

- *a genuine mistake or misunderstanding;*

- *loss or harm is minor;*

- *provocation from the victim, or the victim's group;*

- *influence by others more criminally sophisticated;*

- *expression or regret, or offer of reparation.*

Aggravating factors:

- *offender is ringleader or organiser of offence;*

- *evidence of premeditation;*

- *offence motivated by discrimination against victim's ethnic origin, religious beliefs, gender, political views or sexual orientation;*

- *the victim was particularly vulnerable, or suffered considerable fear, personal attack, or damage or disturbance.*

Reprimands and warnings should never be used for the most serious indictable-only offences such as rape and murder, and only in exceptional circumstances for other indictable-only offences, regardless of the age or previous record of the young person.

One example of such exceptional circumstances might be a child taking another's pocket-money by force (robbery in law), if the specific circumstances show that the violence was minor, that there is remorse, and that there is little likelihood of repetition.

Other offences, less grave in themselves, may nevertheless be too serious for a reprimand or warning to be appropriate, even where there is no statutory bar to using one.

If a first offence is not so serious as to warrant a warning yet a police officer considers that professional help is required the young person should be referred immediately to the youth offending team or to an appropriate local agency or scheme for advice and help.

A reprimand or warning should be given in person by a police officer, of the rank of inspector or above.

As this is not always practicable, a sergeant or a constable with special training in this work may also administer the warning/reprimand.

Where the young person is aged under 17, the reprimand or warning must be given in the presence of a parent or guardian or other appropriate adult, and any written information, must also be issued to the adult.

The term 'appropriate adult' has the same meaning here as in PACE 1984.

The police officer should issue the reprimand or warning orally. This should always be supplemented with written information which explains clearly the implications of the reprimand or warning.

A warning leads to a referral to a youth offending team for assessment and participation in a rehabilitation programme if considered relevant, to rehabilitate the offender, change his behaviour and prevent him from re-offending.

Where a warning is given for a non-recordable offence, the young person, the police officer and, where applicable, the appropriate adult must sign a form at the point the warning is given to confirm that all parties agree that the warning was administered for the offence(s) indicated.

This form will be important in any subsequent proceedings as the court will need to know of any previous warning (whether for a recordable or non-recordable offence) because of the restrictions on the availability of conditional discharge in these circumstances.

If an offence is committed within two years of a warning, the court shall not order a conditional discharge unless exceptional circumstances justify its doing so – this is an added incentive to a person to stay out of trouble as they will face more significant punishment.

For any record of an offence to be cited in court, there must be proof. In respect of warnings for recordable offences, this proof is supplied by finger-prints. In respect of warnings for non-recordable offences, the proof will be provided by the signed form.

All reprimands and warnings for all offences should be recorded as soon as possible after they are administered.

This may mean chief officers prioritising record keeping in relation to cases involving juveniles.

Records of reprimand and warnings will need to be obtained for up to seven years, to ensure the effective operation of the scheme (which applies to young people aged 10–17 inclusive and which will affect those aged 18 and 19 if they appear before a court within two years of receiving a warning). In future therefore:

- *the record of a young person who receives a reprimand or warning aged 10 or 11 must be kept, even in the absence of further offending behaviour, until he turns 17;*

- *other records can be shredded after five years, in the normal way, in the absence of further offending behaviour.*

The legislation provides that reprimands, warnings and failures to participate in a rehabilitation programme may be cited in court in the same circumstances as convictions. In practice, this means that they should be made available to the court.

Unless different agreements are negotiated locally, it is the responsibility of the police to provide the information on records of failure to comply with rehabilitation programmes via the CPS to the courts in any future proceedings, alongside information on antecedents (previous reprimands, warnings and convictions).

Breach of a rehabilitation programme carries no sanction. Failure to comply may be taken into account in sentencing.

There is only one exception to the rule that reprimands and warnings replace cautions, and that is in respect of prostitutes' caution.

In such cases, the initial response will be the prostitutes' caution. Unlike a reprimand or final warning, this does not depend on a admission of guilt. A prostitutes' caution should be accompanied by a specific warning that she will be treated as an offender if the behaviour continues.

REPRESENTATIONS AS TO LEVEL OF CHARGE

You may be able to persuade the police to charge your client with a lesser offence.

If you are satisfied that there is sufficient evidence to charge and convict your client, it may be worth considering giving information to the police about the offence and making representations to persuade the officer to charge your client with a lesser offence.

Charging standards

Guidelines are available, which have been agreed between the CPS and the police, for some types of offences. Under these charging standards you may be able to argue for a lesser charge. Charging standards have been published for driving offences (March 1996), offences against the person (April 1996), and public order offences (April 1996).

Charging standards are agreed criteria upon which the police will charge and the CPS will prosecute. The agreed criteria will enable a custody officer to charge a defendant with the appropriate charge at the earliest opportunity. This is intended to reduce the number of occasions when the CPS changes a charge upon review of the papers and should provide greater consistency and speedier disposal of cases. As public documents, the charging standards are enforceable by judicial review. However, they allow for some flexibility in charging and they are not intended to be prescriptive or to take precedence over the Code for Crown Prosecutors (see Appendix 14).

Driving offences charging standard

The standard sets out an approach to areas of law in which some categories of driving may be prosecuted for a number of different offences. The charging standard links these different categories to particular offences, ensuring greater consistency in charging practice throughout England and Wales.

The charging standard focuses on the following driving offences:

- careless/inconsiderate driving;
- dangerous driving;
- causing death by careless driving when under the influence of drink or drugs;
- causing death by dangerous driving;
- manslaughter; and
- causing bodily harm by wanton or furious driving, etc.

Guidance is provided on the sorts of driving which constitute each of these offences. Specific examples are given, though it is important that these are read in context. The objective test for carelessness and dangerousness is emphasised and factors are identified which are irrelevant when deciding whether or not an act of driving was careless or dangerous, such as the age/experience of the driver, or the death of any person. The charging standard also emphasises that it is important to put the facts of the case in the context of the circumstances in which the driving took place. Driving which is not criminal in some circumstances may amount to careless or dangerous driving in other circumstances. For example, driving which is lawful in good weather may become careless or dangerous in bad weather.

The following are examples of driving, given in the charging standard, which may support an allegation of careless driving when caused by more than momentary inattention and where the safety of road users is affected:

- overtaking on the inside;

- driving inappropriately close to another vehicle;

- driving through a red light; and

- emerging from a side road into the path of another vehicle.

The following are examples of driving, given in the charging standard, which may support an allegation of dangerous driving:

- racing or competitive driving;

- prolonged, persistent and deliberate bad driving;

- speed which is highly inappropriate for the prevailing road or traffic conditions; and

- overtaking which could not have been carried out safely.

The standard contains guidance on the approach to be taken in road traffic fatality cases when there is a family or close relationship between the deceased and the accused driver, often referred to as 'nearest and dearest' cases, and reflects guidance that has evolved since at least the mid-1970s. In general, this approach means that in certain cases a charge should be preferred which does not include death as an ingredient, e.g. dangerous driving and not causing death by dangerous driving.

Offences against the person charging standard

The offences against the person charging standard lists, for example, the injuries which should normally be prosecuted under s.47 OAP rather than s.39 CJA 1988 (common assault):

- loss or breaking of tooth or teeth;

- temporary loss of sensory functions (may include loss of consciousness);

- extensive or multiple bruising;

- displaced broken nose;

- minor fractures;

- minor, but not merely superficial, cuts of a sort probably requiring medical treatment (e.g. stitches);

- psychiatric injury which is more than fear, distress or panic (such injury will be proved by appropriate expert evidence).

Public order charging standard

The public order charging standard offers advice on general principles of charging practice and on a series of specific offences including:

- riot;

- violent disorder;

- affray;

- ss.4, 4A and 5 Public Order Act 1986;

- racially motivated crimes;

- subsidiary offences.

REPRESENTATIONS TO THE CPS

It may be possible to influence the decisions which police officers make by persuading them to seek advice from Crown Prosecutors, either present at an ASU or at the CPS branch.

This would help to:

- get the charge right;

- terminate weak cases early;

- save police resources: not going for lost causes.

You may need to help the officer to identify a case in which advice should be sought.

National guidelines[15] give examples of when the police are likely to need to seek advice, e.g.

- when difficult questions of evidence occur, such as hearsay, similar fact, corroboration;

- when there is a contested identification or possible breaches of PACE;

- when foreseeable defences are likely to cause difficulty;

- where the defendant was acting in self-defence or defending another or property;

- where there are a large number of suspects and possible offences;

- where there has been a use of surveillance, an informant or an *agent provocateur*;

- where there are complex disclosure issues, such as evidence in the hands of third parties.

Any advice given will be put in writing and an advice file opened by the CPS.

If a case file is later produced, the written advice will be put in that file.

REPRESENTATIONS FOLLOWING CHARGE

Bail

You should make appropriate representations including the offering of suitable bail conditions. A client appearing on bail has significant advantages in the later handling of the case.

Facts

It may be possible to agree with the police how the factual background to the charge will be explained. This may avoid a Newton hearing.

Procedure

If your client is to be charged, certain factors will determine the future course of the case:

- whether the first hearing is:
    - an EFH with a designated caseworker (DCW);
    - an EAH;
    - an EFH with a Crown Prosecutor;
    - a normal court with a full bench.

81

- what type of police file is prepared:
  - a remand file;
  - an expedited file;
  - a full file;
- what funding is available:
  - a 'duty solicitor of choice' may represent the defendant and be paid as a duty solicitor at an EFH or EAH only;
- which procedure is followed;
  - s.51 indictable-only, sent to Crown Court;
  - plea before venue/committal proceedings available.

For further details about these procedures see Chapter 14.

End notes

1 *R. v. Condron* [1997] Crim LR 215; *R. v. Bowden* [1999] 1 WLR 823.
2 But *cf. R. v. Western* [1997] 1 Cr App R 478 (*per* Butterfield J).
3 s.76 PACE.
4 s.78 PACE.
5 *R. v. Roble* [1977] Crim LR 449.
6 s.38 CJPOA 1994.
7 *R. v. Argent* [1997] Crim LR 346.
8 *R. v. Pointer* [1997] Crim LR 676; *R. v. Gayle* [1999] Crim LR 502 but *cf. R. v. McGuiness* [1999] Crim LR 318; the mere existence of a *prima facie* case is not enough.
9 *R. v. Popat* [1998] Cr App R 208.
10 Until the full implementation of CDA 1998 those provisions apply to offenders of all ages. In the case of a juvenile offender, officers are reminded that if the option is 'pivotal' or 'high probability of prosecution', a file must be sent to the Youth Referrals Office to determine the final case disposal.
11 The Government is currently reviewing this position.
12 The final warning scheme is being piloted in the London Boroughs of Hammersmith and Fulham, Kensington and Chelsea, and the City of Westminster, Hampshire, Southampton and Portsmouth (jointly); Wolverhampton, Sheffield and Blackburn.
13 If the police officer expressly asks your client whether he has a previous conviction, you should advise your client that if he lies in his answer you will have to withdraw from representing him.
14 The gravity factors for those over 17 appear on pages 71–2.
15 *Manual of Guidance for the Preparation, Processing and Submission of Files.*

CHAPTER 7

Funding the case

LEGAL AID

You are not required to advise, assist or represent a client unless and until appropriate funding is in place. You must consider whether he is eligible for legal aid and give appropriate advice.[1]

The *Legal Aid Handbook* has been published annually by Sweet & Maxwell. It was prepared by the Legal Aid Board and was an indispensable guide for those seeking legal aid. It contained not only the relevant legislation and regulations, but also notes for guidance issued by the Board. It is about to be replaced by the Legal Services Commission's manual. The Board's quarterly newsletter *Focus* also contains essential updating material. LAFQAS requires that the newsletter is available for reference by your fee-earning staff.

Police station and duty solicitor at court

Advice in the police station and from a duty solicitor in court is available free of charge to all suspects and defendants in the circumstances prescribed by the Legal Aid Board.

Defence representation at Early First Hearings (EFHs) and Early Administrative Hearings (EAHs)

1. The court duty solicitor will be available, or

2. Defendants can be represented by any other solicitor of their choice:

    (a) by obtaining an adjournment (the solicitor is not available or legal aid is being applied for);

    (b) who is available at court and legal aid has been granted; or

    (c) who is currently a duty solicitor on any court or police station scheme or is a solicitor who is also a duty solicitor representative (called the 'duty solicitor of choice') to the extent that a court duty solicitor could assist.[2]

Payment for the 'duty solicitor of choice' will be made under contract or at the court duty solicitor rate. Reasonable travel will also be payable. (Area offices will be given guidance on claims from 'duty solicitors of choice' who will be asked to justify why local duty solicitor agents were not instructed.)

'Duty solicitors of choice' will be entitled to claim waiting time, paid at the same rate as advice and representation under the court duty scheme.

Duty solicitors of choice are paid to advise and represent defendants at any subsequent EFH or EAH even though they have already advised at a previous hearing.

It is possible for other solicitors to apply for a Legal Aid Order. If a defendant wishes to apply for legal aid at the EFH to be represented by his own solicitor, then it is a matter for the court, in exercising its discretion, applying the normal interests of justice test, to decide whether an adjournment is appropriate and whether to grant legal aid.

Duty Solicitors/ABWOR

Where ABWOR is available it may only be granted when it is in the interests of justice to do so and it is reasonable for the individual applicant to receive ABWOR.

Anti-Social Behaviour Orders/Sex Offender Orders

The legal advice and assistance scheme is available in the usual way for the provision of initial advice (subject to financial eligibility), although it is not usual for the costs limit to be extended.

The scope of the duty solicitor scheme in magistrates' courts has been extended to enable the duty solicitor to provide advice, assistance and representation, where appropriate, where an application is made for an Anti-Social Behaviour Order (ASBO), or Sex Offender Order (SOO), or to vary or discharge such orders. Duty solicitors are not precluded from appearing in a contested hearing because these are civil proceedings.

ABWOR is, in appropriate cases, also available. An application for ABWOR should be submitted to the Board prior to the first hearing on Form APP4 unless delegated franchise powers can be used.

For ABWOR a separate financial eligibility test applies. A costs limitation must be imposed. ABWOR may be refused for hearings in magistrates' courts where it appears unreasonable or it is not in the interests of justice.

ABWOR should be granted in preference to duty solicitors in magistrates' courts where a case raises complicated issues of fact, law or procedure, e.g:

- application – individual suffering from mental disorder;
- contested ASBO hearing involving disputed evidence from a professional witness;
- contested ASBO hearing raising statutory defence of reasonableness;
- contested ASBO hearing against a group of named individuals.

The length of the hearing may mean it is unsuitable for a duty solicitor, e.g.:

- application contested and evidence to be called;
- adjournment necessary.

Consider also whether the drafting of an ASBO/SOO does not require assistance under ABWOR.

An appeal against the making of an ASBO/SOO is to the Crown Court. ABWOR is available (but not under delegated powers).

Parenting Orders

For parenting orders:

- legal advice and assistance is available for initial advice;
- when an ASBO or SOO has been made in respect of a child, or a child/ young person is convicted of an offence in the youth or adult magistrates' court:
    - Board granted ABWOR is available (franchise powers cannot be used); or
    - the duty solicitor available in the magistrates' court may provide advice and representation;
- where a child has been convicted of an offence in the Crown Court:
    - Board granted ABWOR alone is available.

Legal advice and assistance

The appropriate application form should always be signed if your client is eligible, so as to cover all the work prior to the grant of the Legal Aid Order.

Your claim is initially limited to the equivalent of two hours' preparation work, but you can consider an extension if necessary.

Whether or not your client is eligible for advice and assistance, you can claim for work done before the date of the Legal Aid Order under regulation 44(7) of the Legal Aid in Criminal and Care Proceedings (General) Regulations 1989. This requires work to be deemed to be done under a Legal Aid Order in the following circumstances:

- the interests of justice required that the representation or advice be provided as a matter of urgency;

- there was no undue delay in making an application for legal aid;

- the representation or advice was given by the solicitor who was subsequently assigned under the Legal Aid Order.

Completing the legal aid forms

Take immediate steps, when a defendant first comes to your office, to apply for legal aid. Do not delay doing this until you have the time to take instructions at a formal appointment.

In your application for magistrates' court legal aid you should take particular care when answering the questions asking why it is in the interests of justice that legal aid should be granted. Be familiar with the relevant law and general and local policies: see the Guidance on the Interests of Justice Test for the Grant of Legal Aid in Appendix 14 and *Part 2, Criminal Legal Aid: A Guide to Eligibility* (Lord Chancellor's Department, 10/97) set out in Appendix 15.

The forms

Complete the legal aid application form carefully and include details under each relevant heading. The fullest possible information should be given in response to each question in the form to avoid the possibility of the application being refused on the basis of inadequate information. In a complex case, a supporting letter describing the difficulties in some detail may be appropriate. You may wish to send a copy of the completed form to your client, asking him to check it for accuracy.

CASE DETAILS

Q.2(a) Describe briefly what it is you are accused of doing, e.g. 'stealing £50 from my employer', 'kicking a door causing £50 damage'.		For court use only

Make sure that the information you give accurately reflects the seriousness of the charge against the defendant.

CO-DEFENDANTS/CONFLICTS

Q.2(b) The following other person(s) is/are charged in this case. Q.2(c) Give reasons why you and the other persons charged in this case, if any, should not be represented by the same solicitor.		

Legal aid may have already been granted to another firm for a co-accused. Complete this part of the form with details of conflicts or other reasons for separate representation. The issue of conflict is a live one throughout the case and the service of prosecution evidence may disclose conflicts between defendants; be prepared to act on this and inform the court of any developments which require an amendment of the Legal Aid Order.

Conflict of evidence: if defendants disagree on their presence and/or involvement, consider separate representation. There may be a reason other than conflict why a co-accused requires separate representation by you. You may, for example, be representing him already in other cases and it is likely that he will be sentenced for all outstanding matters together, or you may hold particularly detailed information about the client from an earlier case.

Conflict as to personal circumstances: defendants with different personal backgrounds or histories of offending should be treated with care. Your duty is to act in your client's best interest. Consider whether representing one client could lead you to be critical of another. Consider separate representation or the use of more than one advocate.

A detailed contemporaneous note as to the reasons for the use of more than one advocate will assist to justify your decision.

Reasons for wanting legal aid

Q.7(a) It is likely that I will lose my liberty *(You should consider seeing a solicitor before answering this question.)*		For court use only

Consider whether the court is likely to deprive the accused of his liberty on conviction, e.g.:

1. Seriousness of charge(s):

    (a) violent or sexual offences;
    (b) breach of trust;
    (c) extent of injuries or losses.

    A court may aggregate all the offending for the purpose of assessing seriousness and this may have the result of taking the offender past the custody threshold.

2. Seriousness factors:

    (a) planned; organised teams; adult involving children; committed over period; casting suspicion on others; sophisticated; deliberately frightening others; group offence; soiling; ransacking; ram-raiding; organiser or distributor; stolen to order; special equipment; gross disregard for police authority; vulnerable victim; victim public servant; offender in position of authority; weapon; people put in fear; busy public place; commercial production and/or cultivation.

    See the 'seriousness indicators (aggravating and mitigating factors)' in *The Magistrates' Association Sentencing Guidelines* (see Appendix 16) and consider the 'Features relevant to individual offences' in the *Mode of Trial Guidelines* at Appendix 17. Note also racial aggravation or offence whilst on bail.

3. Seriousness for defendant:

    (a) previous convictions;
    (b) subject to suspended sentence;
    (c) breach of previous court order;
    (d) failure to respond to previous sentences.

    When considering the seriousness of any offence, the court may take into account any relevant previous convictions of the offender or failure to respond to previous sentences.

4. Committal or transfer to Crown Court likely:

   (a) TICs.

Q.7(b) I am subject to a:		
suspended or partly suspended[3] prison sentence		
conditional discharge		
supervision order		
probation order		
deferment of sentence		
community service order		
care order		
(Give details as far as you are able including the nature of offence and when the order was made.)		

Obtain this information, if possible, from a record of your client's previous convictions as you cannot always rely upon your client to give you accurate information. He may be confused about the difference between a suspended prison sentence, conditional discharge and deferred sentence. Remember to include details, as requested, about the nature of the offence which led to the order being made and whether the order was made by a magistrates' court or Crown Court.

Q.7(c) It is likely that I will lose my livelihood		

Consider:

- risk of disqualification from driving when licence necessary to do job (and 'special reason' if disqualification is mandatory);

- conviction for dishonesty of someone whose normal work puts them in position of trust;

- conviction for sexual offence of someone whose normal work is as a teacher or social worker.

Q.7(d) It is likely that I will suffer serious damage to my reputation		

Consider:

- loss of good character;
- defendant may be well known or hold a position of trust in the local community.

Q.7(e) A substantial question of law is involved *(You will need the help of a solicitor to answer this question.)*		

Consider:

- interpretation of the law needs to be argued (particularly if an ECHR argument is being raised);
- a legal point is involved in the defence, e.g. meaning of 'dishonesty' or 'possession', or a general defence is to be raised;
- an attempt will be made to exclude evidence;
- legal arguments as to proportionality and thresholds for community sentences and custody, or as to the appropriate community plea;
- a Newton hearing may be required.

Q.7(f) I shall be unable to understand the court proceedings or state my own case because: a) my understanding of English is inadequate b) I suffer from a disability *(Give full details.)*		

Consider:

- language difficulties;
- illiterate;
- mental disorder;
- other relevant disability;
- drink/drug problem.

Q.7(g) Witnesses have to be traced and/or interviewed on my behalf *(State circumstances.)*		

Consider:

- for trial or mitigation;
- photographs or plans required;
- number of witnesses;
- witnesses unwilling to co-operate;
- prosecution refuse to give witness's name and/or address, requiring application to the court;
- expert witnesses required, e.g. medical, scientific. This alone will normally justify the grant of legal aid.

Q.7(h) The case involves expert cross-examination of a prosecution witness *(Give brief details.)*		

Consider:

- prosecution calling expert evidence (although it is the cross-examination which is required to be expert; not the witness);
- prosecution calling a number of professional witnesses, e.g. police officers;
- defendant not capable of conducting own case.

Q.7(i) It is in someone else's interest that I am represented		

Consider:

- it is in the interests of someone other than the defendant that he be represented, e.g. inappropriate for defendant to cross-examine witness (personal or intimate details to be disclosed);
- relationship between defendant and complainant, e.g. family or neighbour element.

Q.7(j) Any other reasons: *(Give full particulars.)*		

Consider:

- committal or transfer to Crown Court for trial likely;
- defendant will seek trial in the Crown Court;
- facts unusually complex (provide some detail);
- co-defendants legally aided;
- complex features (e.g. mistaken identity).

This information may need to be supplemented during the progress of the case.

Advise your client what the relevant form of legal aid funding will cover. [54.1]

Evidence of means

Once the relevant provisions of the Access to Justice Act 1999 are brought into force legal aid will be granted on the interests of justice test alone[4] without regard to means. However, a Crown Court judge may order the defendant to pay or make a contribution towards the defence costs.[5] Clients should be advised to this effect and given an estimate of the amount involved at the outset and every six months. Remind the client of the possible consequences should their means change.

Extension of order

Until contracting is fully introduced, if an expert's report or other unusual expenditure is required, apply to the Legal Aid Board for prior authority on Form APP7: see Appendix 3. Applications are processed by the Board in accordance with reg. 54 Legal Aid in Criminal and Care Proceedings (General) Regulations 1989 which states:

'(1) *Where it appears to a legally assisted person's solicitor necessary for the proper conduct of proceedings in a magistrates' court or in the Crown Court for costs to be incurred under the legal aid order by taking any of the following steps:*

(a) *obtaining a written report or opinion of one or more experts;*

(b) *employing a person to provide a written report or opinion (otherwise than as an expert);*

(c) *bespeaking transcripts of shorthand notes or of tape recordings of any proceedings, including police questioning of suspects;*

(d) *where a legal aid order provides for the service of solicitor and counsel, instructing a Queen's Counsel alone without a junior counsel; or*

(e) *performing an act which is either unusual in its nature or involves unusually large expenditure;*

he may apply to the appropriate area committee for prior authority so to do.'

(2) *Where an Area Committee authorises the taking of any step specified in paragraph (1) (a), (b), (c) or (e), it shall also authorise the maximum fee to be paid for any such report, opinion, transcript or act.'*

Exception to 'no top-up' rule

Until contracting is introduced and if prior authority is not granted, you can arrange for your client to pay privately for the preparation of an expert's report. It is one of the exceptions to the restriction on private payment in reg. 55 Legal Aid in Criminal and Care Proceedings (General) Regulations 1989 which states:

'Where a legal aid order has been made, the legally assisted person's solicitor or counsel shall not receive or be a party to the making of any payment for work done in connection with the proceedings in respect of

which the legal aid order was made except such payments as may be made:

(a)   out of the legal aid fund or by the Lord Chancellor; or
(b)   In respect of any expenses or fees incurred in:

   (i)   preparing, obtaining or considering any report, opinion or further evidence whether provided by an expert witness or otherwise; or
   (ii)   bespeaking transcripts of shorthand notes of tape recordings of any proceedings, including police questioning of suspects;

where an application under regulation 54 for authority to incur such expenses or fees has been refused by the Area Committee.'

Through order

If the case will result in proceedings in the Crown Court, ask the court to grant your client a 'through' legal aid order as early as you can (at the first hearing in an indictable-only case and after mode of trial hearing in an either-way case).

With a 'through' legal aid order you can carry out preparation before committal/transfer and charge for it in your Crown Court bill. The Justices' Clerks' Society has advised its members to grant 'through' orders when requested (*JCS News Sheet* 95/6 14 February 1995).

'The increasing number of Crown Courts that are adopting the plea and directions hearings in accordance with recommendation 92 of the Royal Commission (sic) report has brought to attention the benefits to be gained by Courts making Through Legal Aid Orders at the earliest possible occasion when a matter is to be sent to the Crown Court. The advantages of making such an order are that the legal representatives for the defence can commence their preparation work for the Crown Court prior to the committal proceedings taking place. This has the effect of increasing the chances of the plea and directions hearing having a positive outcome and of speeding the whole process. Where such an order can be made at the beginning of the proceedings (that is in indictable-only cases), it would also have the advantage of reducing the number of legal aid orders to be prepared in our offices.

'The Society would, therefore, encourage justices' clerks to remind their staff of the powers to make such orders and of the desirability of making them as soon as lawfully possible, in appropriate cases.'

Reg. 11 Legal Aid in Criminal and Care Proceedings (General) Regulations 1989 has been amended to confirm that justices' clerks can make such orders, as well as magistrates.

Court determining officers shall pay for this work (Directions to Determining Officers IC.2(a)) so long as they are satisfied that the work was reasonably done and related directly to Crown Court proceedings.

Legal Aid Order received

Where a Legal Aid Order is made, you should advise your client:

- whether or not he will have to make any contribution to the case [55.1] and, if so, the duration of payments; [55.1.1][6]
- that he is under a duty to report any changes in financial circumstances and that these may affect eligibility and/or contribution status; [55.2]
- the nature and consequences of withdrawal and revocation. [55.3]

Check you have received the order and the date of grant, as well as confirming that the order is in your firm's name and covers all the offences charged.

What if legal aid is refused?

Advise your client that application can be renewed in open court before magistrates or on appeal made to the Legal Aid Area Committee and of the prospects of success of the appeal. [56.1, 56.2]

An appeal to the Legal Aid Area Committee can only be made if:

- the charge is triable 'either-way' or 'indictable only';
- an appeal is made within 14 days of refusal;
- the original application is made at least 21 days before the final hearing date.

You must send the information requested on Form APP5.

Whilst an appeal is pending, you may seek an adjournment of the next hearing.

If the application is refused but the case proceeds to the Crown Court, apply afresh to the Crown Court immediately after the committal.

Advise your client that a new application can be made if circumstances change [56.3].

Billing

Until contracting takes effect:

- make full use of the powers to make payments on account of profit costs and disbursements to ease cash flow; and

- lodge your bills promptly (be aware of the time-limits for submission of claims for costs) and make a diary entry for the last date by which you can do this.

PRIVATE CLIENTS

It is a professional duty to advise your client of the availability of legal aid.[7]

If it is not possible, in the interests of justice, to obtain legal aid, the person who is responsible for the client/case, and has the necessary overview, will need to:

- fix a price for the work or give a best estimate; otherwise, quote an hourly rate;

- regularly review the estimate;

- remember that factors outside their control may increase costs;

- confirm their price or estimate or hourly rate in writing in a 'client care' letter, explaining the basis on which they charge; the factors which may affect the cost; and that they are responsible for the client/case;

- obtain money in advance;

- submit interim bills to help cash flow.

Refer to Rule 15, Solicitors' Practice Rules and Solicitors' Costs Information and Client Care Code. For this, and examples of how solicitors can provide client care and costs information to their client see Chapter 13 of *The Guide to The Professional Conduct of Solicitors 1999* and the [1999] *Gazette,* 21 April, published by The Law Society.

In the event of your client being acquitted, or the allegations withdrawn or discharged, you will wish to apply for any private costs paid to be recovered from central funds. The court considering your bill will require clear evidence of the terms of business agreed with your client.

End notes

1 *The Guide to the Professional Conduct of Solicitors 1999,* Principle 5.01. The Law Society.
2 Para. 50 Legal Aid Board Duty Solicitor Arrangements Rules 1997.
3 Partly suspended sentence may no longer be imposed.
4 s.17 Access to Justice Act 1999.
5 s.17(2) Access to Justice Act 1999.
6 This will become redundant upon the implementation of the Access to Justice Act 1999
7 Principle 5.01, *The Guide to the Professional Conduct of Solicitors 1999.* The Law Society.

CHAPTER 8

The defendant in custody

BAIL APPLICATION

Objection to bail

If there are objections to bail or the court may raise concerns, you should obtain adequate instructions to deal with the objections, and bring these together in a single document:

- if bail has been withheld in the present case by a court, how many applications have been made, to whom, what are the reasons for refusal [58.1] and have your client's circumstances changed since then or are there new arguments as to fact or law?

- confirm with your client what bail conditions may be acceptable to him and to the court. [60.1]

The following sets out information you may require, related to any objections to bail which the prosecutor raises and possible relevant bail conditions.

Likely to abscond

ADDRESS

Obtain the following information:

- how long there? Proposed address on bail? [57.1]
- staying with a friend/squatter/licensee/lodger/tenant or owner occupier?
- cannot return there, alternative address?
- bail hostel place appropriate and available?

SURETIES

Obtain from any proposed surety details of:

- name, address, date of birth and employment;
- criminal convictions;
- length of time known to defendant;
- nature of association;
- frequency and means of regular contact;
- knowledge of current charge and antecedents of defendant;
- employment;
- financial position: income and savings;
- precise nature and form of monies offered to support suretyship – savings or easily realised assets of own, e.g. home owned by surety may not be acceptable to some courts.

Tell the surety of the nature of the allegations against the defendant; and (with client's consent) of his previous convictions; of the obligations of a surety; and of the consequences of the defendant's failure to attend court, i.e. risk of forfeiture of recognisance.

Make enquiries if you suspect that the surety is not bona fide, financially worthy and willing to stand surety. Obtain evidence of assets, e.g. building society passbook. Obtain full information about recent deposits because the court will be suspicious. You must have reasonable grounds to believe that the surety can afford the recognisance into which he is entering.[1]

SECURITY

Does your client have, or have access to, money or items of value which may be deposited as a security?

COMMUNITY TIES

Obtain the following information:

- where born and brought up?
- married or co-habitating? If so, for how long and do they still live together?

- children? If so, how many, what ages and are they still living with your client?

- otherwise, who does your client live with at the above address?

- where do parents/girlfriend/boyfriend/other friends or relatives live?

- present job is? [57.2] If none, how long unemployed and what are job prospects? [57.3.1]

OUTCOME

Consider the following:

- if guilty or convicted, why an immediate custodial sentence is not inevitable;

- if not guilty, what is the strength of the evidence against him:

    - location and date/time of alleged offence;

    - goods or weapon recovered from defendant, home or family;

    - witnesses referred to by police;

    - means and nature of apparent identification; identification parade: number of witnesses attending; number of positive identifications;

    - forensic evidence sought or obtained;

    - admissions made;

    - possible inferences from silence;

    - co-defendants implicating defendant?

- be aware of the circumstances in which a conviction would lead to an obligatory life or minimum term prison sentence under the Crime (Sentences) Act 1997.

BAIL RECORD

Consider the following:

- does your client have convictions for failing to appear in court? If so, when and why did he not appear? [57.5.1]

- has your client been granted bail since then?

- has your client answered to bail in the past when a custodial sentence was likely or imposed? If so, how long was he on bail for each time and what were the conditions? [57.5.2]

SUGGESTED BAIL CONDITIONS

What bail conditions would make absconding less likely:

- sureties;

- a residence condition;

- a security;

- a condition that your client surrenders his passport and does not apply for a duplicate or travel documents; or

- reporting to the local police station;

- curfew.

On bail when alleged offence committed

This is a reason why the court need not grant your client bail (Sched. 1, Pt I, para. 2A Bail Act 1976). Check new offence is indictable-only or either-way.

Is your client already on bail to a court for another offence? If so, what is the offence; when was it allegedly committed; what stage has been reached in the proceedings; when is he next due in court; what will the plea be; and what are the conditions of bail?

If your client will plead not guilty to the present offence, you could argue that he/she denies committing an offence (the present offence) whilst on bail for another offence.

PREVIOUS BAIL RECORD

If your client has been on remand on bail before, did he commit offences whilst on bail? The longer the period that your client was on bail for, without committing offences, the better.

Likely to commit further offences

PREVIOUS CRIMINAL CONVICTIONS [57.4]

Look at your client's previous criminal convictions:

1. How long is it since his last offence (not sentence)? It may be some time, with long gaps between his previous offences (not sentences). You may be able to argue that the criminal record shows that your client is somebody who can stay out of trouble for long periods of time, much longer than the time that he will be on bail for in the present case.

2. Does your client have convictions for the offence he is charged with now? If not, how can the prosecution show that your client is likely to commit another offence of the present type if he is granted bail?

3. If your client's previous convictions are for a less serious type of offence, the risk must be that he will commit an offence on bail of the type that would not justify his being remanded in custody to protect the public.

4. Always check the list of previous convictions with your client. If it is factually inaccurate to his advantage you are not obliged to correct the list. If you consider it in your client's best interests to correct it, seek his consent. You should not be asked by the court to confirm the accuracy of the list. The Justices' Clerks' Society has advised its members that you should only be asked whether you have seen the list of your client's previous convictions. If you have, the court will assume that you will make representations if the list is wrong to your client's disadvantage. You must not, however, mislead the court by saying what you know to be untrue about your client's character. If he insists you do so, withdraw. If either you or the court want reports from the probation service, the true record is likely to be discovered in any event in due course.

CHANGE OF CIRCUMSTANCES

How have your client's circumstances changed since he committed the present offence (if pleading guilty), or past offences?

If you can link the offences with something tangible, such as a family crisis or drug taking, which no longer exists, you can argue that the fact of your client's committing the present or past offences has no bearing on the likelihood of his committing offences in the future.

What bail conditions would lessen the risk of further offending:

- a curfew, if the offence was allegedly committed in the evening or at night;

- a condition not to go to the area where the offence was allegedly committed or where offences of a similar nature often occur;

- if the offence is drink related, not to enter an off-licence or public house?

- not to approach the complainant.

Try to ensure that any condition is drafted with clarity and is no more restrictive than is necessary.

Interference with witnesses

Which witnesses do the prosecution allege that your client is likely to interfere with? Do the prosecution allege that he has actually made a threat against this witness? If so, what and when? What does your client say about this? If not, why is this case different from any other criminal case involving witnesses who are not police officers?

Has the witness made a statement in the case to the police? If so, it would be difficult for the witness to change his evidence at this late stage as a result of interference from your client. Does your client know the witness's present address? If not, interference with the witness is less likely.

How important is the evidence that this witness can give? If the case does not depend on it, it is unlikely that the defendant would risk committing a serious criminal offence by trying to persuade the witness not to give evidence or to give perjured evidence.

SUGGESTED BAIL CONDITION

A condition of bail could be imposed that your client does not approach the witness, contact him directly or through others or go within a specified distance of the witness's home address.

Other objections to bail appear in Sched. 1, Pt I, Bail Act 1976. Objections to bail in non-imprisonable cases are more restricted: see Sched. 1, Pt II, Bail Act 1976.

Bail information scheme

Your court may have a bail information scheme. Bail information scheme officers interview defendants in custody and gather information, obtaining verification from a third party, address the police objections to bail, mobilise resources and provide the information to the defence and the CPS. The object of these schemes is to enhance the independence of the CPS by enabling its advocates to refer to information other than that which is supplied to them by the police. There are also prison schemes which support the court-based schemes.

Duty psychiatric schemes

Many courts have access to duty psychiatric schemes where mental health trained doctors or community psychiatric nurses attend to see those referred to them. The schemes have led to the significant diversion of the mentally ill away from the criminal justice system.

Indictable-only offences

A defendant may be sent to the Crown Court on bail or in custody.[2] One purpose of the preliminary hearing is to allow the magistrates to make the first decision as to bail or custody in a s.51 case. The expectation is, therefore, that the magistrates will hear a full bail application in such cases, and they may adjourn the preliminary hearing for that purpose if the requisite information is not available.

If the magistrates have heard and refused a bail application, it is nevertheless open to them to adjourn the preliminary hearing if it appears likely that before the case would otherwise have reached the Crown Court the accused would be in a position to make a further application with a better chance of success (e.g. where a hostel place is being sought for a defendant of no fixed abode, or where there is a prospect that the defendant would be able to offer recognisances).

Although a defendant who is refused bail by the magistrates is normally entitled to make a second application to them, the effect of s.51 is that once a case has been sent to the Crown Court no further application for bail can be made to the magistrates. A defendant who is sent in custody will anyway have the opportunity of making an application to the Crown Court within a few days.

Bail conditions: interview with legal representative

The power to require a defendant, as a condition of bail, to attend an interview with a legal representative,[3] addresses a particular concern about the number of adjournments sought, and granted, for the purpose of seeking legal advice and sorting out legal representation.

The power is to enhance the court's ability to deal with a defendant who is being particularly obstructive in this regard.

The objective is to try to ensure that a defendant receives legal advice and decides on the response to the allegation in the charge in advance of his next court appearance.

Home Office guidance states that legal advisers will not be expected to report the non-attendance of a client in breach of such a condition which would in any event be to disclose confidential information.

The requirement can be imposed at any relevant stage of proceedings, including at an EAH (but only by a justices' clerk with the consent of the prosecution and the defence).

This power does not apply to the police.

It does not remove the defendant's right to represent himself if he so chooses. If he indicates that he does not wish to have legal representation, it would be inappropriate for the condition to be imposed.

Breach of this condition is unlikely to lead to the defendant's arrest. The breach is more likely to come to light at the next hearing when, for example, the defendant requests an adjournment to seek legal advice.

If it becomes clear at the next hearing that a defendant has not sought legal advice, needs legal advice and there is no reasonable excuse for not having complied with the condition, the court is advised to insist that he seeks an interview with the duty solicitor there and then. A duty solicitor will only be able to assist if the defendant wishes him to do so.

Restrictions on the grant of bail

In cases where there are statutory restrictions on the grant of bail, be ready to assist the court in giving reasons why the restrictions should not apply.

Bail may only be granted in exceptional circumstances if a defendant is charged with murder, attempted murder, rape, attempted rape or manslaughter and has already been convicted of any one of those offences.[4] Identify the exceptional circumstances on which you rely and give the court suitable reasons for the grant of bail.[5]

CHILDREN AND YOUTHS

The courts may decide to bail a 10–16-year-old with or without conditions, or remand him to local authority accommodation, again with or without conditions.

Secure remands

The local authority may apply to the court to hold the 10–16-year-old in secure accommodation under s.25 Children Act 1989.

From 1 June 1999, ss. 97 and 98 of the CDA 1998 amended s.23 of the Children and Young Persons Act 1969 to give the courts power to remand certain categories of 12–16-year-olds direct to local authority secure accommodation: all 12–14-year-olds; 15 and 16-year-old girls; and 'vulnerable' 15 and 16-year-old boys: in each case if a place has been identified in advance. Alternatively, courts may remand 15 and 16-year-old boys direct to prison accommodation. In all these cases, the criteria in s.23(5) of the 1969 Act have to be met. Eventually courts will have power to remand all categories of 12–16-year-olds to local authority secure accommodation.

S.23(5) criteria:

- the child or young person is charged with, or has been convicted of, a violent or sexual offence, or of an offence punishable, in the case of an adult, with imprisonment for a term of 14 years or more; or

- the child or young person has a recent history of absconding while remanded to local authority accommodation, and is charged or has been convicted of an imprisonable offence alleged or found to have been committed whilst he has been so remanded;

and in either case:

- the court must be of the opinion that only remanding the child or young person to local authority secure accommodation/prison accommodation would be adequate to protect the public from serious harm from him.

106

THE NUMBER OF BAIL APPLICATIONS

A full bail application may be made at the first hearing and at the hearing which next follows it. For these purposes hearings at which the defendant is not produced[6] and at which bail is refused for lack of information[7] do not count as hearings. Thereafter (even if no application was made at the first hearing) bail applications may only be made if you raise a new argument as to fact or law or the court gives leave for a further application.[8] If you forgo your right to make the first two bail applications, you can choose when to make an application.

Where bail is granted, advise your client of:

- the importance of answering to bail; [61.1]

- any conditions, security or surety imposed; [61.2]

- the consequences of breaching any bail conditions. [61.3]

APPEALS IN RELATION TO BAIL

To vary conditions of bail imposed by the custody officer at the police station

CJPOA 1994 enables custody officers to grant conditional bail to persons charged with an offence and to vary conditions granted by other custody officers. Under s.43B MCA 1980 a defendant may seek to vary those conditions of bail by application to the magistrates' court.[9]

The application must:

- be in writing;

- contain a statement of the grounds upon which it is made;

- specify the reasons given by the custody officer for imposing or varying conditions of bail; and

- specify the name and address of any surety provided by the applicant before his release on bail to secure his surrender to custody.

A copy of the application must be sent to the custody officer for the relevant police station. The clerk to the justices will then fix the time of the hearing, not later than 72 hours after receipt of the application, no account being taken of Christmas Day, Good Friday, any Bank Holiday or any Sunday.

When the court considers the matter it has powers to vary the conditions to grant unconditional bail or to refuse bail altogether.

An example of a form of application is document 3.7 in Appendix 3.

Alternatively, you can apply to the same or a different custody officer at the original police station. He may vary the bail conditions but cannot withhold bail.

Against a refusal of bail by a magistrates' court

If bail is refused, advise your client of the possibility of an appeal or future application and its prospects of success. [62.1, 62.2]

If the case has not been committed/transferred/sent to the Crown Court, you must obtain a certificate of full argument. Complete a notice of application (see Appendix 3, document 3.5) and lodge with the certificate of full argument and copy record of convictions 24 hours before the hearing with the Crown Court and the prosecution.

Applications should specify:

- details of defendant;
- solicitor;
- charges;
- history of bail applications;
- proposed bail conditions;
- proposed sureties (who should attend).

Consider the effect of too early an application. Consider whether the length of time the client has spent in custody will amount to a change in circumstances justifying a further application.

A solicitor can make the application and will be covered by his precommittal/transfer Legal Aid Order. The defendant will not be produced at court for the application. Tell your client when the application will be made and what the result is.

If the magistrates grant your client conditional bail, but he cannot meet the conditions, you cannot apply to the Crown Court before committal to vary the conditions. You may, however, apply to the High Court (see below).

High Court

If a Crown Court judge refuses to grant your client bail, you can apply to a High Court judge in chambers. You cannot obtain criminal legal aid. Civil legal aid can be sought but will only be granted in exceptional circumstances in this situation. It is possible to apply directly to the High Court, without making a Crown Court application first.

A variation of bail conditions which your client cannot meet, prior to committal, can be sought in this way and civil legal aid, usually on an emergency basis, is regularly granted.

The application to the High Court is made by claim which calls upon the prosecution to show cause why the defendant should not be granted bail or the conditions, if bail has already been granted, should not be varied.

The procedure is set out in the amended RSC Ord. 79, r.9. The claim is supported by a statement of truth or witness statement in which you set out the prosecution's objections and the grounds of your application. The claim and supporting evidence must be served on the prosecutor at least 24 hours before the hearing.

A solicitor can make the application which is heard in chambers and again your client will not be produced at court for it.

Against the grant of bail

Bail (Amendment) Act 1993

The Act gives the prosecution a right of appeal against the decision to grant bail in certain cases.

The right of appeal against bail granted by the magistrates' court is limited to an offence punishable by a term of five years' imprisonment or more (or where, in the case of a child or young person, the offence is so punishable in the case of an adult), or an offence under s.12 (taking a conveyance without authority) or s.12A (aggravated vehicle taking) Theft Act 1968.

Where they wish to appeal, the prosecution must give oral notice immediately the bail hearing finishes and before the defendant leaves court, and serve a written notice on the court and the defendant confirming the intention to appeal, within two hours.

The appeal is to a Crown Court judge and the Crown Court hearing must begin within 48 hours from midnight on the day that oral notice was given (not including weekends or public holidays). The hearing will usually be in chambers without the defendant present.

CUSTODY TIME-LIMITS

You must make careful records of the custody time-limit which applies in a particular case. You must not warn the prosecution if they fail to notice that a limit is about to expire.

Magistrates' court

For either-way offences the time-limit is 70 days unless the court has accepted jurisdiction within 56 days, when the limit is 56 days.

For indictable-only offences the time-limit is 70 days.

For summary-only offences the time-limit is 56 days.

In the youth court, if the court accepts jurisdiction within 56 days in a case which for an adult would be indictable-only, the time-limit is 56 days.[10]

Crown Court

The time-limit following transfer or committal is 112 days. *Where s.51 CDA 1998 is in force the time-limit is 182 days from bail being refused in the magistrates' court.*[11]

Expiry

The time-limit ceases to apply at the start of committal proceedings, plea or trial. A PDH is not such a hearing.

Extension

To obtain an extension the Crown must apply within the time-limit and the court shall not grant the application unless it is satisfied:

- that the need for the extension is due to:
    - the illness or absence of the accused, a necessary witness, a judge or a magistrate;
    - a postponement which is occasioned by the ordering by the court of separate trials in the case of two or more accused or two or more offences; or
    - some other good and sufficient cause; and
- that the prosecution has acted with all due diligence and expedition.

You should seldom concede that an extension is appropriate.[12] Applications for extensions of time-limits should not be regarded as routine but should be challenged whenever possible.

Appeals

Both the defence and prosecution have rights of appeal from the magistrates' court to the Crown Court against the grant and refusal of an extension of the custody time-limit: see Appendix 3, document 3.9(c). Appeals from decisions made during Crown Court proceedings are by way of judicial review.

Bail

If a time-limit has expired, bail shall be granted, without application of the exceptions referred to in s.4 Bail Act 1976. Bail conditions may be imposed, but the court cannot require sureties; nor security; nor conditions to be met before release.[13]

COMMUNICATING WITH A DEFENDANT IN CUSTODY

TV links

CDA 1998 (which is being brought into force in stages) allows preliminary hearings in a magistrates' court or Crown Court (any hearing before the beginning of the prosecution evidence at trial)[14] to take place in court where a defendant in custody sees the court, and is seen by the court, over a video link rather than being physically present in court. In practice the defendant will always be produced at court for the first hearing.

A court may direct that the accused be treated as present if:

- *it has heard representations;*
- *he is in custody;*
- *he is able to see and hear and be seen and heard;*
- *the Home Office have notified availability;*
- *it is before the start of the trial.*

The Act creates a presumption that video links will be used.

At the first hearing in the magistrates' court, when the case is adjourned, magistrates will hear any representations from the defence about why subsequent hearings – a further bail application, plea before venue, mode of trial, the taking of a plea or a committal for trial – should not take place over the video link.

There are no statutory criteria to form the basis of the decision but it is in cases where the defendant is vulnerable that the magistrates are most likely, having given reasons, not to make a video link direction. When the provision was before parliament, the Government indicated that 'good' reasons for requiring the defendant to come to court might include:

- *the need for an interpreter;*

- *the defendant is nervous and unable to communicate through that medium;*

- *the defendant has a psychiatric history;*

- *the defendant has a fear about the use of technology.*

Other reasons that might form the basis of an application for the defendant to be brought to court include:

- *multi-handed or very complex case;*

- *the defendant has poor literacy skills and documents need to be considered;*

- *the defendant suffers from a mental health problem or visual or hearing or learning difficulties;*

- *it is not possible to take instructions from the defendant on material to be served by the prosecutor at the hearing;*

- *the defendant has been unable to see his legal adviser in person at the prison;*

- *the defendant needs to be interviewed by a bail information officer at the court.*

You will wish to make representation if your client might be prejudiced by an unwillingness (because of his perception of a lack of confidentiality) to provide critical information to you over a video link or if there will otherwise be unnecessary visits to the prison at public or private expense.

Consultation booths with video link equipment are available at the court and the prison to allow a conference to be held before or after the video link hearing. However, solicitors in the pilot courts complained about a time lapse which made communication on this out-of-court equipment difficult.[15]

The absence of the defendant may result in an adjournment if you require a signed authority from your client as to your handling of the case and there is insufficient confidentiality in the use of fax connections.

You should keep under review the need for your client to attend the court in person.

Communication – correspondence

It is important that any legally-privileged correspondence from solicitors to prisoners does not contain cash. A solicitor needing to send a prisoner money should send it to the prison governor instead, with an explanation of what the payment is for, and the money will be credited to this prisoner accordingly.

Mail clearly marked 'Prison Rule 39' (or 'YOI Rule 14' if addressed to a young offender) will be treated as legally privileged and passed to the prisoner unopened,[16] unless a governor has reason to suspect that it is not actually privileged.

Governors have power to order suspected letters to be opened: by observing these guidelines, you can ensure your correspondence reaches your client unopened in all but a bare minimum of cases.

End notes

1 *R.* v. *Birmingham Crown Court ex. p Ali* [1999] Crim LR 504.
2 s.52(1) Crime and Disorder Act 1998.
3 s.54 Crime and Disorder Act 1998 amending s.3(6) Bail Act 1976.
4 s.25 CJPOA 1994 (as amended).
5 See para. 9A, Pt I, Sched. 1 Bail Act 1976.
6 *R.* v. *Dover and Kent JJ ex p. Dean* (1991) 156 JP 357.
7 *R.* v. *Calder JJ ex p. Kennedy* [1992] Crim LR 496.
8 Sched. 1, Pt. II Bail Act 1976.
9 The procedure is set out in the Magistrates' Courts (Amendment) Rules 1995 (SI 1995/ 585).
10 *R.* v. *Stratford YC ex p. s.* [1999] Crim LR 146.
11 There are transitional arrangements when this section is first brought into force in a particular area.
12 *R.* v. *Manchester Crown Court ex p. McDonald* [1999] Crim LR 736.
13 reg. 8 of the 1987 Regulations.
14 In the Crown Court the start of trial is defined as the swearing in of the jury.
15 Swindon, Manchester and Bristol magistrates' courts took part in six-month pilots which ended during April 1999.
16 See page 47 for further details.

CHAPTER 9

Determining if there is a case

INVESTIGATING THE EVIDENCE

Before you can advise a client how to proceed you must be able to judge whether the prosecution have admissible evidence that will be available at trial to make out any, and if so which, charges. Identify all the points to prove for each offence and the evidence relevant to each issue.

You must investigate the evidence available which may come from a number of sources:

- the police station;
- police files;
- evidence served;
- unused material.

You must then be satisfied that there are no procedural bars to the prosecution proceeding.

Investigation at the police station if you attend the police station

You may have available sufficient information to advise whether there is a case to answer and possibly on plea.

You will have investigated the police case and assessed its strength:

- what evidence has been disclosed;
- how strong is that evidence;
- is it admissible;
- will it be available at trial;

114

- are there any admissions already made (in a signed pocket book entry or an earlier interview);

- which defences have been raised.

If you did not attend the police station or the information obtained there is insufficient or unreliable, you will have to consider other sources.

Material available – police files

The amount of information available from the CPS is dependent upon the type of police file prepared.

The police case is submitted to the prosecution in a file, which is prepared in accordance with the national *Manual of Guidance*. The *Manual* sets out the standard content of police files. These are listed in Appendix 18. An explanation of how cases are classified for listing at an EFH or EAH is given in Chapter 14.

File content for an early first hearing (EFH): expedited file

Straightforward guilty plea cases are listed for an EFH. An expedited file will normally be prepared. The file standard is broadly the same as that for the ordinary abbreviated file. The file will contain the following core documents:

- MG1 – file front sheet;

- MG4 – charge sheet;

- MG11 – key witness statements;

- MG15 – short descriptive note of interview (SDN).

The remaining elements of an expedited file should be included where applicable and available, e.g. previous conviction details and compensation forms.

If witness statements are not typed for the first hearing because of time constraints (ideally they should be), they must be clearly legible.

If the defendant is in custody, the MG7 remand application form should also be included.

File content for an early administrative hearing (EAH): remand file

The category of cases listed for an EAH includes anticipated not guilty plea cases, plea not known cases and guilty plea cases which are not straightforward.

The police will not have a full file, which will take three to four weeks to prepare. A remand file will be submitted which must include the following documents:

- MG4 – charge sheet;
- MG5 – summary of case;
- MG7 – remand application.
- MG11 – key witness statements.

The remaining elements of a remand file should be included where applicable and available. Documents may be handwritten due to time constraints but must be clearly legible.

The case can only be progressed at the first hearing by requesting an indication of plea before venue or accepting a guilty plea if the prosecutor has copies of any key witness statements in order to be able to review the case. Copies of any key witness statements taken should thus be included, in addition to a summary of the case in order to be able to review the case.

In not guilty plea cases, full files will be required for any pre-trial review (PTR) required by the court following an EAH.

At an EAH, first listing in the magistrates' court of an indictable-only case, and in every Crown Court hearing, the prosecutor will be expected to supply accurate estimates for the length of the adjournment required, with full reasons. This information can be provided on a revised MG7.

File content for indictable-only cases following the implementation of s.51 CDA 1988: remand file

This is the same as for an EAH (see above).

Where the court is considering sending a related either-way or summary case to the Crown Court, defence practitioners will need to ensure that they obtain sufficient information from the prosecution to enable them to dispute the relationship, if appropriate, on an equally informed basis. This will preferably be a copy of such statements as are available.

Indictable-only cases will be listed for appearance before a Crown Court judge within a short time of being sent from the magistrates' court.

Full file preparation will already have commenced but it is likely that the court will want to know when the papers can be served on the defence and the court.

Advance information

In an either-way case, if insufficient evidence has been made available, take steps immediately to obtain advance information. This includes not only advance information but also a copy of any document to which reference is made.[1] Do not delay doing this until you have had the time to take your client's instructions at a formal appointment/interview.

Advance information must be served by the CPS on the defence promptly to avoid unnecessary adjournments. The court 'shall adjourn' the proceedings if there has been a failure to disclose 'unless the court is satisfied that the conduct of the case for the accused will not be substantially prejudiced by non-compliance.[2]

In a straightforward guilty plea case at an EFH, a copy of the whole file may be made for advance information purposes. The CPS require the key witness statements in order to review the file before a decision can be made about whether to accept a plea. Key witness statements should always be available, and if CPS guidance is followed correctly they should be served on the defence as advance information instead of the police summary.

In summary-only cases, the CPS, although under no duty[3] to do so, may be prepared to disclose their case, or some of it, as otherwise the defence cannot be satisfied about the quality of the prosecution evidence. Recommended practice is for the CPS to serve copies of the prosecution witness statements on the defence if requested to do so, following a plea of not guilty.

Unused material

Consider whether the prosecution or a third party may possess information which would materially affect the outcome of the prosecution. If so, you may wish to consider that information before deciding whether there is a case to answer. A guilty plea deprives your client of the statutory rights to any unused material[4] but the common law right to enforce fair disclosure remains.[5]

PROCEDURAL BARS

The following is only a summary. If relevant issues may arise, you should refer to detailed sources.[6]

117

Invalidity

Examine the written charge or summons for possible invalidity:

1. Does it fail accurately to describe an offence known to law? It must contain a brief description of the offence using non-technical language and identify the statute and section contravened, or identify the offence correctly as being against common law.

2. Is it out of time? The general rule is that there are no time-limits in criminal cases, but there are important exceptions:

   (a) if the offence is summary only, a court may not try an information unless it was laid at the magistrates' court within six months of the offence.[7] There are exceptions to this rule including vehicle excise offences and a list of examples of these appears in *Stone's Justices' Manual*, para. 1–62;

   (b) some statutes creating either-way offences contain special time-limits, e.g. Sched. 2 Sexual Offences Act 1956, (unlawful sexual intercourse girl 13–16, one-year limit);

3. Is a summons not properly signed? The signature on the summons must be that of a JP or the justices' clerk or delegated officer. In practice ordinary court clerks check summonses and use signature stamps to sign the documents.

4. Does it fail accurately to describe the informant and give his address?

5. Did the court issuing the summons exceed its commission area? The law is complex, and a magistrates' court may deal with any indictable offence committed in England or Wales. The general principles relating to summary offences are that:

   (a) the offence must be committed or suspected to be committed within the administrative county of the court; or

   (b) the defendant must reside or be believed to reside in that area; or

   (c) a trial with another defendant in the area is necessary or expedient; or

   (d) the defendant is already appearing before the court in relation to another offence; or

   (e) jurisdiction is specifically conferred by statute. Jurisdiction to try a defendant is based on his appearance before the court in answer to a summons or following arrest, defects in process notwithstanding. There is no requirement that the defendant attends only in response to a lawful summons. An invalid summons, however, should, on due enquiry, be dismissed.

6. Has a necessary consent been overlooked?

    (a) Some statutes require the consent of the Attorney-General or DPP to the bringing of the prosecution, e.g. bribery, terrorism, official secrets. A Crown Prosecutor is empowered to provide the consent of the DPP.

    (b) Note: ss.1(7), 25 and 26 POA 1985.

7. Is it duplicative?

    (a) Each charge or summons may allege only one offence unless they arise out of a single activity.

    (b) Alternative allegations of what is essentially a single offence are permitted.

    (c) Alternative allegations of different offences are not permitted (even if created by the same statutory provision).

    (d) But note: two or more defendants may be jointly charged with having committed an offence jointly.

8. Is it vexatious? Are these 'defences' relevant: *res judicata*, estoppel, *autrefois* acquit or *autrefois* convict?

Abuse of process

In the exercise of the court's discretion, a case may be dismissed for:

- prosecution misconduct which deprives the defendant of a protection provided by the law or enables the prosecution to take advantage of a technicality; or allows a trial to proceed when it would not otherwise have done so;

- unjustifiable delay by the prosecution coupled with prejudice to the defendant (which may be proved or inferred from the delay).[8] Arguments based on delay should be raised at the earliest opportunity.

Action to be taken with your client

Your client will need to know:

- how long the case is likely to take; [72.1]

- what steps you are going to take on his behalf; [72.2]

- how strong his case is; [72.4]

- when he will see you next and what will happen then. [72.5]

You should confirm any advice given in writing. [72.3]

End notes

1 r.4(3) Magistrates' Courts (Advance Information) Rules 1985.
2 *Ibid.* r.7(1).
3 There is no duty on the CPS to provide the evidence in summary-only cases, but it is desirable that they do so: *R.* v. *Stratford JJ ex p. Imbert* (1999) *The Times*, 25 February; *R.* v. *Kingston upon Hull JJ ex p. McCann* (1991) 55 JP 569.
4 s.1(1) CPIA 1996.
5 See page 167. *R.* v. *DPP ex p. Lee* [1999] 2 All ER 737.
6 e.g. *Wilkinson's Road Traffic Offences*, Chapter 2, contains a useful summary of jurisdictional and procedural points.
7 s.127 MCA 1980.
8 *R.* v. *Norwich Crown Court ex p. Belsham* [1992] 1 WLR 54 QBD.

CHAPTER 10

Representations to the CPS

THE ROLE OF THE DEFENCE IN CPS REVIEW DECISIONS

All cases submitted to the CPS are subject to initial and then continuous review in accordance with the *Code for Crown Prosecutors* (see Appendix 14). The initial review takes place before the first hearing. There will be a further review before mode of trial. A full review by a lawyer, takes place after mode of trial in either-way cases on receipt of the full file up to three to four weeks later. The caseworker may already have begun preparation of the Crown Court case. Although information is supplied by the police, review decisions can be influenced by information from other sources. The Code states that it is the duty of the Crown Prosecutor to ensure that all relevant facts are given to the court.[1] It also states that 'Crown Prosecutors must be fair, independent and objective'.[2] Information from the defence need not be limited to the public interest test. The evidential test of the Code requires prosecutors to consider what the defence may be, and how reliable the evidence is.[3]

It is quite proper to request the prosecution to reconsider the decision to prosecute. In an appropriate case, much worry, time and expense may be saved. The reconsideration should be sought as early as practicable, but may be done at any stage before trial or guilty plea.

CODE FOR CROWN PROSECUTORS

The criteria for prosecution are set out in the DPP's *Code for Crown Prosecutors* (June 1994), some of which is reproduced below (set out in full in Appendix 14).

You may be in possession of information personal to the defendant (illness, recent bereavement) not available to the prosecution. Similarly you may consider that a prosecution is unlikely to succeed because of the strength of the defence case.

Unless inappropriate (e.g. terminal illness not known to the client) discuss contacting the prosecution with your client first. If you propose making a detailed disclosure of the defence case, advise on the disadvantages (alerting the prosecution to weaknesses in their case which they may remedy). If your client agrees, obtain written instructions in confirmation of this. Be aware that material disclosed may be used by the prosecution at trial if they proceed.

Consider the availability of an alternative to prosecution, e.g. administering a formal caution by the police or, in the case of those under 18, a reprimand or warning.

The evidential test

Crown Prosecutors must be satisfied that there is enough evidence to provide a 'realistic prospect of conviction' against each defendant on each charge. They must consider what the defence case may be and how that is likely to affect the prosecution case.

A realistic prospect of a conviction is an objective test. It means that a jury or bench of magistrates, properly directed in accordance with the law, is more likely than not to convict the defendant of the charge alleged.

When deciding whether there is enough evidence to prosecute, Crown Prosecutors must consider whether the evidence can be used and is reliable. There will be many cases in which the evidence does not give any cause for concern. But there will also be cases in which the evidence may not be as strong as it first appears.

The public interest test

Some common public interest factors against prosecution

A prosecution is less likely to be needed if:

- the court is likely to impose a very small or nominal penalty;

- the offence was committed as a result of a genuine mistake or misunderstanding (these factors must be balanced against the seriousness of the offence);

- the loss or harm can be described as minor and was the result of a single incident, particularly if it was caused by a misjudgement;

- there has been a long delay between the offence taking place and the date of the trial, unless:

- the offence is serious;

- the delay has been caused in part by the defendant;

- the offence has only recently come to light; or

- the complexity of the offence has meant that there has been a long investigation;

• a prosecution is likely to have a very bad effect on the victim's physical or mental health, always bearing in mind the seriousness of the offence;

• the defendant is elderly or is, or was at the time of the offence, suffering from significant mental or physical ill health, unless the offence is serious or there is a real possibility that it may be repeated. The CPS, where necessary, applies Home Office guidelines about how to deal with mentally disordered offenders. Crown Prosecutors must balance the desirability of diverting a defendant who is suffering from significant mental or physical ill health with the need to safeguard the general public;

• the defendant has put right the loss or harm that was caused (but defendants must not avoid prosecution simply because they can pay compensation); or

• details may be made public that could harm sources of information, international relations or national security.

Youth offenders

Crown Prosecutors must consider the interests of a youth when deciding whether it is in the public interest to prosecute. The stigma of a conviction can cause very serious harm to the prospects of a young offender or a young adult. Young offenders can sometimes be dealt with without going to court. But Crown Prosecutors should not avoid prosecuting simply because of the defendant's age. The seriousness of the offence or the offender's past behaviour may make prosecution necessary.

CIRCULAR ON CAUTIONING

The criteria for cautioning adults are set out in the Home Office Circular 18/1994, *The Cautioning of Offenders*, which is reproduced in Appendix 10. It states that there should be a presumption in favour of not prosecuting certain categories of offender, such as elderly people or those who suffer from some sort of mental illness or impairment, or a degree of physical illness. The Home Office has issued guidance on the final warning scheme. See Chapter 6 for further details about this scheme.

MENTAL DISORDER

Home Office Circular 66/90 deals with mentally disordered offenders and states that it is Government policy that alternatives to prosecution should be considered before deciding that prosecution is necessary.

Circular 18/1994 states that:

> 'Where it is considered that a mentally disordered person may have committed an offence, consideration should be given – in consultation with the Crown Prosecution Service where appropriate – to whether any formal action by the police is necessary, particularly where it appears that prosecution is not required in the public interest in view of the nature of the offence . . . If the criteria for a caution are not met, the police should consider whether any action need be taken against the suspect. In some cases the public interest might be met by diverting mentally disordered persons from the criminal justice system and finding alternatives to prosecution, such as admission to hospital . . . or to guardianship . . . or informal support in the community by social services departments.'

Circular on inter-agency working

The Home Office Circular on services for mentally disordered suspects or offenders issued in May 1995 (12/95) supplements Circular 66/90. It offers guidance on when it may be appropriate to charge and prosecute a mentally disordered suspect. The Circular does not use the term 'diversion', in order to stress that diversion and prosecution are not necessarily mutually exclusive. It emphasises that the existence of mental disorder should not be the only factor considered, and the police and CPS should not feel inhibited from pursuing a prosecution if this is considered necessary in the public interest, particularly if the offence is serious or there is a risk to public safety. Where a prosecution takes place, the treatment and care needs of the individual must still be met.

An accompanying booklet, *Mentally Disordered Offenders: Inter-Agency Working*, gives examples of good practice as well as setting out the main responsibilities of those working in the criminal justice system, including the police, probation service, the courts and the prison service. It also recognises that solicitors, particularly those acting in the defence of mentally disordered suspects, have an important role to play in effective inter-agency working and they are encouraged to become involved in local schemes. As well as assisting mentally disordered suspects to obtain the care and treatment they need, you must ensure that they have the same rights and opportunities as any other suspects to clear their names against wrongful allegations, and where appropriate to take responsibility for their actions. With these aims in mind, the booklet contains a separate section giving advice on the role of legal representatives, which was prepared in conjunction with the Law Society's Mental Health and Disability Sub-Committee.

LEVEL OF CHARGE

The CPS and police have agreed a series of charging standards in an attempt to ensure fairness to individual defendants, consistency of charging policy and to avoid overcharging. Three standards have so far been published: on assault; public order; and driving offences.[4]

It will normally be in a client's interests to ensure that the charge is set at the lowest appropriate level (unless the client wants a jury trial and is prepared to take the risk of sentence). In appropriate cases you will wish to bring relevant provisions of the standards to the attention of the prosecutor who must have proper regard to them or be susceptible to judicial review. *The use of the standards is particularly important when an indictable-only charge has been prepared and may justify an adjournment rather that the immediate sending of the case to the Crown Court in areas where s.51 CDA 1998 is in force.* In other areas the issue will need to be considered at an early first or administrative hearing and pursued as further information becomes available.

End notes

1 The *Code for Crown Prosecutors*, para. 2.2.
2 *Ibid.* para. 2.30.
3 *Ibid.* paras. 5.1 and 5.3.
4 See page 77.

CHAPTER 11

Advising your client to plead guilty or not guilty

ADVICE ON PLEA

You are required to:

- explain to your client what the prosecution will have to prove; [68.1]
- discuss the evidence in the case; [68.1]
- advise your client about plea. [68.2]

The decision is crucial and should not be rushed. For procedural issues, see Chapter 9.

Your client must take the decision; you must assist him to reach it by advice. Be aware that failure to make adequate investigation of the proposed plea can result in a serious miscarriage of justice. Especial care must be taken if your client is mentally disordered or of poor understanding. Guides to the availability of sentences and the early release of offenders are set out in Appendices 11 and 12 respectively. If your client has decided to enter a guilty plea, this should be indicated to the court at the earliest proper opportunity to earn the maximum available credit under s.48 CJPOA 1994. That provision requires the court to confirm when passing sentence the extent to which it has taken into account the stage and circumstances in which the defendant indicated an intention to plead guilty.

Consideration before entering a guilty plea

Each case has to be considered on its own merits but there are strong arguments for care before rushing to enter a guilty plea, and your client should be advised about these. [71.1]

The following will be relevant considerations.

- Has there been a sufficient CPS review as to whether it is in the public interest for the matter to proceed?

- Is the level of charge correct?

- Is there sufficient evidence to satisfy the defence lawyer that a plea of guilty is proper?

- Is there sufficient material then available on which properly to mitigate on the defendant's behalf?

- Is there a need for unused material which could only be obtained by a not guilty plea or a committal for trial?

The defence are entitled to advance information in either-way offences and rule 7 of the Magistrates' Court (Advance Information) Rules 1985 is of particular importance. This states that, 'the court shall adjourn the proceedings pending compliance with the requirement [to disclose] unless the court is satisfied that the conduct of the case for the accused will not be substantially prejudiced by non-compliance with the requirement'.

RESEARCHING THE LAW

Before giving advice you must clearly identify each point to prove in relation to each allegation and all possible defences, both special and general.

INVESTIGATING THE DEFENCE CASE

Interviewing the defendant

Just as a criminal prosecution relies upon a complete and reliable investigation of the prosecution witnesses by the police officer, a well prepared defence requires a similarly professional approach to the defendant and the defence witnesses by you. You need to be aware of what experts can teach you about how these interviews should be conducted.[1]

The aims should be:

- to help the witness to give the fullest possible report of his experience;

- to enable the interviewer to create a mental representation as well as a full and faithful written representation of the witness's disclosure;

- that the account should give sufficient detail to enable the interviewer to re-create mentally the sequence of events and descriptions reported by the witness and to follow the witness's line of reasoning or logic. There should be no missing steps in a narrative sequence.

To minimise the risk of preventing, obstructing, influencing, distorting or displacing the witness's account, interviewing should be a two-phase process:

- uninterrupted free narration by the witness;

- probing, to expand and to test the details of the narration and subsequent responses.

Free narration

Invite the witness to give the fullest possible account at his own pace, reporting everything in his mind or mind's eye, editing out nothing and including even the apparently inconsequential. The witness must not be interrupted when narrating. If the witness stops momentarily or for even longer, you must resist the urge to interrupt.

A free-narrative phase elicits approximately 35 per cent of the total accurate information gained from the interview as a whole.

Interruption

Interruption:

- prevents completion of what the witness wanted to say;

- disrupts concentration, the essential requirement for effective and fuller retrieval;

- discourages concerted effort at retrieval, resulting in more superficial responses;

- leads the witness to give shorter, less detailed, responses to fit the reduced talking time.

Create a detailed image in your mind's eye of what is being asserted. Re-create, e.g. by role play, to test out the reality of what is being asserted.

Probing

- Pause after each question and after the witness's answer to remove pressure, help recollection of thoughts and facilitate retrieval.

- Key individuals must be identified when reference is made to them.

- Any verbal exchanges which took place should be referred to. Both sides of the conversation should be reported.

- If an outcome is described, or a reaction, then the triggering cause should also be stated.

- Refer to sensations, feeling and emotions.

Do not topic hop. Move logically from one topic to another, leaving a topic only when it has been exhaustively probed. After a series of connected topics it is wise to give a staged summary, checking back with the witness the sum total of his replies before moving on.

Ask open-ended questions (e.g. 'how', 'why') or closed identificatory questions ('who', 'what', 'when', 'where', 'how', 'which') with minimal supportive prompts ('and', 'then') to give maximum latitude for responding and encourage expansion, creating more detail for probing.

Avoid leading, option or multiple questions. They trigger short, frequently affirmative answers and involve less concentrated retrieval.

Use closed confirmatory questions ('yes', 'no') with care, particularly resisting using these early in the interview.

On completion of the interview give an overall summary, having invited feedback on its accuracy.

If your client admits the offence

Do not necessarily accept your client's admissions at face value: enquire as to his reasons. Challenge the basis of a suspect plea: it may be based on anxiety; poor understanding; outside pressure; the desire to protect another; or a mistake as to the law. Give clear advice.

If appropriate, explain that you cannot go behind the plea and mitigate on the basis that your client 'didn't really do it'.

If your client properly admits the offence but insists on entering a not guilty plea, he is entitled to put the prosecution to proof but explain the professional limitations on your conduct carefully, including your duty not to mislead the court.

You may:

- challenge the court's competence;

- challenge the form of the charge;

- object to inadmissible, irrelevant or prejudicial evidence;

- cross-examine prosecution witnesses to test their credibility or reliability;

- make a submission of no case to answer;

- if that fails, address the court solely on the failure of the prosecution to prove their case.

You may not:

- by your questions put forward any defence which involves an assertion of your client's innocence;

- suggest that a third party may be responsible;

- allow the defendant to give evidence or call a witness to mislead the court, i.e. mount a positive defence.

If your client does not accept these limitations, you must withdraw.

Exceptionally your client may tell you that he is 'innocent' but insist on pleading guilty and ask you to represent him. It is not improper to continue to act, but unwise. Discuss carefully and, if appropriate, try to persuade your client to plead 'not guilty'; but if you fail, advise your client fully and, in particular, that, in mitigation, he cannot assert his innocence. If that is accepted, you may continue, but confirm your advice in writing. If in doubt withdraw.

If your client admits the offence but disputes the evidence

Explain the procedure for a Newton hearing and discuss the evidence. The court will normally sentence on the prosecution's opening or evidence.[2] If, after discussion with the prosecution, this is not accepted by the defence, formal notice should be given and then the court must sentence on the defence version save to the extent that the Crown proves by admissible evidence to the criminal standard that their version is correct.

If your client denies the offence

Do not necessarily accept your client's denial at face value: enquire as to his reasons. If the prosecution evidence appears strong, challenge your client with it. Cross-examine him as robustly as appropriate, taking care to explain why you are doing so ('only a foretaste of things to come'). Do not let your client think you are hostile or no longer on his side. Give clear advice as to the risks and consequences of losing a trial, i.e. if your client's evidence is disbelieved he risks possible destruction of any mitigation. Give clear time to reflect. If a denial is maintained, carry on to consider mode of trial.

If you remain doubtful, strive to avoid pre-judgment and to remain detached. If you think your client is guilty, that does not prevent you from fully defending him. Your opinion may be erroneous and, in any event, it is not your function to judge your client. However, the relationship of solicitor and client is based on mutual trust: if quite exceptionally your belief that your client is guilty is so strong that it prevents you properly representing your client, you should withdraw.

Your client, while denying the offence, may give inconsistent accounts to you. Challenge your client with these and seek his explanation. If your client's explanation is acceptable you may continue to act.

If your client does not know how to plead

You will have to face the difficult question 'what would you do?' Stress that the decision is the client's but give clear advice. Weigh up the strengths and weaknesses of the prosecution and defence cases and the factors your client considers important. If in real doubt, advise that he puts the prosecution to proof.

Confirmation

You should write confirming your client's instructions. When the instructions are against your firm advice, you should:

- set out the reasons for your advice and, if appropriate, invite him to reconsider;
- put your client's instructions in writing and have him sign them.

SENTENCE

Before seeking a client's final instructions on plea you should give realistic advice as to the likely sentence as appropriate in the event of:

- a plea;

- an adverse Newton hearing;

- a conviction in the magistrates' court;

- conviction in the Crown Court.

You must be familiar with:

- the Magistrates' Association Sentencing Guidelines;

- any local variations;

- relevant guideline decisions of the higher courts;

- the circumstances in which obligatory sentences must be imposed and the limited exceptions available in relation to:

    - serious offences;

    - drug trafficking;

    - domestic burglary.

You should adjust this advice to take account of mitigating factors known to you. A table of sentences available to the court and a chart explaining the calculation of early release dates can be found in Appendices 11 and 12.

Such advice may encourage clients whose guilt is likely to be proved but sentence will be below their expectation, to enter a proper guilty plea. Such advice may encourage clients who are not guilty to avoid a guilty plea.

FITNESS TO PLEAD

The Home Office Circular 93/91 on the Criminal Procedure (Insanity and Unfitness to Plead) Act 1991, gives guidelines to all relevant agencies on this issue. The magistrates have no jurisdiction to try an issue of fitness to plead, but for imprisonable cases see below. If your client is apparently unfit to plead the following choices arise:

- discuss with the prosecution the discontinuance of proceedings or reduction of charges so as to allow summary trial wherever the sentencing powers of magistrates are sufficient: see the *Code for Crown Prosecutors* in Appendix 14;

- the use of s.37(3) Mental Health Act 1983 (MHA). This can only be used if the defendant is suffering from mental illness or severe mental impairment. It cannot be used if the defendant is suffering from psychopathic disorder or mental impairment which is not severe;

- for a summary offence, advise the court of the position; the court will enter 'not guilty' pleas and order a trial;

- the magistrates may be persuaded to order a report on the question of fitness if there is a possibility that the defendant may recover in the near future. Alternatively, an extension of legal aid could be sought for a report to be obtained. If someone is unfit to plead but with appropriate medication and treatment can become fit to plead within a reasonable time then adjournments should be sought until that point is reached.

Home Office Circulars 66/90 and 12/95

Reference should be made to the above circulars. Circular 66/90 sets out the powers available for dealing with cases involving mentally disordered offenders and emphasises that it is Government policy that the mentally ill should normally be diverted away from the criminal justice system. Circular 12/95 provides information about central and local initiatives and developments in inter-agency working and advises against diversion from the criminal justice system where the offence is serious or the defendant represents a danger to the public.

You should try to arrange the most favourable course of action for the defendant, having regard to the following:

- the urgency of obtaining treatment;

- the seriousness of the offence;

- whether a lesser charge would suffice;

- whether a defendant is in custody, or on bail;

- whether a hospital is available and is willing to offer treatment.

Note that, in discussing an appropriate disposal, the prosecution may request sight of a copy of any medical report. Beware the potential dangers of disclosing confidential or damaging information; obtain the views of the psychiatrist. If medical reports are required you will retain control if you obtain the report rather than allowing the court to order one.

It is essential to establish where your client last lived or usually lives. In case of difficulty you can contact the regional forensic psychiatry advisor at the regional health authority. Courts can assist by requiring the authority to provide information about possible arrangements.

BAIL

Conditions can be imposed requiring co-operation with arrangements to obtain medical reports: s.30(2) MCA 1980. Clients should not be remanded in custody merely because they are mentally unwell.[3]

SUMMARY TRIAL OF SUMMARY OR EITHER-WAY OFFENCES

Problems

The trial of the defendant who is mentally ill and incapable of giving proper instructions may present you with practical and ethical difficulties. You can only take your client's instructions as you find them, and make the court aware of the position.

It may be that a defence can be established upon the absence of *mens rea* at the time of the offence.

Non-imprisonable

If the offence is non-imprisonable, the court must convict before it can order medical or other reports or decide upon disposal.

Imprisonable

If the offence is imprisonable, the court may deal with the defendant without proceeding to full conviction providing it is satisfied that the defendant 'did the act or made the omission charged', but to do so it needs to be aware of the defendant's apparent illness. If satisfied that the necessary conditions are met, the court may then make a Hospital Order: s.37(3) MHA 1983.

NON-SUMMARY CASES

The magistrates have no jurisdiction to handle indictable-only crime, or either-way offences where the court does not use s.37(3) MHA 1983 and declines jurisdiction. These cases will be committed, transferred or sent to the Crown Court.

Crown Court

At the Crown Court the fitness of the client to plead will, in appropriate cases, be tried by a separate jury as a distinct issue. (See the Criminal Procedure (Insanity) Act 1964, as amended, and Home Office Circular 93/91 referred to above.) Careful preparation and detailed medical advice will be required. You should obtain the necessary authority to incur the relevant expenditure and give instructions to your experts at the earliest opportunity. You should seek to obtain disclosure of all relevant medical records.

If a client may be acquitted of the offence you should not raise the issue of fitness to plead until the judge has held that there is a case to answer.

Remember that insanity is a defence if the defence can prove McNaughton insanity to negative the necessary mental element. You should refer to an appropriate practitioner text on this.

If the client is found unfit to plead or acquitted by reason of insanity, the court may impose:

- an absolute discharge;
- a hospital order, with or without restrictions, without limit of time or for a specified period (except in cases of murder);
- a guardianship order;
- a supervision and treatment order.

End notes

1 Shepherd, E and Milne, R, 'Full and faithful: ensuring quality practice and integrity of outcome in witness interviews', (1999) *Analysing Witness Testimony.* Blackstone Press.
2 *R. v. Newton* (1983) 77 Cr App R 13; *R. v. Tolera* [1998] Crim LR 425. Although the court is not bound to do so and may itself direct a Newton hearing. In this situation the defendant cannot change his plea: *R. v. Beswick* [1996] Crim LR 62.
3 Home Office Circular 66/90 para. 7.

CHAPTER 12

Choosing a place of trial

If your client is charged with an either-way offence, you will have to advise him about plea before venue and if appropriate mode of trial.

PLEA BEFORE VENUE

If your client is pleading guilty it will usually be advantageous to enter the plea in the magistrates court at the plea before venue hearing. In the Crown Court greater sentences are generally imposed.

If the magistrates have sufficient sentencing powers, after allowing for discount, they should retain the case. Be aware of the *Magistrates' Association Sentencing Guidelines* summarised in Appendix 16.

If the contents of a pre-sentence report or a Newton hearing may result in the magistrates having sufficient sentencing powers they should order a report or hold a Newton hearing before deciding whether to commit for sentence.

If a defendant is on bail prior to the plea before venue hearing, that bail should continue.[1] You should, however, consider with a client in custody the impact of the conviction on his prison status, and balance this against any possible loss of discount for a later entry of a guilty plea.

The procedure

The procedure applies to those facing either-way charges[2] who are 18 and over at the date the procedure begins. If a defendant is willing to indicate that he will plead guilty, there will not be any representations by either party as to the place of trial and the magistrates are not able to decline jurisdiction. The case will proceed to sentence. However, within their jurisdiction, the magistrates have power to commit the defendant to the Crown Court for sentence under the provisions of s.38 MCA 1980. The primary advantages to the defence of this procedure is that magistrates are not limited at the early stages to hearing the Crown's version of events; indeed the reverse is true as *R. v. Newton* (1983) 77 Cr App R 13 applies in full force. Thus the court has to sentence on the basis of the version of the facts indicated by the defence unless the Crown has proved another version to the criminal standard. Furthermore, the defence is able to place before the court all personal mitigating circumstances. This enables some thousands of cases to be concluded within the magistrates' court jurisdiction rather than be committed for sentence.

If a defendant wishes to indicate a not guilty plea or to indicate no plea at all, then the prosecution makes representations as to the place of trial and the defence have the same opportunity.

The consequences of using the procedure

However, it is necessary to advise defendants of the practical consequences of using the procedure. [71.1] The following questions are critical:

- Will the court be willing to order a pre-sentence report within its own jurisdiction rather than by immediately committing for sentence, allowing the report to be obtained at the Crown Court stage?

- In custody cases will the defendant be content to lose privileges as occurs immediately upon conviction?

A defendant who pleads guilty before the justices to an offence triable either-way and is committed to the Crown Court for sentence should normally be entitled to a greater credit on sentence than a defendant who delays making such a plea until appearing on indictment in the Crown Court. Such a guilty plea does not normally alter the position as to the defendant's bail or remand in custody. In the usual case, when a person who had been on bail enters a guilty plea at that stage, the practice should be to continue his bail, even if it is anticipated that a custodial sentence will be imposed by the Crown Court, unless there is good reason for remanding him in custody.[3]

If he is in custody, then after entering such a plea at that stage, it would be unusual, if the reasons for remand in custody remained unchanged, to alter the position. The defendant would, however, have the benefit of a greater discount than if he had delayed his plea until the Crown Court.

Where the defendant pleads guilty to some either-way offences but elects trial in relation to other related offences, that is offences which could have been placed on the same indictment, s.38A MCA 1980 requires that the court shall adjourn the cases where the guilty plea is entered until the committal of the other matters. At that stage the court has a discretion to commit for sentence even if its own powers would have been sufficient to deal with the matter. The Crown Court can then deal with all sentencing at the same time.

File standards

In cases committed for sentence all evidential material on the expedited file must be typed. Where a defendant has been committed for sentence on a remand file, this must be upgraded to an expedited file.

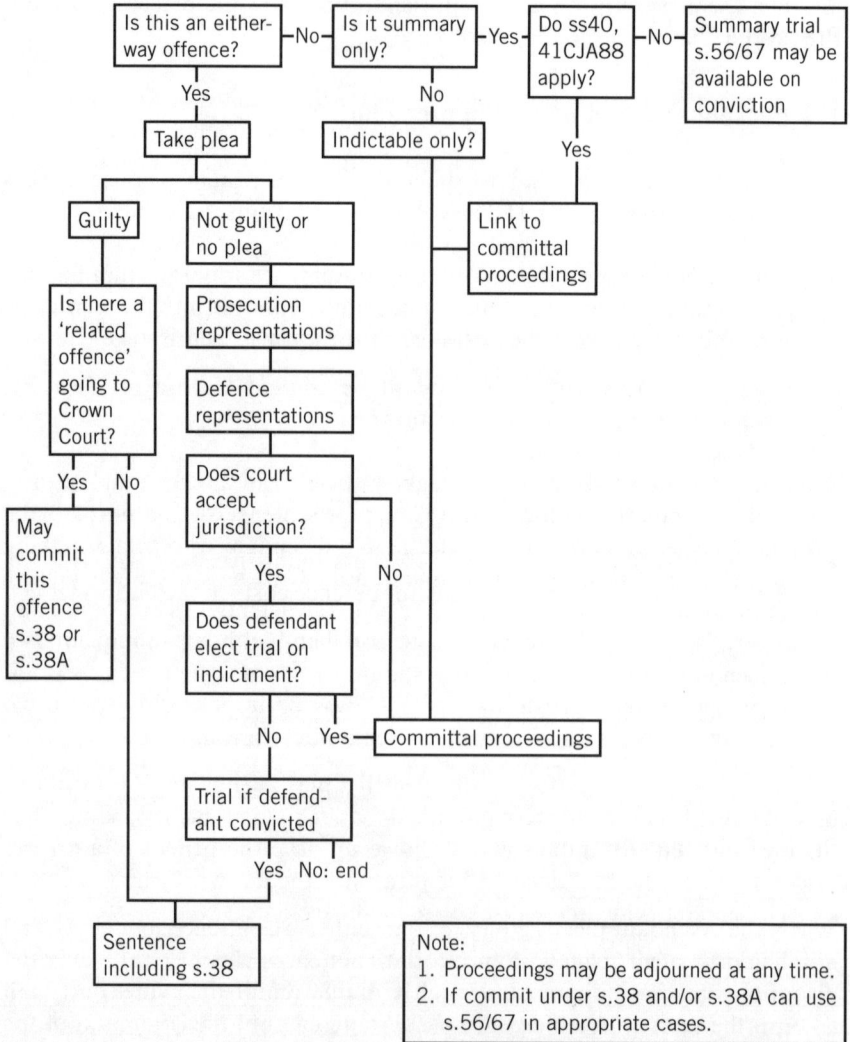

Figure 12.1 A summary of the procedures in either-way cases

Table 12.1 The Crown Court's sentencing powers

Committals under	Court powers
s.38 MCA 1980	Full powers of the Crown Court
s.38A MCA 1980	Full powers of the Crown Court unless acquittals in all matters on indictment in which case magistrates' powers
s.56 CJA 1967	Magistrates' court powers
s.40 CJA 1988	Magistrates' court powers
s.41 CJA 1988	Magistrates' court powers.

Pressures

If your client is pleading not guilty, be aware that, whatever the immediate pressures on your client, with hindsight your client would, in most cases, choose the tribunal most likely to acquit him. Bring to bear your experience of the local courts. Perhaps there is a greater likelihood of acquittal in the Crown Court, but not for every type of case.

If you consider the Crown Court most appropriate, but your client favours trial in the magistrates' court, ask your client his reasons and discuss them in detail. Your client may be worried about the delay before trial; try and put it in context and remove exaggerated concerns.

Summary trial advantages

- Usually less delay before trial.

- Less prosecution costs and when Access to Justice Act 1999 in force, client may only be ordered to pay for defence costs in the Crown Court.

- No duty to have a defence statement (when secondary disclosure not required).

- Lesser sentencing powers and lesser sentence likely.

- Less intimidating surroundings.

Crown Court advantages

- The greater and timely disclosure of the evidence.

- The pace of the trial is slower, for the benefit of the jury, providing the opportunity for a more thorough examination of the evidence.

- Perhaps a greater prospect of acquittal by the jury, e.g. where the prosecution case depends entirely on police evidence.

- The judge is a qualified lawyer who will readily understand any legal issues raised by the defence and be able to deal with them in the absence of the jury, e.g. a disputed confession or a disputed inference from silence in the police station is dealt with by a *voir-dire*.

- Better forum for dealing with expert evidence and complex issues.

Arguments

If you wish to argue for summary trial be aware of the relevant provisions of the mode of trial guidelines (Appendix 17). They recommend that all either-way cases should be tried summarily unless there are specific arguments to the contrary. The absence of an aggravating factor is a powerful, if not decisive argument in favour of summary trial. Your client should be advised about the procedure. [71–2]

YOUTHS

Those under 18 do not normally have a right to elect jury trial but issues can arise as to the preferred place of trial for them.

You should be aware of your client's age at all stages:

- if a youth attains 18, a case may be remitted from the youth court to the adult magistrates' court. Consider relevant arguments;

- if a youth is jointly charged with an adult, they may appear in the adult magistrates' court: be aware of the limitations this imposes on sentence without remittal to the youth court;

- if a youth is jointly charged with an adult who is committed, transferred or sent to the Crown Court the youth may also be committed, etc., if it is in the interests of justice. Consider with your client the preferred place of trial and relevant arguments;

- if a youth faces a grave crime consider:[4] whether the magistrates' or youth court may decline jurisdiction because they may not have sufficient sentencing power; your client's preferred place of trial; and all relevant arguments. In the event of a guilty plea it will be usual to seek to have the matter tried at the summary level as this significantly limits the court's sentencing powers.

End notes

1 *R.* v. *Rafferty* [1998] Crim LR 433.
2 See Appendix 18.
3 *R.* v. *Rafferty* [1998] Crim LR 433.
4 Those crimes listed in s.53 Children and Young Persons Act 1993.

CHAPTER 13

Preparing for sentence: plea of guilty or conviction

Whether your client is pleading guilty or not guilty it will be essential to prepare, at the earliest opportunity, as much as possible of a statement, for use on entry of the plea or in the event of a conviction. This information should be added to the core information about your client (see Chapter 5).

STATEMENT: FOR GUILTY PLEA OR CONVICTION

Remember that for sentencing there can be no specimen charges.[1] The court may only sentence matters which are charged or TICd. Careful consideration should therefore be given to the evidence in support of a TIC before advising a client to accept it in court. A plea in mitigation will normally be structured in three stages:

- offence mitigation;

- offender mitigation;

- recommendation as to outcome(s).

This approach is adopted by the *Magistrates' Association Sentencing Guidelines*. In preparing a mitigation the following are among the relevant issues.

Reasons for the offence/the offence itself

1. Try to find a cause for why your client committed the offence.
2. If the crime was opportunistic, why was he tempted?
3. If this was your client's first offence, why did your client do it when he has managed to resist the temptation before?
4. What does your client think about it, and himself, now?

5. You will need to relate the information above to the instructions you already have about his drink, drugs, psychiatric or gambling problems.

6. If you know, from what your client has told you, that he has such a problem, find out what this means for him on a daily basis.

7. Were there financial problems? If so, how did they begin and why could they not be brought under control?

8. Explain why your client committed the crime in a way that puts the act in the context of his life generally.

9. Was your client related to the victim and acting out of revenge or in retaliation?

10. At best you can establish a chain of events, each apparently outside his control at the time, ending with a situation where the crime was irresistible.

11. Was your client influenced by others?

12. The court will want to try to understand your client and why he committed the offence.

13. Be receptive to all the signals about your client that he is giving out, consciously and unconsciously.

14. Think about the sort of information the advocate will want – the factors which make the offence more serious and those which help the mitigation. [84.1, 84.2]. See the 'aggravating and mitigating factors' in the *Magistrates' Association Sentencing Guidelines* at Appendix 16 and the 'aggravating factors' listed in Chapter 7 relating to obtaining legal aid: Table 13.1 shows an abbreviated list of these.

Table 13.1 Abbreviated aggravating factors

Aggravation	Mitigation
Degree of loss caused or planned	
Person in authority	Minor role
Premeditated	Under influence of another
Seriousness	Provocation
Use of weapons	Triviality
Public place	Distress
Vulnerable victim	Impulsive
Organised	Personal use
Length of time	Restitution/recovery
Breach of trust	Financial pressure
Breach of bail	
Racial aggravation	

15. Consider the 'Features relevant to individual offences' in the *Mode of Trial Guidelines*: see Appendix 17.
16. Pay particular regard to any aggravating factors so that you can minimise them as far as possible and put them in context.
17. Where others were involved, consider how your client was influenced by them and the extent of your client's role. [83.1]

Attitude to offence

- Did your client admit the offence to the police?

- Did your client plead guilty or was he convicted?

- Did your client tell the police about offences which they could not otherwise have proved against him?

- Did your client help the police recover stolen property or provide other information of value?

- Did your client show distress, regret or remorse? [85.2]

Consequences of offence

Think of ways in which your client has been punished already.

- How has the offence affected his personal relationships?

- Has your client waited a long time to be sentenced?

- Has he spent time in custody, on remand? [86]

- Was this your client's first time in custody? What was it like? If you can use his own words it is more likely to get the court's attention.

- Has your client lost his job? [89] How difficult will it be to find another one?

- It may be your client's first conviction – losing his good name.

Positive steps awaiting sentence

- How has your client spent his time waiting to be sentenced? Has your client kept out of trouble?

- Has your client taken positive steps to tackle the problems which led him to commit the crime?

- How have your client's circumstances changed for the better?

- If appropriate, advise him to save up money to pay a fine or compensation.

- Make sure that the advocate knows the history of the case and whether your client pleaded guilty or was convicted.

- What is your client's income and its source at the time of sentencing? [88]

Consequences of sentence

What are the detrimental effects of the likely sentence:

- on your client?

- on others?

PERSONAL MITIGATING FACTORS

You will also need to consider personal mitigating factors such as:

- age;

- character;

- mental disability or illness;

- physical disability or illness;

- family relationships;

- employment history;

Your statement of core information should contain most of the details.

MITIGATION AS TO PENALTY

Be aware of the primary sentences and secondary sentences which are available to the court which will sentence your client. A schedule of the availability of primary sentences appears at Appendix 11.

You should keep your recommendations close to, but below the likely penalty and should consider how a primary penalty may be lessened if a secondary penalty is attached. You should always seek your client's instructions before advocating a particular secondary penalty.

Secondary penalties include:

- compensation;
- disqualification (from driving or company directorship);
- exclusion/banning (exclusion or banning orders in relation to association football/exclusion from public houses);
- deprivation;
- forfeiture;
- restitution;
- confiscation;
- costs;
- deportation recommendation;
- Restraining Order;
- Reparation Order.

Custody threshold

In cases approaching the custody threshold courts will have particular regard to:

- admissions and genuine remorse;
- youth and immaturity;
- attempts to overcome addiction;
- physical or mental disability;
- character;
- family responsibilities;
- the fact (if such is the case) that it could amount to a first prison sentence.[2]

Credit for guilty plea

Be aware that the courts should give credit for a guilty plea related to the stage of the proceedings at which a guilty plea was entered. They are

146

required to indicate the extent to which they have done so when announcing their decision.[3]

Welfare

You should be aware of any problems (such as drink, drugs, debts, family, housing, employment) from which your client suffers and refer to the relevant agency. It may assist in a guilty plea to show that constructive efforts are being made to deal with the problem. You should then actively liaise with the agency.

PREPARATION

Consider with your client, as appropriate, the obtaining of references, medical or pre-sentence reports; if an endorsable offence, inform your client that his driving licence will be required at court.

WITNESS TO CHARACTER

Consider obtaining a letter of reference from your client's school, youth club, work or elsewhere. For an impressive character witness whom you may call to give evidence at court obtain details as follows:

- name and address;

- occupation, employment, positions of responsibility, qualifications;

- relationship to client: personal, employment, other, and how long/how well known;

- opinion of client's character and trustworthiness;

- opinion as to effect on client of offence, court hearings and potential penalty;

- practical offer of help or employment.

Before calling a character witness, ensure he is aware of the precise charges; the defendant's previous convictions; the nature of the prosecution case; the nature of the defendant's account; and the potential sentence.

An unrealistic or overprotective character witness will not be persuasive.

Make a note of the availability of a character witness on the file. [87.2]

EXPERTS

Consider obtaining authorities for any medical or other expert's reports you need for your mitigation. This may avoid causing unnecessary adjournments for the court to order a report and you will retain control of the report.

TAPES OF INTERVIEWS

It may not be necessary to listen to the tape in the case of an unequivocal guilty plea in a straightforward case where the short descriptive note of interview accords with the client's instructions. In all other cases it may prove beneficial to listen to a tape to check the accuracy of the prosecution's records and to identify further mitigating factors. If your client is mentally disordered or of poor understanding, you should routinely listen before considering the plea.

See page 163, *Listening to tape-recordings of police interviews with defendants* – guidance from the Criminal Law Committee of the Law Society.

MENTAL HEALTH

Disposal

Consider the best disposal at each stage.

1. Remand to hospital. The court has the power if remanding a defendant in custody to remand to a hospital for reports.[4]
2. Interim Hospital Order. Upon conviction for any imprisonable offence, in order to assist the court in deciding whether to make a Hospital Order, an Interim Hospital Order may be made to enable the defendant's condition and response to be evaluated.[5]
3. Psychiatric Probation Order. If the court makes a Probation Order, it may attach a condition that the defendant submits to psychiatric treatment.[6]
4. Hospital Order. Upon conviction for an imprisonable offence or after finding the defendant did the act or made the omission charged, a Hospital Order may be made requiring the defendant to be detained in a suitable hospital for treatment: the order does not enforce attendance for a set period and the date of release is determined by doctors.[7]

5. Guardianship. As an alternative to a Hospital Order, but under the same provisions, a Guardianship Order may be made where appropriate by which the defendant is placed under the guardianship of the local social services authority. The purpose is to ensure care and protection is provided. The guardian has powers to require the defendant to live where directed, attend for medical treatment, education, training, etc.[8]

6. Restriction Orders. The magistrates have no power to make Restriction Orders under s.41 MHA 1983, but may commit in custody to Crown Court for sentence for that purpose.[9]

7. Hospital Direction and Limitation Order. This is a new form of Hospital Order (under s.45A MHA 1983) attached to a period of imprisonment. The court must be satisfied:

(a) on the evidence of two medical practitioners (one of whom must give evidence orally);

(b) that the offender is suffering from a psychopathic disorder, that the disorder is of a nature or degree which makes it appropriate for him to be detained in a hospital for medical treatment; and

(c) that some treatment is likely to alleviate or prevent a deterioration to his condition.

An offender who is sentenced to a term of imprisonment with a Hospital and Limitation Order will be conveyed to a specific hospital and treated as if he had been sentenced to imprisonment and transferred to hospital. If the offender ceases to be in need of treatment before the expiration of the sentence, he will be liable to be returned to prison.

If he is still in hospital when the sentence expires, he will cease to be subject to restriction and will remain in hospital as if detained under s.37 MHA 1983. He will be eligible for release on the decision of the responsible medical officer.

The power is only available in the Crown Court.

INFORMATION ON HOSPITALS

In finding hospital accommodation for a mentally disordered defendant, it is essential to establish where your client last lived or usually lives. Health authorities will not normally accept responsibility for a patient from outside their area.

Health authority services

1. **Local psychiatric hospitals** These are run by mental health NHS trusts. Local health authorities are the commissioning 'purchaser'. They provide facilities for patients who may from time to time need treatment and care in hospital, sometimes in a secure setting. The provision of secure wards for patients who are disruptive or difficult to contain in open wards varies greatly. Health authorities or trusts provide detailed information about provision of local psychiatric services.

2. **Medium secure units** These provide treatment and care in a secure setting for patients whose disruptive or possibly harmful behaviour constitutes a risk to others. Generally a period of up to 18 months' or two years' treatment is provided. Detailed information is available from regional forensic psychiatry advisors.

Private health services

There are psychiatric hospitals in the private sector, known as registered mental nursing homes, whose facilities and services fill gaps in the state scheme. It may be that a regional authority will pay for the cost of providing accommodation at a private hospital for a patient within its responsibility whose needs cannot be otherwise met.

Special hospitals

There are three special hospitals, run by Broadmoor, Ashurst and Rampton Hospital Authorities which provide special security for patients subject to MHA 1983 detention because of their dangerous, violent or criminal propensities. Generally, they will only admit those who cannot be accepted anywhere less secure.

Court order

If you have a client who has been diagnosed by one doctor (perhaps at the prison) as suffering from a mental disorder which justifies a Hospital Order, but you cannot find a psychiatric hospital which is willing to admit him, you should contact the regional forensic psychiatry advisor at the regional health authority.

In the event of a failure to respond, or a conflict between hospitals or authorities as to responsibility for your client, consider applying for an order from the court.

If a court is minded to make a Hospital Order or Interim Hospital Order, it may require the regional health authority to provide information upon hospitals in its region or elsewhere at which arrangements could be made for his admission.[10]

End notes

1 *R.* v. *Kidd Conovan and Other* [1997] Crim LR 766.
2 *R.* v. *Howells* [1998] Crim LR 836.
3 s.48 CJPOA 1994.
4 s.35 MHA 1983.
5 s.38 MHA 1983.
6 s.3 Powers of Criminal Courts Act 1973.
7 s.37 MHA 1983.
8 ss.37, 40 MHA 1983.
9 s.43 MHA 1983.
10 s.39 MHA 1983.

CHAPTER 14

Preparing for different types of hearing in the magistrates' court

SUMMARY AND EITHER-WAY OFFENCES

Date of first appearance in bail cases

S.46 CDA 1998 (by amendment of s.47(3) PACE 1984) requires defendants to be bailed after charge to the first court able to accommodate the case (the 'next available court').

What is expected to happen at the 'next available court'?

For defendants either bailed to the 'next available court', or produced from custody normally two types of court are organised. These are Early First Hearings (EFHs) for straightforward guilty pleas, and Early Administrative Hearings (EAHs) for cases where a not guilty plea is expected, the plea is unknown or there is a guilty plea which is not straightforward.

Staff are available in Administrative Support Units (ASUs) at police stations to assist in early file preparation. Crown Prosecutors and designated caseworkers (DCWs) undertake the early review of cases which they can be expected to present at the next available court.

The need for full and sufficient information is vital in order for the court to make the appropriate decision on where the case should be heard following plea, or to pass an appropriate sentence for the offence taking into account the interests of the victim, and for the defence to advise on plea; and mitigate if a plea is entered.

In cases where a guilty plea is anticipated by the police in either-way cases, advance information will be prepared for service at court, if not before, in the hope that the duty solicitor, or 'duty solicitor of choice', can deal with the case before three justices at an EFH.

Early first hearings – EFHs

- Full bench required.

- Summary/either-way cases where a straightforward guilty plea is anticipated may be prosecuted by a DCW with a duty/own solicitor defending.

The *Trials Issues Group Manual of Guidance* Editorial Board[1] has produced criteria for straightforward guilty plea cases, for which an expedited file can be prepared. These are:

- Guilty plea anticipated (i.e. the defendant admits all the elements of the offence or the offence was witnessed by a police officer and the defendant has given no indication of an intention to deny the matter).

- Straightforward – no complicated or contentious issues of fact or law involved, and no aggravating public interest issues involved which require in-depth consideration.

- Generally, a maximum of two defendants.

- Generally, a maximum of three key witness statements.

- Capable of being dealt with at the first hearing (note: some cases may require an adjournment to resolve straightforward issues in relation to sentencing – for example a pre-sentence report, or for compensation or previous criminal history issues to be resolved).

Straightforward guilty plea cases will be suitable for review and presentation by DCWs where the following criteria[2] also apply:

- the offence before the court is summary or triable either-way but suitable for summary disposal;

- the case involves only adult defendants;

- the accused is on bail and there is no objection to its continuance, or the accused has been remanded in custody by the court following a guilty plea.

In appropriate cases you should consider with your client whether an adjournment should be sought. Do not be pressurised by the court into advising your client to plead guilty against your better judgement. See the checklist 'Considerations before entering a guilty plea' in Chapter 11, p. 126.

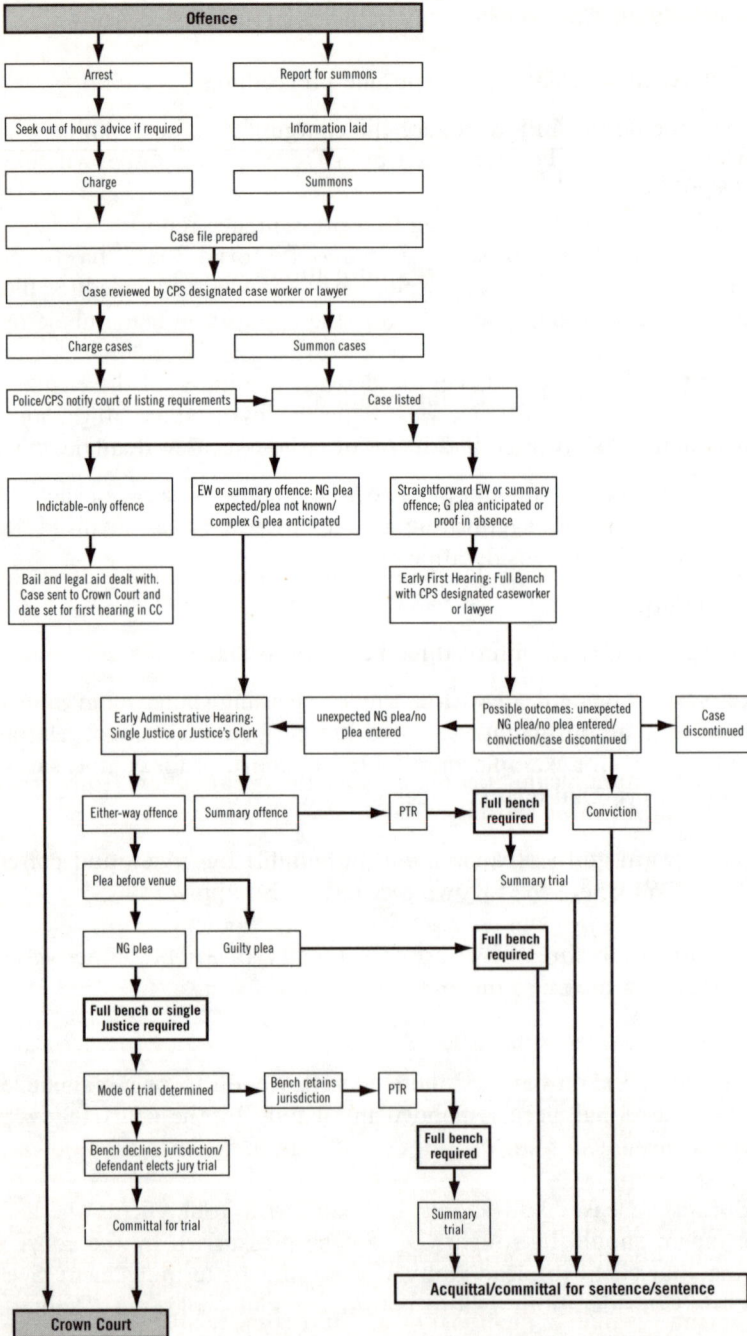

Figure 14.1 Cases in the magistrates' court: the procedure

Reasons why an adjournment may be necessary are listed below:

- to persuade the CPS to discontinue proceedings;
- to persuade the CPS to reduce the charge;
- to obtain unused material;
- to obtain information leading to a pre-sentence report;
- to obtain information to verify mitigation;
- to be represented by own solicitor (the application being made by the duty solicitor);
- to obtain further advance information;
- it is necessary to trace and interview witnesses before advice on plea can be given;
- to obtain a medical report;
- to obtain a report on diversion as a disposal (including diversion of juveniles);
- advance information served is too bulky to take instructions on;
- an SDN shows an admission which the client denies, and there is a need to listen to the tape;
- cannot communicate at court because the client suffers from a mental health problem or learning disability;
- the client has difficulty communicating in English and an interpreter is not available;
- the client is in a state of emotional turmoil;
- the client is drunk or under the influence of drugs.

It may be adjourned to another EFH, or to an EAH or ordinary court list if some complexity has been identified so that it is no longer classified as a straightforward guilty plea case. What may be straightforward from a prosecution point of view may not be straightforward in terms of defending that person.

The readiness of the defence solicitor to advise on plea and mitigate at the first or an adjourned hearing, without further preparation, will depend upon the extent to which he was available to take instructions in the police station (time available; facilities) or at court (time available; facilities).

If the defence solicitor wished to persuade the CPS to discontinue the prosecution, the case would normally be adjourned from the EFH to an EAH.

There will be cases that the court adjourns for further information, e.g. a DVLC print-out, an up-to-date CRO, a PSR or details of compensation.

Early administrative hearings – EAHs

Case management

S.49 CDA 1998 provides that a range of magistrates' courts' powers may be exercised by a single justice or, under rules of procedure provided for by MCA 1980, by justices' clerks. A justice will be required if the defendant is produced from custody.

S.50 CDA 1998 indicates that where a person has been charged with an offence (other than an indictable-only offence), a single justice or, under rules of procedure provided for by MCA 1980, a justices' clerk may deal with legal aid and may also exercise their powers to sit as a single justice.

EAHs:

- may take place before a single justice or justices' clerk;
- occur when:
  - the plea is not known;
  - a contested case is anticipated; or
  - guilty pleas which are not straightforward (summary/either-way) require case management.

A CPS lawyer will prosecute with a duty solicitor/own solicitor defending.

Routinely:

- pleas are entered;
- a PTR date set;
- legal aid is considered;
- the case is adjourned;
- bail conditions are considered.

If 'PTR type' directions are given, these are usually:

- to the prosecution: to give primary disclosure;
- to the prosecution: to serve a copy of the interview tape;
- to the defence: to obtain full instructions from the client;
- to liaise with other parties to agree s.10 CJA facts and serve a joint written statement on the court.

The single justice or justices' clerk may:

- remand in custody (justices' clerks cannot);
- determine/grant legal aid;
- extend bail, or impose or vary conditions of bail (justices' clerks can only do so with the consent of the parties);
- mark an information as withdrawn;
- dismiss any information, or discharge an accused in respect of an information where no evidence is offered by the prosecution;
- request a pre-sentence report following a plea of guilty, and give an indication of the seriousness of the offence for that purpose (justices' clerks cannot give seriousness indication);
- request a medical report, and for that purpose remand the accused in custody or on bail (justices' clerks may not remand the accused in custody or on bail with different conditions unless the parties consent);
- make an order for the payment of defence costs out of central funds;
- remit an offender to another court for sentence;
- where a person has been granted police bail to appear at a magistrates' court, appoint an earlier time for his appearance;
- give a direction prohibiting the publication of matters disclosed or exempted from disclosure in court (justices' clerks may not);
- extend, with the consent of the accused, a custody time-limit or an overall time-limit;
- give, vary or revoke orders for separate or joint trials in the cases of two or more accused or two or more informations (justices' clerks may not do so without the consent of the parties);
- where an accused has been convicted of an offence, order him to produce his driving licence;

- give directions for the conduct of the trial, including:
    - the timetable of the proceedings;
    - attendance of the parties;
    - service of documents (including summaries of any legal arguments relied upon by the parties);
    - the manner in which evidence is to be given.

INDICTABLE-ONLY OFFENCES

The preliminary hearing in the magistrates' court

CDA 1998 makes provision (in ss.51 and 52, and Schedule 3) for adult defendants charged with an offence which is triable only on indictment to be sent straight to the Crown Court for trial, following a preliminary hearing in a magistrates' court. The purpose of this hearing is to determine whether there is an indictable-only offence charged and whether there are related offences which also fall to be sent under s.51, to decide the defendant's remand status, and to deal with legal aid.

Cases to which s.51 applies

Offences triable only on indictment

*S.51 covers not only those offences which are invariably triable on indictment, but also those which **in certain circumstances** are so triable, including offences of trafficking in a Class A drug or a domestic burglary where the accused has two previous convictions for such an offence (ss.3 and 4 Crime (Sentences) Act 1997), and an either-way offence which is charged with an offence under s.17 Firearms Act 1968.*

Adult defendants

An adult accused falls to be dealt with under s.51 where the offence in respect of which he is appearing:

- *is indictable only; or*
- *is an either-way offence (or a summary offence which is imprisonable or carries disqualification) which is related to an indictable-only offence in respect of which he is sent to the Crown Court under s.51; or*

158

- *is an either-way offence with which he is jointly charged with another defendant who is sent to the Crown Court in respect of a related indictable-only offence.*

*An adult accused appearing on an indictable-only charge **must** be sent forthwith to the Crown Court to be tried for that offence. There is, likewise, no discretion in respect of any related offences for which he, or any other person who is jointly charged with him for a related either-way offence, appears at the same time.*

*But the court does have a discretion whether to send to the Crown Court under s.51 a defendant who appears charged with either-way offences which are related to an indictable-only offence for which he has **previously** been so sent, or another person who is jointly charged with such a defendant.*

Juveniles

Juveniles charged with an indictable-only offence are not liable to be sent to the Crown Court in their own right. But where a juvenile is charged jointly with an adult with any indictable offence in respect of which the adult is sent to the Crown Court under s.51, the magistrates may send the juvenile to the Crown Court as well if they consider that it is in the interests of justice for him to be tried jointly with the adult defendant. Where they do so, the magistrates may also send the juvenile to the Crown Court to be tried for any related offences.

Listing

The preliminary hearing in a case to which s.51 applies should be listed before two or more justices.

Adjournments

S.52(5) provides that the hearing in the magistrates' court may be adjourned. But it is envisaged that, given the limited nature of the court's function under s.51 it will seldom be considered necessary to adjourn. Circumstances in which it might be necessary to do so are set out below.

Bail applications

Normally only the first bail application will be made in the magistrates' court. However, if there is a lack of essential information, it may be appropriate to adjourn for long enough to obtain it.

Further consideration of charges

The court need only satisfy itself that the defendant is an adult who is charged with an indictable-only offence. It is not the purpose of the preliminary hearing for the magistrates to determine whether there is a prima facie case. The Crown has the option of withdrawing if it is clear that the indictable-only charge cannot be sustained. Where there is doubt, it would not normally be appropriate to seek to adjourn the hearing unless a short adjournment (of days, not weeks) is likely to resolve the issue.

It may be appropriate to adjourn the preliminary hearing where the prosecution request further time to investigate alleged related offences and it is desired to invoke the power to commit the accused to police detention under s.128(7) MCA 1980 to allow them to do so.

EITHER-WAY CASES: APPLICATION TO DISCHARGE AT COMMITTAL

When a defendant is to be tried in the Crown Court (on either-way offences *or, until s.51 CDA applies offences triable only on indictment*) you will need to consider whether the prosecution evidence discloses a case to answer. If the evidence is strong you should consider again with your client whether a plea might be entered in the magistrates' court to any either-way offence. This will necessitate an application under s.25 MCA 1980. This will normally be granted, particularly if the defendant has not formally entered a plea.[3]

If the case is to continue to trial, you should then consider with your client whether applications should be made to discharge the defendant from all or any of those offences. There are tactical issues to bear in mind. If raising the matter will merely give the prosecution notice of an error which they can easily correct, or result in the substitution of another offence triable on indictment, it may be better not to do so. In that event it is good practice to obtain your client's written consent. If, however, the case will be discharged or the prosecution persuaded to discontinue or substitute a lesser charge, a submission should be prepared. Submissions as to the admissibility of evidence may be made at a committal hearing but not if they raise issues under ss.76 or 78 PACE 1984 as such argument may only be raised at trial. Defence evidence may not be called. Documentary hearsay may be introduced for the prosecution on a certificate from the prosecutor.

You must not agree to commit a case for trial until you have had time to fully consider evidence and to discuss in confidence with your client any tactical issues arising. You should, if necessary, seek an adjournment so that proper consideration may be given to these issues.

End notes

1 Guidance issued 4 June 1999.
2 *Ibid.*
3 Consider *R.* v. *Warrington JJ ex p. McDonagh* [1981] Crim LR 629.

CHAPTER 15

Preparing the case for a plea of not guilty

THE NEED FOR TIMELY PREPARATION

Preparation of a criminal case should begin in the police station and proceed with as much speed as possible. You should not delay obtaining material from the prosecution, or defence evidence, until after the mode of trial hearing or entry of a not guilty plea.

In particular:

- obtain and listen to tapes of interview;

- obtain and consider custody records;

- consider the need for a defence statement and begin work on it;

- consider the need for supporting evidence such as videos which may be 'wiped' if not obtained early. You may need, with your client's authority, to bring such material to the attention of the police.

- in cases which will go to the Crown Court obtain a through Legal Aid Order to enable preparation of the Crown Court case even ahead of committal.

INVESTIGATING THE PROSECUTION CASE: TESTING THE EVIDENCE

The first stage of preparation for trial is to test thoroughly the prosecution case.

To do so, you will first wish to ensure that there has been full and sufficient disclosure – information about unused material is given by the police to the prosecution on the MG6 series of forms, see Appendix 19. If you are seeking to cast doubt upon the prosecution's case and/or build an alternative case theory, you will need:

- all evidence on which the prosecution rely;[1]
- all tape-recordings of interviews with the defendant, co-defendant and other witnesses (some of these may be unused material);
- all relevant custody records;
- all relevant charge sheets;
- disclosure schedules and appropriate disclosure.

The police investigation

Do not assume that the police investigation is thorough or complete. *Active Defence*[2] gives advice on:

- the manner of the police investigation;
- what prevents effective and ethical investigation by the police;
- forensic investigation on behalf of the police: theory and practice;
- how the police investigation is recorded.

Investigating material which has been disclosed to you

Active Defence gives advice on:

- identifying problematic evidence;
- spotting missing evidence;
- analysing prosecution witness statements;
- analysing antecedents to prosecution witness statements;
- analysing tape-recordings of PACE interviews;
- analysing video recordings of witness interviews;
- analysing contemporaneous notes;
- analysing written records of tape-recorded interviews.

Tape-recordings

The Law Society has issued guidance on listening to tape-recordings of police interviews with defendants.

They are guidelines only, and your decision whether it is reasonable to

163

listen to a tape-recording of an interview calls in each case for the exercise of professional judgement based on the facts known to you at the time that decision is made. You should listen to the tape-recording if, after considering these guidelines and any other relevant factors, you remain in doubt about whether or not to do so, but it will usually be advisable to record in writing why it was necessary to listen to the tape-recording in those particular circumstances.

Applications to the police for tapes of interviews should be made expeditiously to avoid delay.

If there is a delay in a record of interview being made available enquiries should be made as to when the record will be received by the solicitor. If, as a result of those enquiries or in the absence of a meaningful reply, the solicitor believes that the record will not be received in time to prepare the case properly and the solicitor has a tape of the interview, the solicitor will have to listen to the tape instead.

A solicitor attending a police station should take as full a note as possible of a tape-recorded interview. However, these interviews often take place at a speed which makes it difficult for a solicitor to take a comprehensive note. There may be facilities available for providing copies of tapes on the spot following charge. In stations where these do not exist, police are encouraged to make 'every effort' to ensure that a copy of the tape is forwarded to the defendant's solicitor as soon as possible. The Circular 24/98 confirms that there is nothing to prevent a solicitor from making his own audio recording of the interview with the suspect. The request to do this may only be refused if there are individual circumstances specific to the case which may prejudice the course of the investigation.

A solicitor's main aim should be to ensure that the interview is conducted fairly. But the solicitor should also be able to note at the time, or if necessary, immediately after the interview:

- whether the client exercised his right of silence and, if so, whether the client remained entirely silent or not;

- whether there were any problems of 'tone', timing, phrasing, intonation or other matters which might affect the interpretation of the interview; and

- whether there were any points of mitigation.

If a solicitor was present during the interview, when deciding whether it is necessary to listen to all or part of a tape-recording of the interview the solicitor should first and, so far as practicable, consider any notes of the interview which are available and the extent to which they accord with the formal record of interview.

The police written record of taped interview (ROTI) is a summary intended to be 'a balanced account of the interview including points in mitigation and/or defence made by the suspect'. Research published in 1992 and 1995[3] showed that little reliance could then be placed on these written records. Solicitors should use their present experience of written records (ROTIs and SDNs) in deciding to what extent to place reliance on them.

If the solicitor doubts the reliability of these types of written record it will be necessary to listen to the tape-recording in the following circumstances.

1. When the client:

    (a) instructed the solicitor to do so; or
    (b) is unable to confirm the accuracy of the contents of the summary; or
    (c) is a juvenile or a mentally disordered or mentally handicapped person.

2. If the client is uncertain about how to plead or intends to plead not guilty:

    (a) where the written record is materially disputed and resolution of the dispute is relevant to the conduct of the case;
    (b) where the client complains of oppression or circumstances tending to create unreliability in the confessions made by the client;
    (c) where the solicitor is informed by the client, or the solicitor present at the interview, that the 'tone', timing, phrasing or intonation in the interview, as would be disclosed by the tape-recording, is relevant to the conduct of the defence and is not apparent from the written record;
    (d) where the Crown Prosecution Service and/or prosecuting counsel has listened to the tape in the course of preparing the prosecution case.

3. In the case of a guilty plea where the solicitor has reason to believe that there may be mitigating factors which are not revealed in the written record.

The Lord Chancellor's Department has been consulted about this guidance and is content with what is proposed.

Note that a written record is not intended to be a complete record of what was said in the interview and it will at times, be necessary for the solicitor to prepare a transcript of part or all of the interview.

Custody records

You have the right to receive you own client's custody record and an early request should be made to the relevant ASU. [64.3]

Other connected custody records should appear on the schedule of unused material.

It will record:

- whether your client attended the police station voluntarily or under arrest; [37.1]
- whether your client requested [37.2.1] and received [37.2] legal advice and who the former adviser was; [37.2.2]
- whether your client was interviewed or questioned. [37.3]

Close scrutiny of the custody record may reveal points of significance in both what is recorded and in what is omitted. It should, therefore, be a golden rule of defence preparation that your client's custody record is obtained as soon as possible after you have been instructed.

The front page of the custody record will reflect the state of the investigation shortly after your client's arrival at the police station. Check the information recorded therein against the facts alleged by the police witnesses, paying particular attention to the following:

1. Reason for arrest. Does the reason for arrest bear a proper relation to the offence charged at the conclusion of your client's detention?

2. Request for legal advice. Is this section completed in accordance with your client's instructions? If the suspect requested legal advice and then changed his mind, is the inspector's agreement to the interview proceeding in these circumstances recorded in the custody record together with an indication of the reasons for the change of mind?

3. Notification to named person. Was this requested? If so, what genuine efforts were made to comply with it? Are there entries showing attempts by the officer to get in touch?

4. Time of arrest and arrival at station. Check that these agree with the times given in the officers' statements.

5. Property. This may help or hinder you, and needs careful scrutiny:

    (a) Did your client appreciate what he was signing?
    (b) The apparent absence of certain items may help your client.
    (c) The presence of some item might assist.

The log: the subsequent page(s) constitutes the 'diary' of a prisoner and should be looked at word for word. Compare the chronology of events in the log with that stated by the officers.

Consider the 'logic' of the enquiry. What would you have expected the officer to have done, when would they have done it? Then ask yourself which entries in the record do not ring true or show up the statements to be unreliable. Pay particular attention to the times and chronology recorded.

Charge sheet

You should obtain from your own client his charge sheet: other connected charge sheets should appear on the schedule of unused material.

DISCLOSURE

Initial disclosure

The CPS must consider from the initial stages of a case whether any unused material should be disclosed to the defence outside the CPIA 1996 scheme:

'the prosecutor must always be alive to the need to make advance disclosure of material of which he is aware (either from his own consideration of the papers or because his attention has been drawn to it by the defence) and which he, as a responsible prosecutor, recognises should be disclosed at an earlier stage. Examples canvassed before us were:

(a) previous convictions of a complainant or deceased if that information could reasonably be expected to assist the defence when applying for bail;

(b) material which might enable a defendant to make a pre-committal application to stay the proceedings as an abuse of process;

(c) material which will enable the defendant to submit that he should only be committed for trial on a lesser charge, or perhaps that he should not be committed for trial at all;

(d) material which will enable the defendant and his legal advisers to make preparations for trial which may be significantly less effective if disclosure is delayed (e.g. names of eye witnesses who the prosecution do not intend to use).

Even before committal a responsible prosecutor should be asking himself what, if any, immediate disclosure justice and fairness requires him to

*make in the particular circumstances of the case. Very often the answer
will be none, and rarely if at all should the prosecutor's answer to that
continuing piece of self-examination be the subject matter of dispute in
this court'.*[4]

Primary disclosure

Under CPIA 1996, on the defendant pleading not guilty in the magistrates'
court or being committed to the Crown Court for trial, the prosecutor is
required to disclose to the accused previously undisclosed material which
in the opinion of the prosecutor might undermine the prosecution case, or
else to give the accused a written statement that there is no such material
(s.3(1)). The Government explained in Parliament that this was intended to
mean: 'material which, generally speaking, has an adverse effect on the
strength of the prosecution case'.[5]

It has always been accepted that, if the accused discloses a defence to the
police during the investigation, the prosecutor should clearly respond by
giving any material which assists that defence on primary disclosure.

What has taken longer to be recognised is that the prosecution case may be
undermined as a result of a particular defence which the defendant may or
may not run and the mere fact that material is in the possession of the
prosecution which raises a new issue in the case which may assist the
defence is sufficient to fulfil the test 'might undermine'.[6]

It is now widely acknowledged that the statutory test for primary disclosure is the same as the test of relevance confirmed by the Court of Appeal
in *R. v. Keane*:[7] documents are material if they can be seen on a sensible
appraisal by the prosecution:

- to be relevant to an issue in the case;

- to raise or possibly raise a new issue whose existence is not apparent
  from the evidence the prosecution proposes to use;

- to hold a real (as opposed to a fanciful) prospect of providing a lead on
  evidence which goes to the above.

This means that, generally speaking, any material which goes to an essential element of the offence(s) charged and which points away from the
accused having committed the alleged offence(s) with the required intent
or would provide material relevant to cross-examination, will have an
adverse effect on the strength of the prosecution case and so ought to be
disclosed to the defence at the primary stage.

In most cases it should be possible for the prosecutor to disclose all necessary material in primary disclosure. The defence is usually known and material, which might assist a different defence than that, falls to be disclosed then anyway. A prosecutor should resist any temptation to wait until he knows the defence before carrying out the disclosure exercise. Secondary disclosure should be a backstop only: for material which the prosecutor could not be expected to identify for himself as disclosable.

As a consequence, defence practitioners must carefully consider such primary disclosure as is made by the Crown. They must critically examine any statement that there is no primary disclosure to be made. They may wish to bring further lines of enquiry to the attention of the prosecution (for example the existence of undisclosed medical evidence at the police station).

The schedule of non-sensitive material

This will be provided to the accused at the same time as primary disclosure.

Examine the schedule with care: consider which other items should appear on the list and be prepared to challenge their absence. Examples of material which lawyers reported were not listed[8] included:

- telephone calls to the police from members of the public reporting the crime and messages between the police control room and individual officers describing the offence and the offender;

- statements made by witnesses whom the prosecution were not calling;

- previous drafts of witnesses' statements and notes of interviews with witnesses.

Identify the true nature of each item listed and consider how it might assist the defence. Be ready to give reasons for its disclosure in a specific request to the prosecution and ensure that the reasons are supported by the defence statement. Examples of material which lawyers reported was not adequately described include:

- the contents of police officers' notebooks;

- the contents of statements of witnesses who were not being called by the prosecution;

- the contents of crime reports;

- the contents of incident report books.

If the schedule of unused material fails to describe the contents of documents adequately, they should be closely examined (by the CPS).

The CPIA Code requires that the description of each item should make clear the nature of the item and should contain sufficient detail to enable the prosecutor to decide whether he needs to inspect the material before deciding whether or not it should be disclosed.[9]

Defence statement

If the case is to be tried summarily and the accused pleads not guilty:

- the prosecutor must make primary disclosure under s.3 CPIA 1996;

- the accused may give a defence statement to the prosecutor and the court which must satisfy the conditions set out in s.5(6): s.6(2).

If the case is to be tried in the Crown Court, when the case has been committed, or a serious and complex fraud or a case involving a sexual or violent offence against a child has been transferred, or a voluntary bill of indictment has been preferred and the prosecutor has made disclosure, the defence must give a defence statement within 14 days or risk an adverse inference being drawn at trial.

Take time in the preparation of the defence statement and you will wish to obtain your client's agreement to the document before it is served on the prosecution and the Court.

You must consider the degree of disclosure to achieve your objectives:

- you should not strengthen the prosecution case by providing evidence to fill a gap in the prosecution case or enabling the prosecution to make further enquiries to remove a line of defence;

- you should provide sufficient detail to ensure that you receive full secondary disclosure;

- you should meet the statutory requirements so as not to raise adverse inferences against the defendant at trial:

  - observe the time limit;

  - do not plead inconsistent defences;

  - ensure that the general nature of the defence is identified;

  - ensure that all matters in issue are identified;

  - identify why they are in issue;

- give details of any relevant alibi and be aware when information about an alibi has to be given;

- identify the names and addresses of alibi witnesses known at the time the notice is served.

Instructing advocates to draft the defence statement

The Bar Council has issued guidance to counsel about the circumstances which should exist before counsel agrees to draft a defence statement. These remind counsel about the significance of this document and the need to obtain the client's informed agreement before it is sent. This guidance is set out in Appendix 21.

Applying for further time

Be ready to apply for further time to file a defence statement when this is required (see Appendix 3, document 3.9(c)).

Investigating unused material

Active Defence gives advice about the unused material which is obtained as part of the police investigation, the information in that material which may be of assistance to the defence and how to formulate the request for secondary disclosure, linking it to the defence statement.

Examples of unused material which lawyers report[10] has not been disclosed under CPIA 1996 include:

- police messages showing an account of the offence or description of the offender which contradicts that given by prosecution witnesses;

- police notebooks showing an initial complaint by a victim which is inconsistent with his later statement;

- crime report showing names and addresses of potential witnesses who were not interviewed by the police and that the victim initially gave a different description of the offender;

- a statement from a witness which is inconsistent with the victim's account;

- a statement from a witness which is inconsistent with that witness's later statement;

- previous convictions of the victim or a witness;

171

- a forensic report showing the detection of fingerprints which were not the defendant's.

Table 15.1 is a checklist of types of unused material which you may wish to request from the prosecution. Tick any item which is likely to support the defence set out in the defence statement. Find out if the prosecutor has inspected the item concerned.

Secondary disclosure

Look back at the wording of your defence statement and ensure that it supports your request for any of this material as further disclosure is limited to prosecution material:

- which has not been previously disclosed;

- which might reasonably be expected to assist the accused's defence as disclosed by the defence statement: s.7(2).

Examine the disclosure made and compare it with your initial request. Keep the matter under review. Be prepared to make an application to the court for further prosecution disclosure (s.8(1)), see Appendix 3, document 3.9(e)).

The Magistrates' Court (Criminal Procedure and Investigations Act 1996) (Disclosure) Rules 1997 and the Crown Court (Criminal Procedure and Investigations Act 1996) (Disclosure) Rules 1997, require the application to be made by notice, in writing, to the appropriate office of the court and to specify:

- the material to which the application relates;

- that the material has not been disclosed to the accused;

- the reason why the material might be expected to assist the applicant's defence as disclosed by the defence statement given under s.5; and

- the date of service of a copy of the notice on the prosecutor.

Third party disclosure

Consider what further evidence may be in the hands of people other than the investigators. Be prepared to approach them to see if they will consent to the inspection and/or disclosure of the relevant material.

Table 15.1 Checklist of unused material you may request from the prosecution

Checklist of types of unused material	✓	MG6(c) no. if referred to in police schedule	Has the prosecutor inspected it?
Operational information Request for a police response Deployment of police officers Requests and reports from deploying and deployed officers Circulation of reports and descriptions by officers Tasking of officers **Crime report information** Offence: finally recorded, legal description Complaint details: time, date, whether discovered by police, reporting officer, investigating officer Complainant details Details of the offence: time, date, location Description of suspect Vehicles seen Modus operandi Property – stolen and damaged Details of offenders Details of enquiries: enquiries at the scene, in the vicinity; actions, details of action, including all persons involved Details of all people spoken to by the police, including those who did not make a witness statement **Police officers' notebooks/incident report book** Verbal exchanges with complainant/ other witnesses Actions taken Suspect description Sketches made **Custody records** **Witness statements** Notes made/drafts/ final versions **CCTV film** **House to house enquiries** Pro-forma questionnaires **Forensic scientist/SOCO** Crime scene examination form			

Table 15.1 continued

Checklist of types of unused material	✓	MG6(c) no. if referred to in Police schedule	Has the prosecutor inspected it?
List of items and CTM collected/ removed			
List of items and CTM submitted for testing (pro-forma); not submitted for testing			
Fingerprints lifted/identified			
Photographs/video recordings/ sketches			
Reports of work carried out by forensic scientists			
Medical examiner/police officer			
Samples taken			
Samples submitted for testing (pro-forma); not submitted for testing			

In the event of refusal, you should consider other ways to obtain the evidence:

- consider inviting public authorities (such as local authorities) to consider their obligations to ensure a fair trial under Art. 6 ECHR;

- consider inviting the police to carry out further investigations under the Code of Practice under the Criminal Procedures and Investigations Act 1996.[11] Once the investigator has examined the material, it must appear on a schedule of unused material. However, this will give notice of the issues to the prosecutor;

- consider the issue of a summons for the production of the material or evidence. In the magistrates' court the application is made under s.97 MCA 1980 and in the Crown Court under the amended s.2 Criminal Procedures (Attendance of Witness) Act 1965. Be aware that such applications must be made as soon as possible. It is necessary in both cases to identify why the evidence or documents are material to the issues in the case. For this purpose clarify what are the issues in the case. In the Crown Court the application must be in the statutory form and be supported by a statement of truth. Consider whether you wish documents to be produced at a time and place ahead of trial. The Crown Court provisions are set out below.

Crown Court summons for a witness to give oral evidence only

The application may be made orally to a judge or in writing specifying:

- the charge on which the proceedings concerned are based;
- a brief description of the evidence;
- the ground for believing that the potential witness is likely to be able to give the stipulated evidence; and
- the reasons why the applicant considers that the potential witness will not voluntarily attend.

Late applications in the Crown Court for documentary evidence

Under s.2 Criminal Procedure (Attendance of Witnesses) Act 1965 (as amended) the application for a witness summons must be made as soon as is reasonably practicable. The court may refuse to issue a summons if the requirements are not fulfilled.

If an application is made within seven days of the trial, the application should be completed as outlined above but should not be copied to the potential witness by the applicant. The appropriate officer should refer the application to the trial judge or other available judge to determine or give instructions which may include copying to the witness.

If an application is made after the trial has begun, the application should be made orally to the judge to determine or give directions. The oral application should include:

- a brief description of the evidence;
- reasons why this is material evidence;
- reasons why the applicant considers that the witness will not voluntarily attend; and
- grounds for believing that the potential witness is likely to be able to produce the document or thing.

Reviewing decisions

Prosecutors are under a duty continuously to review what amounts to primary and secondary disclosure. Be ready to remind prosecutors of their duty as new issues arise.

Table 15.2 Crown Court summons for a witness to produce documentary evidence

Stage	This should contain	Other action
Application is made in writing to the appropriate officer of the Crown Court.	(i) A brief description of the required document or thing.	A copy of the application and supporting statement of truth should be served on the potential witness by the applicant at the same time. It should inform him of his right to make representations in writing and at a hearing, and that he has seven days to inform the court if he wishes to make representations.
	(ii) Reasons why the witness will not voluntarily produce it.	
	(iii) Reasons why the document or thing is likely to be material evidence.	
	(iv) A supporting statement of truth setting out the charge and specifying: – the evidence in a way which will enable the potential witness to identify it; – grounds for believing that the witness is likely to be able to produce the evidence; – grounds for believing that it will be material evidence	
	If advance production is required, provide details of the time and place at which the witness is to produce it.	

Sensitive material

The prosecutor must obtain the court's permission to withhold relevant but sensitive material. This will take place by a procedure similar to that established by the Court of Appeal[12] although the Human Rights Act 1998 may call for amendment to the procedure. The decision to allow non-disclosure must be kept under review. Be ready to bring to the court's attention any change of circumstance.

ASSESSING YOUR CLIENT

Factors

The greater your client's vulnerability, the less likely the court will be to draw an advance inference from your client's failure to mention facts in the police station which are used as part of his defence at trial.

Consider the following factors:

- age/maturity;
- condition at time of interview (tiredness/sobriety);[13]
- mental disorder;
- personality;
- disability;
- illness;
- injuries;
- language;
- psychological vulnerability;
- criminal experience;
- time of interview;

Did your client understand the caution at the time of the interview?

The caution is supposed to inform your client about the significance of the interview in the police station and your client's contribution to it. If it appears that you client did not understand the caution, an adverse inference should not be drawn from your client's failure to mention material facts.

177

Research[14] found the average IQ of suspects to be 82, within the bottom 5 per cent of the general population. One in three was classified as 'intellectually disadvantaged'. Due to extreme distress or mental disorder or drugs 35 per cent were not in a normal mental state. In addition, 6.5 per cent were illiterate, 3 per cent had a learning disability.

These results are similar to those of an earlier study:

> '*In about one-quarter of the cases there was some identifiable mental abnormality (drug-induced abnormalities, mental handicap or mental illness). A substantial group were frightened enough to show visible symptoms (trembling, shivering, sweating, yawning, hyper-ventilation, incoherence). Taking these groups together, nearly half of the suspects were in an abnormal state immediately prior to being interviewed.*'[15]

These abnormalities are not being identified.

The Royal Commission research (1993) found that whilst the police were able to identify juveniles and people with serious mental disorders or disabilities, they were understandably less able in assessing disorders and handicaps of minors. The police had only identified 4 per cent as requiring an appropriate adult, whereas the researchers put the true figure at about 20 per cent. The police most commonly failed to recognise the clinically depressed suspects as vulnerable. They failed to recognise mental handicap in one in three cases.

Research in 1995 found that appropriate adults were called in only 38 instances in a sample of 20,805 custody records. The researchers considered that they were required in a further 446 cases.[16]

It is the person's mental state at the time that he is in police custody which is relevant. To find that you should have:

- asked third parties;
- asked the custody officer;
- asked the police surgeon/forensic medical examiner;
- asked the appropriate adult;
- listened to your client's way of talking;
- watched how your client behaves;
- asked if your client is taking medication; and
- made appropriate records.

The Law Society's *Pocket Reference*[17] gives guidance on assessing your client. It also explains what clues the title of a drug or its proprietary name can give you as to your client's vulnerability by telling you the use of the drug.

Was your client suffering from the effects of a medical condition at the time of the police station attendance? [36.5] If so, was your client examined by the police surgeon? [36.5.1]

In relation to the disclosure which your client made at the police station during questioning, experts inform us that drugs taken may affect a person's memory. As well as illicit drugs, these include sleeping tablets, anti-depressants, tranquillisers and steroids (although the effect will depend upon the individual involved and where a drug reduces the person's anxiety it may increase their attention and concentration). Many physical illnesses cause memory disturbance, such as epilepsy, migraine, thyroid diseases, diabetes and alcohol withdrawal.[18]

INVESTIGATING THE CRIME SCENE

Active Defence gives detailed advice on looking for and reviewing the evidence of the offender having entered or left or been at the crime scene and whether the offender was your client, including:

- entry/exit routes;
- CCTV;
- potential witnesses and house-to-house questioning;
- vehicles;
- contact trace material;
- police surveillance;
- objects.

Remember that 'whenever two objects meet (such as the offender and the crime scene, the victim and the crime scene or the offender and the victim), there is an exchange of material from each to the other'.

Active Defence also advises on assessing the credibility of:

- eye witness evidence,
- ear witness evidence.

INSPECTION, PHOTOGRAPHS AND PLANS

Obtain photographs of your client's relevant injuries urgently. The earlier they are taken the more helpful they will be.

It is particularly useful to visit the locus yourself as part of your investigation and preparation of the case. Consider the need for photographs and a plan of the scene of an incident.

Seek prior authority for photographs and/or plans on APP7 from the Legal Aid Board (see Appendix 3, document 3.2).

Obtain a s.9 witness statement from the person who takes, makes or prints any photographs and plans to confirm the date and time of preparation and what they disclose.

Serve the statement and exhibits, if uncontroversial, upon the prosecution in good time before trial (at least seven days) and request their acceptance. You may prefer the element of surprise, but will need to be able to prove the exhibits at court (by oral evidence or by acceptance of s.9 statements).

WITNESSES

Note whether any witnesses may exist to assist the defence. [33.3] Can they be traced, are they available or willing? Consider whether the prosecution has disclosed details of possible witnesses. Advise your client as to reasonable steps that may be taken, in light of the financial implications and resources available. An enquiry may be required. Leave no room for doubt who is to try and contact the witness. An important witness should be interviewed at an early date.

Obtain a statement [66.1], dated and signed by the witness. Do not interview a witness in the presence of another witness. The statement should include:

- name, address and telephone number; [33.3.1]

- occupation and employment;

- date of birth;

- age and marital status;

- previous convictions: in particular any of dishonesty or of a similar nature to the current charge against the client; any occurring with the client; any custodial sentences;

- relationship to client; frequency of contact;

- account of incident;

- comments on prosecution evidence (including exhibits) where relevant;

- whether interviewed by police; account given to them; consistent or inconsistent with above; explanation for inconsistencies;

- first knowledge of case against client;

- extent of knowledge of case; discussion with client (if any);

- whether willing witness in court; if not, reasons;

- dates when witness available to give evidence;

- any disabilities with which witness suffers.

Beware of calling a witness at court who has previous convictions.

Send a typed copy of the statement to the witness and explain that he should not show it to or discuss it with anyone who may give evidence in the case. Ask the witness to check its accuracy and correct any errors. He should then return it to you for you to amend it and return it to him for signature. Within four working days of being informed of a trial date or the appearance of the case in a Warned List, warn the witness of any court hearing dates when attendance is required. Explain to an unwilling witness the position regarding a witness summons and 'conduct money'. Advise upon court procedures and practice.

Consider obtaining a s.9 witness statement for the purpose of impressing on him the need for honesty and clarity. If it is uncontroversial, consider serving it on the prosecution (see Appendix 3, document 3.3 for an example of a s.9 witness statement).

If it is a child witness, see the witness in the presence, where appropriate, of a parent or social worker; consider whether in court special facilities may be required to protect the child; unless inappropriate, provide a copy of the statement to parents; advise with particular care.

Obtain a witness summons from the court for any witness whom you intend to call and think will not attend court voluntarily. Consider how to serve the summons and whether it is possible to take a statement at the same time, if the witness will allow this and has not made a statement to you already. Consider whether a reluctant witness is worth calling.

Interviewing a prosecution witness

You should give active consideration to the need to re-interview witnesses particularly if their statement is more limited than you would have expected or there are other relevant areas on which they may be expected to speak. They can no longer be cross-examined at a committal hearing.

See page 11 and *Active Defence*.

ADDITIONAL EVIDENCE

If served with additional evidence ensure statement and comments are updated. Make sure you notify the prosecution within the time-limits whether any witness or witnesses whose statements have been served by way of additional evidence are required to attend court to give evidence in person. If in doubt about whether their attendance is required, notify the prosecution that they should attend. You should cancel this requirement if they no longer need to attend.

SENSITIVE STATEMENTS

Ensure your client is aware of all prosecution and defence evidence. You should, however, use your discretion in providing copies of 'sensitive' statements and exhibits relating to a defendant's case, subject to your client's right to have access to material forming part of the case against him. In providing any such material, you should remind your client that the use of papers must be limited to use in connection with the purposes of litigation, and that any misuse of the papers by your client may amount to contempt of court.

GUIDANCE ON PREPARING YOUNG WITNESSES FOR COURT

A handbook has been published[19] by the NSPCC and Childline to prepare young witnesses for court. It has been produced to accompany the 1998 Young Witness Pack.

Arrangements for the preparation of young witnesses, including pre-trial court visits, should be made available on request to young witnesses called by the defence.

Items in the Young Witness Pack series include: *Let's Get Ready for Court*, an activity book for child witnesses aged 5–9; *Tell Me More About Court*, a book for young witnesses aged 10–15; *Inside a Court Room*, a card model of a courtroom with slot-in characters for use with younger witnesses aged 13–17; *Young Witnesses at the Magistrates' Court and Youth Court*, for 9–17 year olds; *Screens in Court*, an information sheet for 9–17 year olds; and *Your Child is a Witness* for parents and carers.

The handbook *Preparing Young Witnesses for Court* is aimed at child witness supporters. They liaise with the criminal justice agencies to ensure that they are aware of the child's needs and that those needs are met. They also ensure that the agencies are committed to expediting the case.

Child witness supporters are independent of the prosecution and defence. The police will arrange a child witness supporter for a prosecution witness. They have only basic information about why a child is going to court and there will be no discussion of the child's evidence or expression of belief in the child witness. Preparation work is not confidential and if a prosecution child witness begins to talk about the evidence, the supporter must notify the police and ask the child to speak to the person who conducted the interrogative interviews.

Child witness supporters should have undertaken training accredited by all the agencies involved and conduct the preparation according to a written programme agreed on an inter-agency basis. The independent supporter is accountable to the court and must be prepared to give evidence about the work undertaken with young witnesses and produce written records if requested to do so.

Local initiatives for child witness preparation have developed under the auspices of the NSPCC, the Crown Court Witness Service, Social Services Departments and Area Child Protection Committees. A defence solicitor can contact any of these organisations to arrange a child witness supporter for a young defence witness. Be familiar with *A Case for Balance*: the good-practice video on court proceedings involving child witnesses produced by NSPCC. Further guidance on child witnesses is given in Appendix 24.

ENQUIRY AGENT

If you are unable to do all the work yourself, you may need to instruct an enquiry agent on your behalf to take photographs, prepare plans, trace witnesses, visit any witnesses who will not co-operate and take statements from them, and make other particular enquiries of an urgent, delicate, or unusual nature or at unusual times or great distances or when you cannot guarantee the security of a member of your staff.

Seek prior authority for this by extension of the Legal Aid Order where practicable; otherwise be prepared to justify the time and costs on taxation.

Ensure such enquiries are relevant and that the agent is properly briefed on your behalf.

OTHER EVIDENCE

Note whether your client has any documents, receipts, letters or photographs. Advise him to deliver them to you speedily for safekeeping.

S.9 CJA 1967

If evidence is to be disclosed before trial, the written statement of a witness for the prosecution or defence should be properly signed, dated and prefaced by a caption in accordance with s.9 CJA 1967, s.102 MCA 1980, and r.70 MCR 1981: Appendix 3, document 3.3.

A witness statement in s.9 form can be served upon the prosecution or the defence. If its contents are agreed and accepted, then the statement may be read to the court and becomes evidence in the same way as live evidence given at the trial. The witness need not attend; cross-examination is not possible. However, acceptance does not prevent the party tendering the evidence from calling the witness to give oral evidence.

Service of statements in your possession should be made within seven working days from entering a not guilty plea in the magistrates' court, to allow proper consideration. A lesser period may be agreed between the parties if the statement is uncontroversial.

An agreed statement is not conclusive, but if the opponent party then calls contradictory evidence, the proponent would normally be allowed to call the witness who made the statement to rebut the contradiction, even if an adjournment is necessary.

Prosecution witness statements served under s.9 CJA 1967 should be considered with careful regard to the defendant's comments upon their contents, if any. The prosecution may be prepared to agree to some editing or addition to such statements, so as to put them into an acceptable form.

Failure to reject the statement within seven days is treated as acceptance. Later application may, however, be made to the court to require a witness to attend and give oral evidence, but you are then at risk of refusal and/or costs.

Consider with care whether service of a defence witness statement, or detailed response to a prosecution witness statement, will disclose too much of your client's defence case. Generally, disclose only what you know is uncontroversial or formal, e.g. photographer; doctor; plan-drawer.

FORMAL ADMISSION – S.10 CJA 1967

At any stage a formal admission of facts may be made, providing conclusive evidence of those facts. Admissions can be made orally at trial or in writing before trial, in accordance with s.10 CJA 1967. This should be made in writing within seven working days of knowledge of the facts.

This is a potentially useful cost-saving device; consider it carefully, with your client as appropriate, before using it. An admission can be withdrawn, but only with leave of the court. You should be slow to make an admission unless you are satisfied that the Crown could, if necessary, prove the relevant facts.

INTERVIEWING YOUR CLIENT

Not guilty statement

It may be useful to keep a 'state of case' pro forma in the file with a brief note of the advice that your client has been given about what to plead, where to be tried and the type of committal (Appendix 4). This will keep anyone looking at the file up to date about the stage that the instructions have reached. The advocate will also know what is expected to happen at the next hearing.

Make sure that the advocate also knows enough about the case at a remand hearing to supply details of the number of witnesses to be called, give a best estimate of the likely length of the trial and consider whether issues in the case can be identified and evidence agreed.

Allow enough time to take full instructions from your client for the trial.

Do not take the statement in the presence of any potential witnesses.

Co-defendants

Take details of whether your client has co-defendants. If he has, record who they are, what they are pleading (if you know), and which firm of solicitors represents each of them. If you act for any of the accused, note why there is no conflict of interest [35.3.1].

Give details of their ages, how your client came to know them [35.1], how friendly he was with them at the time, what he knew then of their criminal records (if anything), and what their role was (if any) [35.2].

Taking the instructions

Relate the events in chronological order. Make sure that you start right at the beginning and set the scene before you deal with the incident itself.

Even if you are taking a statement for a trial, you will need to include full details of the defendant's personal history for use if he is convicted. (See Chapter 18.)

Detail

Try and get down what happened in plenty of detail.

You should be able to follow the events, picturing them in your mind's eye. Take it step by step – one action at a time.

Structuring material

Topics should be grouped together, with separate sub-headings. Each different action or thought merits a separate paragraph in the statement. A separate chronology is often useful.

Ask why

Do not take what your client says at face value – probe until you are satisfied. If he cannot give you a satisfactory answer then show this in the statement.

Use the actual words said

When you can, use the actual words that people said.

Identify people referred to

Ask your client to describe the person. Then if that person is one of a group (of police officers, for example), give that person a reference (Officer 1) to save you having to repeat the description every time you refer to him.

Arrest and interrogation

It is proper to delay taking instructions on the arrest and interrogation until advance information, custody record and tapes are available and the client has had access to these.

If the circumstances of his arrest or interview may be relevant you will need to include:

- Arrest:
    - the circumstances, place, time;
    - all conversations between him and the police officers;
    - identify the officers individually: 'Officer 1', 'Officer 2'; plain clothes, uniformed; car marked, unmarked;
    - words of arrest, were they used, what were they?
    - reason for arrest, was any given?
    - caution, was one given, when?
    - questioning or admissions at the time of arrest or in the police car, details; [37.3]
    - time of arrival at the police station;
    - custody officer, what was said to him by the arresting officer?
    - right to contact a friend/relative, was client told?
    - right to contact a solicitor, was client told?
    - was solicitor asked for [37.2.1], when?
    - did any solicitor attend?
    - who and when?
    - what instructions did he give the solicitor?
    - what advice did he receive? [37.2]
    - did he act on that advice?

187

- did any discussions take place with officers investigating the case in the absence of the solicitor? [37.3] If so, obtain details;

- Interview:

  - deal separately with each interview and its content;

  - note times (approximately);

  - how many interviews?

  - did he answer some/all/no questions in each interview? [37.4]

  - did he give a written statement or prepared oral statement? [37.4]

  - was he medically fit to be interviewed? If not, why not? Were any representations made about this?

  - did he understand the caution?

  - if he remained silent, did the solicitor explain the reasons for this on tape? And that it was as a result of the solicitor's advice?

  - was a special warning given during this interview? If so, did it relate to an object/mark/substance or suspect's presence and how did he account for himself?

  - obtain details of the object/mark/substance or facts of the suspect's presence at a particular time.

  - cautioned appropriately at each stage?

  - how was the interview recorded?

  - asked to sign notes at any stage? Did he? Content of notes and client's endorsement.

  - who was present?

  - was access to legal advice before the interview formally denied?[20]

  - was he asked to confirm a significant statement or silence on tape at the beginning of the interview? If so, did he do so? What was the content of the significant statement? [37.4]

  - what questions were put?

  - what answers did he make, were they the truth; if not, why not?

- Other:

  - any breaches of Code C during your client's time in custody – breaks, meals, etc;

  - was he injured? [37.5]

- were any photographs taken of the injury and, if so, by whom?

- was a police surgeon/forensic medical examiner called: if so, why?

- were non-intimate or intimate samples taken?

- if so, by whom, when? [38]

- did he consent? [38.1]

- when was he charged? [39.1]

- what time was he released?

- were bail conditions attached to his release? [47.2] If so, obtain details;

- did he make any complaint? [37.6] Was he advised to make a complaint? [37.6.1]

- date and time and venue of court hearing [39.11]

Be aware of the fundamental importance attached by the courts to the right of access to a solicitor (s.58 PACE) and that breach of that right and significant and substantial breaches of Code C relating to detention, treatment and questioning may result in the court excluding a confession in the exercise of its discretion.[21]

Be aware too of the court's duty to exclude a confession obtained as a result of oppression or in circumstances tending to render the confession unreliable.[22]

Be aware of the special care necessary when considering the position of those who are mentally ill or have learning difficulties.

Alibi [34.1]

Evidence in support of an alibi is evidence tending to show that by reason of the presence of the accused at a particular place or a particular area at a particular time he was not, or was unlikely to have been, at the place where the offence is alleged to have been committed at the time of its alleged commission.[23]

You need to consider whether the charge allows a defence of alibi to be raised: the time and place of the offence must be specifically defined.

The details which you must obtain, and which must be included in a defence statement, include the name and address of any witness the accused believes is able to give evidence in support of the alibi. [34.2.1]

If the accused does not know the name and address of the witness, the particulars must include any information in the accused's possession which might be of material assistance in finding any such witness.[24]

You should normally:

- take a statement from an alibi witness;
- tell the alibi witness that:
  - the police may seek to interview him;
  - the police should not interview him without notifying you and enabling you to be present;
  - you will contact him if the police notify you that they wish to interview him;
  - he should refuse to allow the police to interview him until the police have contacted you and allowed you to be present.

Taking your client's comments

Observations on evidence

Your client's comments should be taken on the prosecution statements, any unused material disclosed to you and any documentary exhibits [65]. The comments should be in a separate document from his statement to you.

The comments serve two functions:

- the advocate needs to know in great detail which parts, if any, of a witness's statement your client does not agree with so that he can challenge these in cross-examination;
- they enable you, through your client, to raise any evidential matters, contradictions, inconsistencies or other cross-examination points which occur to you in respect of that witness and in respect of that witness's evidence in relation to the others.

Go through each witness's statement line by line with your client. Was something said or not? Did something happen or not? What has the witness left out? Number each comment in the text, against the item it refers to. Keep the comments short and to the point.

Remind your client that he must not discuss the case, or arrange for anyone else to discuss it, with a prosecution witness.

EXPERTS

Consider the need in the course of preparing for a trial for expert evidence, e.g. to explain or rebut prosecution evidence; to support a laced drinks argument or post-driving consumption defence; to establish nature, extent and causation of injuries: see ways of finding an expert below.

It will not always be obvious from the prosecution forensic scientist's written statement what the strengths and weaknesses of the evidence are. There is a danger that if the prosecution forensic scientist gives oral evidence he will strengthen the evidence contained in his witness statement by commenting on the significance of the findings. Scientists in the Home Office laboratories will have looked at thousands of scenes of crimes and exhibits and acquired a 'feel' for what they would expect to see following any given crime.

A forensic scientist instructed by you should be able to warn you of any such risk, in advance. The area that a defence forensic scientist is likely to make most ground in is the interpretation of the evidence in the context of the facts of the case rather than faulting the identification of the sample or its comparison with another exhibit.

Seek prior authority on APP7 by way of extension of the Legal Aid Order: see Appendix 3, document 3.2. You will have to obtain an estimate of the expert's fees. An example of how you can do this is set out in Appendix 3, document 3.4.

Provide your expert with the following (as appropriate):

- prosecution case papers including precise charge;
- prosecution exhibits – plans, photographs, documents, etc;
- prosecution expert's statement or report;
- defendant's proof of evidence and comments;
- witnesses' proof of evidence/statements;
- client's letter of authority for medical report.

If authority is granted, you can then instruct the expert. Your expert may have to examine an exhibit held by the prosecution. The prosecution will not (normally) release exhibits to the expert:

- the expert must go to them at whichever laboratory dealt with the case;

- instructing solicitors must obtain CPS approval for the proposed examination and then, having obtained some documentary proof of that, write to the police and the laboratory concerned. Once all have signalled that they consent, but not until then, there is normally no objection to the expert contacting the scientist direct to work out the details.

Advance notice of expert evidence

In the magistrates' court, expert evidence (except in relation to sentence) may not be given unless advance notice of the evidence is provided to the other parties: the Magistrates' Courts (Advance Notice of Expert Evidence) Rules 1997.

The position is the same in the Crown Court: Crown Court (Advance Notice of Expert Evidence) (Amendment) Rules 1987.

Contamination

Be aware of how forensic evidence can be contaminated. Some examples of possible contaminants are:

- placing a hand or finger inside an exhibit bag;

- folding items containing wet semen or blood, so transferring it to other parts;

- folding items without separating the surfaces, so that the surfaces contact each other;

- a suspect being placed in a cell used by another suspect and sharing the cell blanket;

- a suspect being handled by an officer who was in contact with the 'victim';

- a suspect being placed in a police car which was used to transport the 'victim'.

Forensic science: ways of finding an expert and types of expert

Be aware that there has been no form of regulation of the forensic science profession and you will need to satisfy yourself about the competence and ability of a particular 'expert' to undertake work in an individual case. To remedy this, a Council for the Registration of Forensic Practitioners has been established with support from the Home Office.

You should find out on what basis the person feels qualified to advise in that particular case, including what recognised scientific qualifications the 'expert' has, what practical experience he has of investigating that sort of case and applying scientific techniques to the evidence at issue.

The Law Society's Directory of Expert Witnesses and CD is published annually by Sweet & Maxwell, with supporting telephone enquiry service available to subscribers. Enquiries to: Sweet & Maxwell, tel: 020 7449 1111 or the Law Society Expert Witness Helpline, tel: 020 7320 5710; fax: 020 7831 1687.

Organisations and publications which you may find helpful

The British Academy of Experts

116–118, Chancery Lane, London WC2A 1PP. Tel: 020 7637 0333. Provides the names and addresses of suitable members from their directory for a small charge. The Academy has some 2,000 members.

The British Academy of Forensic Sciences

Enquiries to: The Secretary, BAFS, Anaesthetic Unit, London Hospital Medical College, Turner Street, London E1 2AO. Tel: 020 7377 9201 (Dr P J Flynn, Secretary of the Academy). A body to 'encourage the study, improve the practice and advance the knowledge of legal, medical and forensic science'. It keeps a list of experts, including forensic pathologists.

Forensic Access

Chequers Court, Station Road, Thatcham, Berkshire RG19 4PR. Tel: 01635 866 877. As well as providing forensic science services for solicitors, they maintain a register of expert witnesses. If the enquiry is a routine one they will not make a charge for referring a solicitor to an expert in the appropriate field.

The Forensic Science Service

Priory House, Gooch Street North, Birmingham B5 6QQ. Tel: 0121 666 6606. Fax: 0121 622 3536. Open to prosecution and defence alike. It has a marketing division in Birmingham which solicitors can telephone to find out about the facilities they offer and their charges.

The Forensic Science Society

Clarke House, 18a Mount Parade, Harrogate, North Yorkshire HG1 1BX. Tel: 01423 506 068. Fax: 01423 530 948. An international body whose object is to advance the study of forensic science. It runs a directory of independent consultants.

Different areas of expertise

Which expert you choose will depend upon the area of expertise that is required: forensic biology; forensic chemistry; firearms; document examination; fingerprints; or photographs.

Forensic biology

Biological evidence is material that originates from a living source and is most relevant to the investigation of offences against the person. Examples are:

- hair and textiles fibres;

- bloodstains on clothing and weapons;

- semen on underwear, bedding and swabs;

- saliva;

- clothing.

An experienced forensic biologist should be able to help the defence in a number of ways:

- whether material was cut or torn, how recently the damage was done and whether a particular knife could have caused it;

- the number of matching fibres found on your client's clothing, the number and type of each different fibre at the scene and how representative of them the fibres found on your client's clothing are;

- it might be that the absence of fibres is of significance;

- you would need to look for an alternative source of the fibres;

- you would also need to look at the chain of custody of the exhibit to ensure that it has not become contaminated;

- check the chain of custody of an exhibit from the moment the police take possession of it until it is examined at the laboratory;

- the distribution of blood and size of the splashes will tell a forensic scientist a lot about what actually happened;

- human hair can be distinguished from animal hair;

- dyes, colourings, rinses, spray or lacquers help to identify the owner in comparison with a control sample;

- there is a two-way transfer of hair and fibres when woolly hats, bala-clavas or masks are worn;

- residue from the scene of the crime may be found in the offender's hair.

Once a scientist has found a match between a suspect and the profile of samples taken from a crime scene, a calculation will be made to estimate the rarity of that profile – the random occurrence ratio. This calculation is made by using information stored in a database of DNA measurements created by other DNA work done in the laboratory.

It results in a statement 'it is estimated that the frequency with which the DNA characteristics in the profile is likely to be found in the population at large is one in . . .'.

Forensic chemistry

This is the area of expertise which is used in relation to offences against property, analysing and comparing material from a non-biological source. These are some examples:

- paint;

- oil;

- glass;

- footwear impressions;

- fire debris;

- tyre marks;

- blood, urine and breath alcohol specimens.

Where entry is forced, there may be contact traces on any wood, metal and clothing involved.

Contaminants on glass may help to provide a match.

Forensic pathology

A Memorandum of Good Practice regarding the early release of bodies in cases of suspicious death has been agreed with the Home Office and other criminal justice agencies. It sets out steps which the solicitor should take. See Appendix 22.

Document examination

Document examination can involve:

- disguised handwriting;
- ink analysis;
- typewriting analysis;
- photocopying analysis;
- electrostatic deposition analysis of indented handwriting.

Other experts

Other experts who may be able to help you include:

- the Meteorological Office;
- a forensic accountant;
- a clinical psychologist;
- a psychiatrist;
- your client's General Practitioner;
- a consultant doctor;
- a forensic psychologist;
- a forensic medical examiner (police surgeon);
- drugs experts, such as 'Release' (Tel: 020 7729 5255) will prepare a s.9 witness statement informing you of the street value of named drugs.

Active Defence gives more detailed advice on:

- the theory and practice of forensic science investigation;
- legal aid;
- instructing an expert;
- questioning forensic evidence;
- psychological factors.

End notes

1 In some cases of ABH or common assault the prosecution may not be required to obtain a medical report to prove injury. See Appendix 20.
2 Ede, R and Shepherd, E, *Active Defence: A Lawyer's Guide to Police and Defence Investigation and Prosecution and Defence Disclosure in Criminal Cases.* The Law Society.
3 Baldwin, J, (1992), *Preparing the Record of Taped Interviews*, RCCJ Research Study No. 2. The Stationery Office. Hooke, A and Knox, J, (1995), *Preparing Records of Taped Interviews*, Research Findings No. 22. Home Office Research and Statistics Department.
4 Kennedy LJ, *R. v. DPP ex p. Lee* [1999] 2 All ER 737.
5 Baroness Blatch, House of Lords, third reading, 19 February 1996. *Hansard*, col. 886.
6 See also Sprack, John, 'The Criminal Procedure and Investigations Act 1996: (1) The Duty of Disclosure' [1997] Crim LR 309.
7 [1994] 1 WLR 746.
8 Surveys of solicitors' and barristers' experiences of how CPIA 1996 is working in practice were conducted by the Criminal Bar Association and the Law Society in 1999.
9 para. 6.9.
10 Surveys of solicitors' and barristers' experiences of how CPIA 1996 is working in practice were conducted by the Criminal Bar Association in the Law Society in 1999.
11 CPIA 1996 and its Code of Practice require the police, in conducting an investigation to pursue all reasonable lines of enquiry, whether they point towards or away from the suspect. What is reasonable in each case will depend upon the particular circumstances: s.23(1) (a) and Code of Practice para. 3.4.
12 *R. v. Davis, Johnson and Rowe* (1993) 97 Cr. App. R 110.
13 *R. v. Argent* [1997] Crim LR 346.
14 Research study no.12 by clinical psychologists for the Royal Commission on Criminal Justice (1993).
15 Irving, B, Research study for the Royal Commission on Criminal Procedure (1980)
16 [1997] Crim LR 788.
17 Shepherd, E, *A Pocket Reference* (part of Police Station Skills for Legal Advisers). The Law Society.
18 Lader, M, 'The Influence of Drugs on Testimony', *Analysing Witness Testimony.* Blackstone Press 1999.
19 *Preparing Young Witnesses for Court, A Handbook for Child Witness Supporters.* NSPCC/Childline 1998.
20 See s.58 PACE 1984; inferences from silence may not be drawn in these circumstances: ss.34, 36, 37 CJPOA 1994 as amended by the Youth Justice and Criminal Evidence Act 1999.
21 s.78 PACE 1984.
22 s.76 PACE 1984.
23 s.5(8) CPIA 1996.
24 s.5(7) CPIA 1996.

CHAPTER 16

Preparing for preliminary hearings in the Crown Court

INDICTABLE-ONLY CASES: PRELIMINARY HEARINGS

*The first hearing will take place soon after the hearing in the magistrates' court. Under the Magistrates' Court (Modification) Rules 1998 the notice which is required by s.51(7) of the Act, together with other documents including the information, must be sent by the magistrates' court to the Crown Court within **four days** of sending a person to be tried under the new procedures. Under the Crown Court (Modification) Rules 1998 the first Crown Court appearance must then be listed within **eight days** of receipt of that s.51(7) notice where the defendant is sent in custody, or **28 days** where he is sent on bail.*

Bail

An accused whom the magistrates have sent in custody to the Crown Court may make an application for bail to the Crown Court, and the first hearing affords an early opportunity for him to do so. There is nothing to prevent a defendant from seeking to make a bail application on a date before that fixed for the first Crown Court hearing; it is then for the Crown Court to decide when to allow an earlier hearing. If the court so decides, it will depend on the circumstances of the case whether at that hearing it is possible for the court to determine the timetable for the case (in effect bringing forward the date of the preliminary Crown Court hearing), or whether it will still be necessary to hold a hearing for that purpose on the date originally fixed. If an earlier hearing is arranged, the s.51(7) notice and associated documents should be sent to the Crown Court in time for the date set for the hearing, and the Crown Prosecution Service should be given as much notice of the date as possible.

Where the magistrates decide to send the accused on bail to the Crown Court, it is open to the prosecution to appeal to the Crown Court under the Bail (Amendment) Act 1993 against the grant of bail. Where this is done, the

198

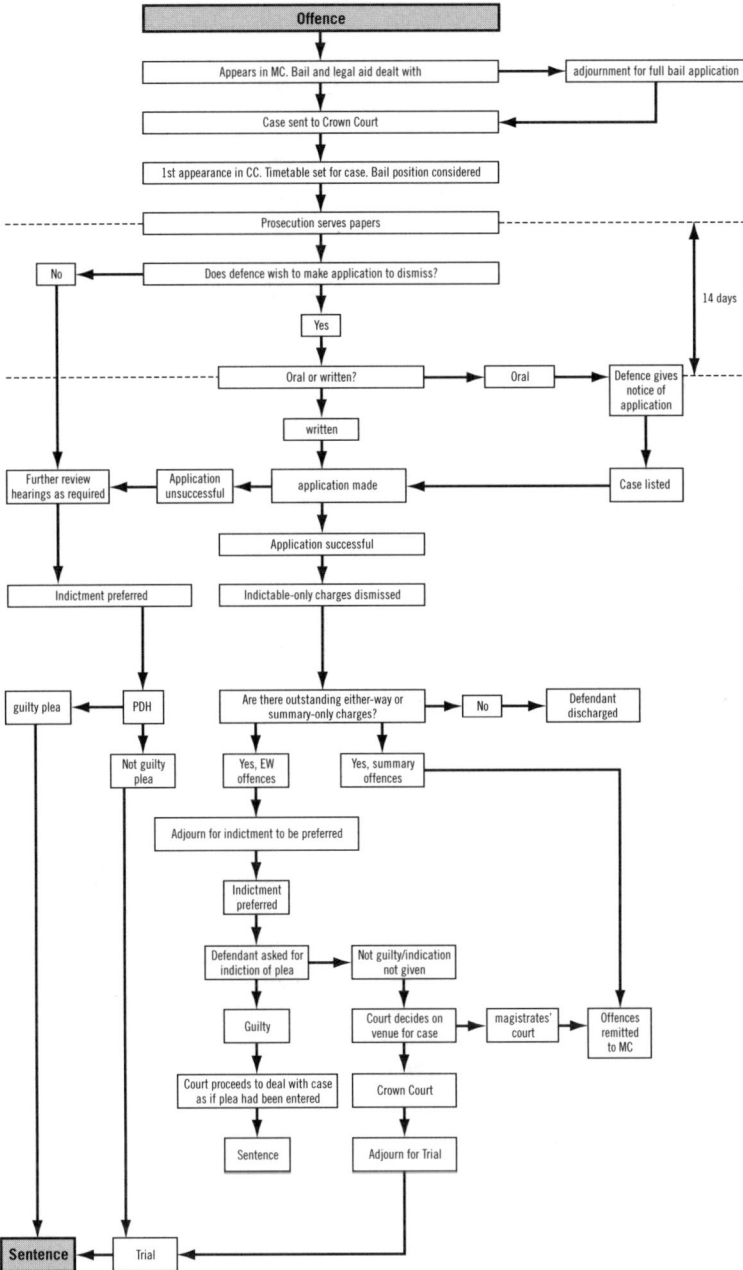

Figure 16.1 Indictable-only cases

appeal must be heard within 48 hours. Again the s.51(7) notice, etc., should be sent to the Crown Court in time for the appeal hearing, although in the time available it may not be possible for the court to do more than to resolve the remand issue.

Crown Court Rule 27 has been modified to allow the preliminary hearing in the Crown Court to take place in chambers, and a Practice Direction has been issued (see below) providing (inter alia) that this hearing (and any others which take place before the prosecution case is served) should normally be heard in open court as chambers, with the defendant present and the court open to the public. The Crown may be represented at this hearing by a Crown Prosecutor and the defence by a solicitor without higher court rights; representatives may appear unrobed.

Rights of audience

A Practice Direction was given by the Senior Presiding Judge for England and Wales on 22 December 1998, about the rights of audience in cases sent to the Crown Court under s.51.

(2)   A preliminary hearing is any hearing which takes place before the prosecution has completed service of its case.

(3)   The purpose of the first preliminary hearing it to:

- *deal with any outstanding bail issues;*
- *set a timetable for the service of the prosecution case;*
- *set a date for the PDH.*

(6)   Preliminary hearings shall normally be heard in open court as chambers, with the defendant present and the court open to the public. Any person who has rights of audience in the magistrates' court may appear in these hearings in the Crown Court unrobed.

(7)   Crown Courts may wish to make arrangements with the magistrates' court so that the magistrates' court chooses the day on which the first preliminary hearing will take place.

(10) Immediately after service of the prosecution case, the current rights of audience in the Crown Court will apply.

The first Crown Court hearing would set a timetable and review the bail/ remand position.

The second Crown Court hearing is after the service of the 'committal papers' (or to find out where they are) and its purpose is to review the paperwork and confirm the PDH date. The timing will be at the judge's discretion.

INDICTABLE-ONLY CASES: APPLICATIONS TO DISMISS

Paragraph 1 of Schedule 3 to the Crime and Disorder Act 1998 requires the Attorney-General to make regulations containing provision for the date by which the prosecution case must be served. The Crime and Disorder Act 1998 (Service of Prosecution Evidence) Regulations 1998 set a long-stop date of one year from the date the case is sent to the Crown Court within which it is for the judge in a particular case to determine the date by which the evidence is to be served.

It is expected that some defendants will wish at an early stage to indicate their intention to plead guilty, although they will not be able to enter a plea until the indictment has been preferred.

The evidence that is served will form the prima facie case. It will generally be convenient for the evidence to be served in one bundle. In a complex case it may be appropriate to serve it as it becomes available, in order to reduce delay. If so the prosecution should notify the defence that more evidence is to be served later. Where the prosecution evidence is served sequentially, the prosecution should advise the defendant and the court whenever the evidence served to date is adequate to constitute service of the prosecution case. This may be before all prosecution evidence has been served.

The date of service of the prosecution case is relevant to the timing of the applications for dismissal, disclosure and the preferment of the indictment. Where the institution of proceedings requires the consent of the Attorney-General or the DPP, it is unlikely that it will be practical for consent to be given until the prosecution case is ready.

Once the prosecution case has been served, the defence may make an application for dismissal under para. 2 of Schedule 3. Detailed provision for this is made in the Crime and Disorder Act 1998 (Dismissal of Charges Sent) Rules 1998. The defence may give notice of intention to make an oral application, or make an application in writing (to which the prosecution may respond with a request for an oral hearing). The notice or written application, accompanied by copies of any material relied on, must be copied to the prosecution, which is allowed 14 days from receipt in which to make comments or adduce further evidence. There is provision for the 14-day period to be extended. The case will be dismissed if the prosecution fails to prove an essential ingredient of the offence or a judge is persuaded that no reasonable jury would convict on the evidence disclosed. Arguments as to admissibility (including under ss.76 and 78 PACE 1984) may be raised.

Like the dismissal rules for transfer cases, the Rules include provision for evidence to be given orally, but only with the judge's leave, which may be given where the interests of justice require. This will often be appropriate in cases where a case has been inadequately investigated and further information may assist the defence in preparing its case, for instance by identifying relevant issues.

If a defendant succeeds in having the case against him dismissed, para. 2(6) of Schedule 3 to the Crime and Disorder Act provides that no further proceedings on the dismissed charge may be brought other than through a voluntary bill of indictment.

S.32A Prosecution of Offences Act 1985 (as inserted by Schedule 8 to the Crime and Disorder Act) allows the prosecution to discontinue a case which has been sent to the Crown Court under s.51, at any time before the indictment is preferred.

The Crown Court will deal with a summary offence only if the accused pleads guilty to it and has been convicted of the indictable-only offence to which it is related; in so doing the court's powers are restricted to those which would have been available to a magistrates' court. In any other circumstances the summary offence will either be remitted to the magistrates for trial or (if the prosecution do not wish to proceed) be dismissed.

Where (following a successful application to dismiss or discontinuance, or for any reason) the indictable-only offence which caused a case to be sent to the Crown Court is no longer on the indictment, but there remain either-way offences for which the defendant has not been arraigned, the procedures for dealing with them are set out in paras. 7–12 of Schedule 3 to the 1998 Act for adult defendants and in para. 13 for cases involving juveniles.

In order to avoid unnecessary transfers between the Crown Court and the magistrates' courts, the Crown Court should deal with outstanding either-way offences where there is a guilty plea, or where the case appears suitable for trial or indictment, or where the defendant elects Crown Court trial. Cases should be remitted to the magistrates for trial only where a not-guilty plea is indicated (or no indication is given), the case suitable for summary trial and the defendant is content to be so tried.

The procedure amounts to an adapted plea before venue/mode of trial hearing, at which the Crown Court determines mode of trial in much the same way as the magistrates would do.

First, the outstanding counts on the indictment which charge either-way offence are read to the defendant and the court invites him to indicate a plea, explaining that if he indicates that he would plead guilty, the court will proceed to deal with him as if he had been arraigned and had actually pleaded guilty.

If the defendant indicates that he would plead not guilty or fails to give any indication, the court must next consider whether the case is suitable for summary trial or trial on indictment, having regard to any representations made by the prosecution or the defendant, the nature of the case, the seriousness of the offence, whether magistrates' sentencing powers would be adequate, or any other circumstances.

If the court decides that the offence is more suitable for trial in indictment, the case will proceed in the usual way. If on the other hand it decides that the case is more suitable for summary trial, the court must give the defendant the option of electing Crown Court trial.

Where the indictable-only offence which caused a case to be sent to the Crown Court is no longer on the indictment, cases involving children or young persons should be remitted to the magistrates' court unless it is necessary that they should be tried at the Crown Court. The circumstances in which the Crown Court should deal with juvenile defendants are where:

- *the accused is charged with an offence which is a grave crime for the purposes of s.53 Children and Young Persons Act 1933 and the court considers that it ought to be possible for him to be sentenced under that provision; or*

- *the juvenile is charged jointly with an adult with an either-way offence, and it is necessary in the interests of justice that they should be tried at the Crown Court.*

Where a young person is charged with an offence which is not a grave crime, there is no provision for the Crown Court to retain the case.

PLEA AND DIRECTIONS HEARING – PDH

Steps prior to the hearing

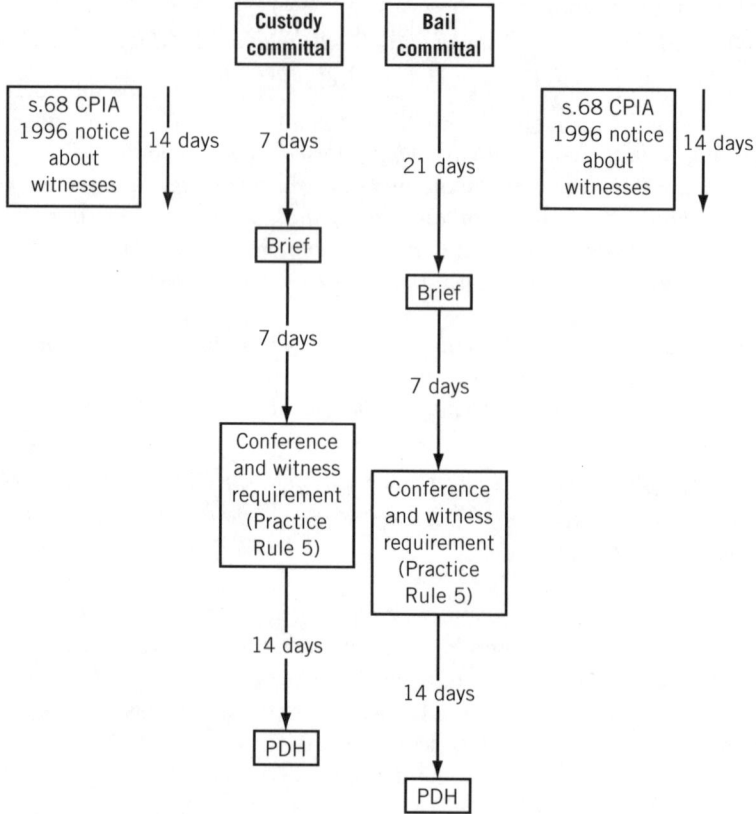

Figure 16.2 Summarising the timescale of the hearing

Actions to take before the PDH

1. Advise the defendant about sentence discount for a guilty plea and inform the probation service about an intended guilty plea not less than 15 days before the PDH.
2. Draft, and obtain the client's consent (if necessary) at committal, to a defence statement for submission under s.5 CPIA 1996.
3. Select a named trial advocate.
4. Send a brief to the trial advocate within seven days of the committal in a custody case and 21 days in a bail case, allowing the trial advocate seven days to read the brief.

5. Hold a conference with the intended trial advocate within 14 days of the committal in a custody case and 28 days in a bail case.
6. Ensure that the brief to the intended trial advocate is sufficiently complete to enable him to advise on all matters relevant to the PDH and contains at least the prosecution committal bundle, the defendant's full instructions, the defence witness statements and the tapes of any interviews with the defendant.
7. In all legally aided cases the Legal Aid Order should be included with the brief as this is the authority for the advocate to be paid from public funds.
8. Submit a list of witnesses required at the trial, having consulted with the trial advocate, to the court and the prosecution not less than 14 days after committal and again 14 days before the PDH.
9. Ensure that if the PDH advocate is not the intended trial advocate, he has clear instructions from the intended trial advocate about conduct of the PDH and the answers to be given to the judge's PDH questionnaire.
10. Ensure that if the PDH advocate is not the trial advocate, he has a note of the intended trial advocate's availability.
11. Decide whether there is a need for the advocate to be instructed during the substantive hearing and if necessary identify the grounds on which the judge may grant a certificate for that purpose.

Identify witnesses to attend trial

S.68 and Sched. 2 CPIA 1996 provide that prosecution witness statements used at committal may be read, instead of those witnesses being called, unless a party objects. If an objection is made, the 'court of trial' may still order the reading of the statement if it is in the 'interests of justice'.

The written statements and depositions of the prosecution witnesses will be read out at trial without oral evidence being given, unless the accused informs the Crown Court and the prosecutor within 14 days of the committal. If notice is not given in time, the accused will lose the right to prevent the evidence only being read, unless the court gives leave to require the attendance of the witness.

Asking about intended pleas

There is an increasing tendency for the Probation Service to ask about intended pleas either in person at committal or in forms handed out at committal or for the Crown Court probation team or Court Administrator to send a form to the solicitor for completion and return before the PDH, requesting the solicitor to notify them about the intended plea(s).

Considering evidence

In co-operation with the advocate consider:

- proofs and observations on evidence and which witnesses will be called;
- s.9 CJA 1967 statements;
- s.10 CJA 1967 admissions;
- what exhibits will be required.

Ensure defence statement and expert evidence notice is served at appropriate times.

Considering pleas

In co-operation with the advocate and as necessary:

- discuss appropriate pleas, bearing in mind the gravity of charge, the weight of the evidence, sentencing options and policy including discount for guilty plea;
- in the event of guilty plea ensure contact with the Probation Service at least 15 days before the PDH so that pre-sentence reports are prepared and that any medical or psychiatric reports are available, and remember to obtain any necessary authorities;
- obtain written consent from the client before suggesting the tendering of alternative pleas to the prosecution;
- consider obtaining written confirmation from your client if he is tendering a plea on a particular version of the facts.

Relevance of statement made in plea and directions hearings

Statements in the course of such a proceeding, which have no force of law, or the contents of the questionnaire should not be used for evidential purposes without the consent of the party affected.[1] What is said at such a hearing is not expected to form part of the material used at trial and it is rarely appropriate to refer to it. Instead hearings are meant for the efficient disposal of business in the Crown Court.[2]

Questionnaire

Copies of the PDH questionnaire and pre-trial checklist for cases involving child witnesses are included in Appendix 23.

Bail issues

Custody time-limits

An appearance at a PDH does not bring a custody time-limit to an end.

Sureties must normally attend a PDH.

Binding rulings before Crown Court trial[3]

A Crown Court judge may make at any pre-trial hearing a ruling as to:

- the admissibility of evidence; and/or
- any question of law.

You should identify any such issue and provide sufficient material for the advocate to argue the case. The judge's ruling is binding unless later discharged or varied in the interests of justice.

However, a party cannot apply to discharge or vary unless they can show a material change of circumstances.

PREPARATORY HEARINGS

Formal preparatory hearings (which are the start of the relevant trial and end a custody time-limit) may be held in cases where the indictment involves a serious or complex fraud case or reveals a case of such complexity or length that substantial benefit is likely to accrue from:

- identifying the material issues;
- assisting the jury's comprehension of the case;
- expediting proceedings;
- assisting the judge's management of the case.

Sureties should attend.

207

At a preparatory hearing the judge may:

- adjourn the proceedings;

- rule on admissibility or law (from which ruling all parties may appeal);

- order a prosecution case statement; the service of schedules and consideration of s.10 requests;

- order a defence case statement.

A case statement will include:

- principal facts;

- witnesses;

- exhibits;

- proposition of law;

- consequences of these;

- giving in 'general terms the nature of the defence and indicating principal matters in dispute';

- objections to the prosecution case statement;

- points of law to be argued;

- indicate s.10 admissions.

The defence need not disclose witnesses (except expert or under the disclosure rules). A case statement under these provisions cannot normally be used as part of the prosecution case.

Attending the advocate at the preliminary Crown Court hearing

A representative may always attend the advocate at preliminary hearings and at the plea and directions hearing. At those hearings, consideration must be given as to whether a representative should attend the trial or sentencing hearing. A judge's certificate will be required in many cases.

End notes

1 *R. v. Hutchison* [1985] Crim LR 730.
2 *R. v. Diedrick and Aldridge* [1997] Crim LR 58.
3 ss.39–43 CPIA 1996.

CHAPTER 17

Preparing for a contested trial – Magistrates' and Crown Courts

Many of the following provisions apply, the more strongly in the Crown Court, but parts (including, in particular, the section on final preparation) apply equally to Magistrates' Court trials.

REPRESENTATION FOR TRIAL

Level of representation

Consider appropriate level of representation:

- most suitable advocate for type of case and personality of client;
- in magistrates' court consider application for certificate for counsel in appropriate cases;
- in Crown Court, if appropriate, consider whether suitable solicitor has rights of audience;
- if not, consider choice of suitable counsel.

A QC may accept instructions in the Crown Court to appear without junior counsel in cases such as:*

- pleas of guilty worthy of silk representation where the plea is certain in advance of the hearing;
- appeals to the Court of Appeal, Criminal Division, worthy of silk representation which can properly be undertaken by a silk alone;
- otherwise straightforward matters which have some sensitive overlay, whether political, local or other;

These rules are under review and likely to be changed on 1 April 2000.

* [1989] Gazette, 25 January.

Conferences

The object of a conference is to enable your client to meet his advocate to establish confidence and to be advised jointly by the trial advocate and solicitor. Conference with the trial advocate should normally be held in the following cases:

- where there is a not guilty hearing;

- where your client needs to be advised about plea(s);

- where the case is complicated by a particular factor or involves serious consequences;

- where the case requires careful consideration of tactics, evidence, plea, experts, exhibits, witnesses.

Your client should be informed of the date and time of the conference. Consider asking your client to attend your office first so as to ensure his attendance at the conference and that time is not wasted waiting unnecessarily for him.

The solicitor should take an active part in the conference and not merely take notes.

Full notes of the conference are essential and should be typed up afterwards and sent to the advocate and to the client in appropriate cases.

At the end of the conference the solicitor should prepare a list of action points to be taken and confirm this with the advocate. These matters should be prepared as soon as possible. If you anticipate any difficulties then contact the court to ensure sufficient time is given.

If your client fails to attend two conferences then consider listing the case before a judge, without attendance of the witnesses, so as to obtain the client's instructions. Solicitors should write to the client to this effect before taking this action.

Brief to trial advocate

A brief to the trial advocate (whether in-house or solicitor advocate/counsel) should contain full and detailed information concerning the case and be prepared as soon as possible after committal proceedings. In the case of any unusual preparation or expenditure it may be prudent to seek the advice and support of the advocate to justify any application for authorities from the Legal Aid Board and ultimately to assist in any problems that may arise on determination. Such advice could cover the cost of transcripts, enquiry agent's fees, expert witnesses and the like, where the solicitor has any doubt that they may be required.

Other relevant documents should be included as enclosures with the brief. Inform the advocate of any amendments made to the Legal Aid Order (reg. 40(5) Legal Aid in Criminal and Care Proceedings (General) Regulations 1989).

The back sheet to the brief should contain the name of the court, name of the case (including co-defendants), the case number (if known), which defendant advocate is instructed to act for, whether remuneration legal aid or fee and the name, address, telephone number and reference of the instructing solicitor.

Information to be included in brief to advocate

1. Committal date/date sent or transferred/date of PDH.

2. Details of charges in indictment

3. Bail history in this case.

4. Periods of time in custody.

5. Witness list submitted (s.68 CPIA 1996) (details of which witnesses should attend court). [73.3]

6. Defence statement (details of any disclosure already made by the defence). [73.7]

7. Pleas to be entered.

8. An outline of the prosecution case.

9. A summary of what each prosecution witness deals with. [73.1]

10. Details of co-accused.

11. Any relationship with prosecution witnesses or co-defendants.

12. Outline of the defence case – possible witnesses and exhibits.

13. Full antecedents.

14. Previous convictions.

15. TICs and any disputes over compensation arising on charges or TICs.

16. Background information on clients.

17. Any particular problems and any particular area on which the advocate's advice is sought.

18. Whether or not a conference is required.

19. Legal aid or private and details of any applications in relation to costs.

20. Always instruct the advocate to advise on appeal at end of case.

Enclosures to be included with brief to advocate

1. Prosecution statements and exhibits (including police station interview tape).

2. Additional evidence.

3. Client's proof and observations.

4. Statements of defence witnesses. [73.2]

5. Expert reports.

6. Indictment.

7. Copy of correspondence with prosecution.

8. Additional background information on client; references, etc.

9. A list of previous convictions. [73.5].

10. A schedule of TICs.

11. Copy of Legal Aid Order. (Inform advocate of any amendments made to the Order).

12. Defence statement (if drafted and submitted).

13. Unused material:

    (a) primary disclosure, with date given, and MG6C schedule; [73.6]
    (b) secondary disclosure (if any, and/or requests for secondary disclosure).

14. Standard brief to unattended advocates.

15. Standard brief in relation to appeal.

Attending the advocate at the hearing

Payment from Legal Aid, for providing support for the advocate at court, can only be authorised where the proceedings, or the personal circumstances of the legally assisted person, fall within one or other of five exceptions, or the litigator has obtained a certificate of attendance to provide support for the advocate at court.[1] The exceptions are:

- the defendant being charged with a class 1 or 2 offence;

- the proceeding having been brought or taken over by the SFO or are before the Crown Court by reasons of a notice of transfer under s.4 CJA 1987 (serious or complex fraud transfers);

- the legally assisted person being a child or young person within the meaning of s.107 Children and Young Persons Act 1933 at the time when the Crown Court acquired jurisdiction of the case (by committal, transfer or otherwise);

- the legally assisted person is unable to understand the proceedings or give instructions because of an inadequate knowledge of English, mental illness other mental or physical disability; or

- the legally assisted person, if convicted, was likely to receive a custodial sentence whether suspended or to take immediate effect. This exemption is only available on the days when a sentence of imprisonment is likely to be imposed.

These changes do not affect the situation where solicitors attend court for a conference with the advocate where a conference is necessary. The Law Society advises that where practitioners are in doubt as to their duty to attend or arrange for the attendance of a responsible representative, a certificate should be applied for.

A certificate may be granted at PDH and after on any ground which satisfies the judge but regulations include examples of suitable situations where:

- there are numbers of defence witnesses;

- there are quantities of defence evidence;

- the defendant is disruptive;

- there is more than one defendant;

- there is a need for note-taking.

Final preparation

Review before the hearing

You should review readiness for the hearing sufficiently in advance to enable steps to be taken if shortcomings are discovered.

Prosecution case

Check receipt (as appropriate) and keep a record of dates of receipt of:

- record of previous convictions;
- advance information;
- tapes of interviews;
- custody records;
- committal bundle; notices of additional evidence;
- prosecution primary disclosure: undermining material and schedule;
- prosecution secondary disclosure: material which may assist the defence case;
- expert's report.

Check CPS have been told:

- which witnesses are required (and confirmed in writing);
- whether the record of interview required editing;
- if tape-recording of police interview is required to be played in court;
- of any agreement as to s.9 statement or s.10 admissions;
- of any expert evidence to be called.

Defence case

Check defendant has been:

- proofed adequately;
- been advised whether to give a defence statement in the magistrates' court; [77.1, 77.2]
- given a defence statement in the Crown Court or warned of the implications of not doing so; [78.1, 78.2]
- warned of hearing date/time/place; [74.1]
- given access to his proof of evidence;
- advised of court procedures, behaviour; [74.2]
- advised whether or not to give evidence [74.3] and the implications of not giving evidence. [76.1]

Check defence witnesses have been:

- proofed adequately;
- warned of hearing date/time/place; [80.1]
- reminded of evidence if appropriate;
- advised of court procedures, behaviour. [80.2]

Check defence statement (if appropriate) has been given to CPS and court.

Brief to unattended advocate

In cases where an advocate is unattended:

- deal with advocate's early arrival at court to see the client;
- include sufficient details about the defendant and any witnesses to enable the advocate to contact them if they do not appear;
- require the judge's comments on sentence to be fully recorded;
- require notes to be provided of the headings of the advocate's speech in mitigation;
- require a telephone report to the solicitor after the case ends;
- require the advocate to deal with witnesses' expenses;
- require the advocate to deal with the client and any relatives who may be present after the case has been concluded;
- require the advocate to find out where the client has been taken if in custody, and pass that information to the solicitor;
- require the advocate to endorse the brief within two days with what oral advice on appeal has been given to the client.

NOTIFICATION OF TRIAL

If a date for trial is fixed notify your client promptly of the name and address of the court and the date and time attendance is required and the date and time of any conference arranged and seek confirmation of receipt by enclosing addressed pre-paid envelope.

If a date is not fixed it will be placed in the warned list. Write a letter to your client informing him of the warned list procedure. Clients may not otherwise understand the procedure.

As soon as you are notified that a case is on the warned list notify your client. Practices as regards notification will vary depending on a client's communicability (distance, telephone, etc.), ask your client to provide a telephone number where he can be contacted, or where somebody else can contact him, at short notice, if possible. It is your duty to take reasonable steps to ensure your client attends court on time. Failure to attend by your client will necessitate further adjournments and could lead to arrest.

Be sure to notify sureties when a trial is listed. They will have to attend.

ATTENDANCE AT TRIAL

1. Where a solicitor or representative attends the advocate, he must be fully appraised of the case.

2. The role of the solicitor is an active one ensuring that the advocate represents the client's case fully at court, and offering assistance when appropriate.

3. Ensure defence witnesses are available/contactable.

4. Take as full notes of evidence as possible and with particular care when the advocate is on his feet. Always make full notes of the judge's comments. The advocate will often require notes of evidence overnight or during the trial. Make them legible and ensure that there are gaps between lines so that the advocate can identify relevant sections.

5. You can and should take instructions from your client during the trial. Be aware your client may wish to speak to you from the dock. You may not however advise your client or otherwise discuss the case from the time he starts giving evidence, until he has left the witness box, without leave of the court. Advise him of this rule in advance. This rule also applies to all other witnesses.

6. Obtain witness expense forms and assist witnesses to fill them in and take them to the Accounts Department.

7. If your client is convicted and/or sentenced to a term of imprisonment or otherwise, ensure that you attend your client with the advocate.

8. Contact the family/friends after the case and with your client's authority inform them of result.

9. When seeing your client who is sentenced to a term of imprisonment ensure he signs relevant documents, i.e. letter of authority regarding any property to be returned or otherwise.

10. Ensure sureties attend court on first day of trial.

End note

1 *The Guide to the Professional Conduct of Solicitors 1999,* Principle 20.04 and Annex 20A. The Law Society.

CHAPTER 18

Action after acquittal or conviction and sentence

ACQUITTAL

Defendant's costs

If privately funded, or pre-legal aid, work has been carried out, and your client is acquitted, or the case is discontinued or withdrawn, remember to apply for costs from central funds. If your client has an old Legal Aid Order and was ordered to pay contributions towards his legal aid, apply to the court for these to be refunded if your client was acquitted.[1]

An order from central funds may be made where a case is not proceeded with or dismissed. An order should normally be made unless there are positive reasons against it:

- if the defendant's own conduct has brought suspicion on himself and misled the prosecution into thinking the case against him is stronger than it is.[2]

Witnesses' costs

The costs of attendance at court of a witness required by the defendant or the court, or of an interpreter, or of an oral report by a medical practitioner, are allowed out of central funds, unless the court directs otherwise.[3]

Such expenses cannot be claimed as disbursements under a Legal Aid Order unless the court refuses to make an order from central funds.[4] The court must, however, expressly order costs out of central funds in favour of a character witness.

Other orders

Apply for restitution of any property seized from the defendant.

Write to the chief constable of the appropriate force area for the destruction of your client's fingerprint record, DNA sample and photograph. Remember the very short time-limit for doing this if your client wishes to be present when this is done.[5]

CONVICTION/SENTENCE

Correcting mistakes

A court may vary or rescind a sentence or other order (including replacing an Invalid Order) on the application of the prosecution or defence or on its own initiative.

In the magistrates' court there is no time-limit provided that it is in the interests of justice.[6]

In the Crown Court the power must be exercised within 28 days from the day the order was made.

These powers should be used, rather than an appeal, when a decision which is clearly wrong has been made.

Immediate advice

You have a duty to advise all clients of their appeal rights. A useful reference guide is published by Justice.[7]

IMPRISONMENT

The advocate (where instructed) and you or your representative should see your client in the cells and provide preliminary advice on the question of appeal and check with your client if any matters need to be dealt with in his life as a result of imprisonment.

You should find out from the clerk of the court in which your client appeared, which prison your client will be taken to. A prisoner's whereabouts cannot be given over the telephone.

You should spend time with the family/friends of your client informing them of the whereabouts of your client, the procedure for prison visits, visiting orders and letters to the prison, and on appeal procedures.

The Prisons Handbook[8] contains full information about all the penal establishments in England and Wales, including their regimes, accommodation and facilities. It also contains penal case law, the Prison Act 1952, the Prison Rules, advice to prisoners and a list of helpful organisations and resources.

Your client and (with his permission) his family should be written to immediately after the court confirming the sentence and any advice, including any given at court.

Your client should have the meaning of the earliest release date and his responsibilities on licence explained.

In the event of later difficulties in locating your client, HM Prison Service may be contacted at Prisoner Location Service, PO Box 2152, Birmingham B15 1SD. You need to write to the Prison Service giving as much information as possible, including your client's:

- name, age and date of birth;
- offence;
- the court where they were convicted/sentenced and the date of conviction/sentence.

APPEALS AGAINST CONVICTION AND/OR SENTENCE

From the magistrates' court to the Crown Court

Appeals may be against conviction and/or sentence and are heard by a judge sitting with lay justices. Appeals against conviction are by way of re-hearing, and fresh evidence may be called. Obtain the notes of evidence given at the magistrates' court trial from the justices' clerk. Note that magistrates' courts are not courts of record and notes kept by the clerk are not a record of the evidence given. There is no obligation on the court to provide such copy notes, although the Divisional Court has ruled that clerks should view sympathetically such requests from solicitors where a proper reason is given. A charge is likely where they are provided.

Warn your client that the Crown Court may award any sentence, whether more or less than that of the magistrates, providing it is not more than the maximum sentence the magistrates could have imposed.

Procedure

This is by notice in writing (see Appendix 3, document 3.6) to the magistrates' court and prosecutor within 21 days of sentence being passed. An appeal against conviction cannot begin earlier. The Crown Court may extend the period, i.e. give leave to appeal out of time, on receipt of a letter setting out the reasons (which will be put before a judge). Your magistrates' court Legal Aid Order will cover you for time spent advising on appeal and completing the notice. An application for a new Legal Aid Order should be made promptly for the appeal itself.

Bail pending appeal

If your client is sentenced to custody, an application to the magistrates' court for bail pending appeal cannot be made until notice of appeal is served on the court and the prosecution.

Consider a possible appeal with your client and if you are so instructed file notice of appeal. Apply with speed, otherwise you may prolong your client's time in custody. The notice can be lodged and application made the same day on which the sentence is passed.

If the application fails, make an application to a judge in chambers at the Crown Court on the prescribed form to be served on the Crown Court and prosecution; there is no time-limit for making such an application. At least 24 hours' notice is normally required.

Even if bail is refused, the court may agree to expedite the appeal hearing.

Abandonment

Abandonment should be notified in writing to the magistrates' court, Crown Court and prosecution at least three days before the hearing.

High Court

Right to appeal by way of case stated to the High Court[9] is available to.

- a party to magistrates' court proceedings (defence or prosecution);
- any person aggrieved by a conviction, order, determination or other proceedings.

It is available to challenge the proceedings on grounds of:

- error in law; or

- an excess of jurisdiction.

Procedure

The case is drawn up at the request of a party or aggrieved person by the clerk to the justices.

The time-limit for application is: within 21 days of conviction or, only if case adjourned for sentence, of sentence. The Divisional Court has no power to extend this time-limit, but a defective application, made in time, may be corrected later.

Apply to the magistrates' court in writing, specifying grounds.

The magistrates' court may state a case conditionally on the applicant entering into a recognisance to pursue the matter.

It is important to appreciate that your client loses the right of appeal to the Crown Court if he applies for case stated.

In appropriate cases you will wish to consider whether judicial review is an alternative remedy. This does not carry with it the loss of the right to appeal to the Crown Court.

Appeal from the Crown Court[10]

An application for leave to appeal against conviction or sentence must be sent to the Crown Court within 28 days from conviction and/or sentence. The time-limits are separate.

Within 14 days the advocate should have prepared a written advice in favour of or against appeal.

Within a further seven days your client should be sent a copy of the advocate's advice and if it is negative your client should be advised that he can pursue the appeal but it unlikely to succeed as a result of the advocate's advice.

An advice in favour of appeal and confirming the grounds of appeal should be included with the application for leave to appeal.

If the single judge refuses leave, your client is entitled to pursue his appeal to the full court and must do so within 14 days of receipt of the notice of refusal from the single judge.

You will be sent a copy of the notice of refusal. You should write to your client informing him of your advice on the refusal and advise if the matter is pursued and fails at the second stage that the appellant can forfeit up to a maximum of 90 days if the full court considers the appeal was without merit. This power is unlikely to be used if the appeal was renewed on the advocate's advice and in practice the court tends to direct that only a maximum of 28 days shall not count towards the sentence.

Always advise your client and family that the appeal procedures take a long time.

The Legal Aid Order will cover advice as to whether to lodge an appeal and whether to renew an application for leave after refusal by the single judge. It can also include a prison visit in an appropriate case.

You should be familiar with *A Guide to Proceedings in the Court of Appeal Criminal Division*, which is available free of charge from all Crown Court centres. After setting out the initial steps to be taken at the conclusion of the case, it goes on to deal with the settling of grounds of appeal, the obtaining of transcripts, the perfection of grounds and the procedure which then follows. It contains useful information about legal aid, extension of time limits, bail pending appeal, abandonment and costs. Most of the guide is set out in the latest edition of *Archbold*.

Appendix 1 of the guide, which sets out specific instructions to the advocate to give advice and assistance on appeal in the event of a conviction and again following sentence, should have been included with every brief.

RE-TRIAL FOLLOWING TAINTED ACQUITTALS

The prosecution may apply to the High Court to quash a tainted acquittal if a witness in the case is later convicted of perverting the course of justice or anyone is convicted of an offence of interference and the court finds there was a real possibility that the defendant would otherwise have been convicted; and that the matter is not so old or any other reason that it is not in the interests of justice to allow a re-trial.[11]

CRIMINAL CASES REVIEW COMMISSION

The Commission has taken over the functions of the Home Secretary and Northern Ireland Secretary to refer cases to the relevant Court of Appeal.

Its jurisdiction includes referrals in respect of sentence as well as conviction.

It may also refer convictions or sentences made or imposed in the magistrates' court to the Crown Court.

There are conditions to be satisfied before the Commission can decide to refer a case to Court:

- there must be a real possibility that the conviction, verdict, or sentence would not be upheld;

- conviction cases: there must be evidence or argument not previously raised (unless there are exceptional circumstances);

- sentence cases: there must be information or an argument on a point of law not previously raised;

- there must have been a determined appeal or a refusal of leave to appeal (unless there are exceptional circumstances).

Court of Appeal investigation

The Court of Appeal may itself direct that the Commission investigate a particular matter 'in such manner as the Commission thinks fit'. This extends to any matter which the Commission thinks is related and relevant to the determination of a case by the Court of Appeal.

Case must have been through the normal appeal process

The case must have been through the normal appeal process. Exceptionally, application and reference may be entertained even though the appellate process was not invoked, e.g. material on which an appeal might have been based may not come to hand until years later. 'Exceptional' has a clear, ordinary meaning and is not defined by the Criminal Appeal Act 1995.

Where it is possible to appeal out of time that route should be taken first.

'Real possibility'

The Commission is not to refer a case unless it considers that there is a real possibility that the conviction, finding or sentence would not be upheld were the reference to be made – could the new material cause the Court of Appeal to think the conviction unsafe?[12]

The 'real possibility' must be judged (save in exceptional circumstances, e.g. flagrantly incompetent advocacy; e.g. counsel takes a decision in defiance of your client's instructions) on the strength of an argument or evidence not raised at trial, or on appeal, or on an application for leave to appeal as it should not give the defence the opportunity to run two different defences through appeal.

The review is not limited to fresh evidence. It is wider, as it can look at evidence available at the previous hearing but not used. Is there a reasonable explanation for failure to produce the evidence? What if the advocate failed to cross-examine a witness properly so that certain evidence did not come out?

Sentence

In the case of a sentence the Commission must be able to point to an argument on a point of law, or information about the circumstances of the offence or the offender, which was not raised at trial.

Points of law include: 'wrong in principle'; failure to give a discount for early plea; a sentence which did not fall within the jurisdiction of the court imposing it; an erroneous interpretation of a statutory power.

Adherence to tariff or disparity between offenders for equivalent offences is not a point of law, even if the tariff has changed over the years.[13]

When referring a case

The Commission must provide the court to which the reference is made with a statement of the Commission's reasons for making the reference.

The Commission must supply a copy to every person likely to be a party to any proceedings in the appeal rising from the reference.

When not referring a case

The Commission must give reasons for a decision not to make a reference to the person making the application.

Application form

The Commission has produced an information pack which includes an application form. This is available from the Criminal Cases Review Commission, Alpha Tower, Suffolk Street, Queensway, Birmingham B1 1TT; DX 715466 Birmingham 41.

They do not insist that a completed form is submitted or that it is completed in full.

Material has been well presented by lawyers where there is a summary at the front backed up by the documentation in a folder, with a clear indication of what they think the issues are and what the next steps should be.

The Commission would prefer you to use the form to 'front up' an application, just so they can be sure that they have all the information which they need.

The Commission welcomes telephone calls seeking advice and guidance as to what other information or documentation would be beneficial (tel: 0121 366 1800). The Commission is happy to discuss a potential application.

Your role

Your role is to:

● advise on an application to the Commission;

● prepare an application (including taking witness statements, obtaining experts' reports and opinions);

● continue to advise and do work for that client whilst the Commission is reviewing the case.

There is no particular limit on your role while the investigation and review is being undertaken.

The Commission encourages legal representation of applicants. You can emphasise the strengths of an application whilst ignoring irrelevant detail. You should emphasise to your client that the Commission's role is investigative and that an adversarial approach at this stage is unlikely to assist.

A key role of yours is to advise the CCRC on the merits of the application. You should be realistic in your assessment of what points raised by your client and identified by you – even if resolved in your client's favour – are likely to make a difference to the safety of the conviction; process failure does not automatically make a conviction unsafe. Don't be afraid to put forward meritorious grounds just because they cannot yet be supported by evidence; the Commission has an investigative role.

You should identify the issues of concern:

- in what respect is it suggested that the conviction is unsafe?

- what evidence is (or may be) available to support that contention?

- if there are a number of issues, assess their relative weight and pertinence.

You should obtain your client's case papers from the solicitors who have previously represented him in the case so that you can confirm the instructions which he gave them and see what investigations they undertook and decisions they made.

A well constructed and well supported application in which the grounds are clearly identified and argued and the case mapped out for the Commission will help your client. An application which is structured similar to the way in which the Commission prepares a statement of reasons in support of its conclusion is very helpful: summary of the prosecution and defence case at trial; the appeal history (date, grounds and outcome); and the grounds of application to the Commission. Use of chronologies, summaries and skeleton arguments in support of the grounds is encouraged by the Commission.

In relation to the incident giving rise to the conviction, you should set out your understanding of the sequence of events and give details of the witnesses involved and the extent of their involvement, their full names, contact addresses, or last known location and the role (if any) played by the client.

Although there is no entitlement to have information received by the Commission disclosed to you while the Commission investigates and reviews the application, where the Commission recognises that it is dealing with a solicitor who understands its independent role and responsibilities and criteria for referring a case to an appeal court, it is more likely to consider it of value to actively involve you.

If the Commission is going to interview someone, you may want to attend the interview.

You should respond promptly to correspondence and keep your client informed about the work being done on his case.

You should manage your client's expectations; explain at the outset the Commission's work position.

There are criteria by which individual cases can be assessed for priority ranking. The Commission is happy to explain them as they are at any given time. If there may be grounds for priority ranking, representations about this may be prepared for submission with the application.

In your application, make clear whether there was an application for leave to appeal or a full appeal and whether the appeal was against conviction/ sentence or both.

Alert the Commission to where pertinent documentation can be found including forensic tests conducted – when they were conducted and location and availability of material the Commission may wish to test.

Legal aid

Assistance is available to clients under the Legal Advice and Assistance Scheme.

The LAB's devolved guidance for miscarriage of justice applications is that you may normally allow 10 hours' work and you can in appropriate cases grant an extension on that for all relevant activities.

This guidance applicable to a CCRC application is separate from advice and assistance given in respect of the original trial and any other appeal.

End notes

1 Legal Aid in Criminal and Care Proceedings (General) Regulations 1989, reg. 35.
2 s.20(3) Prosecution of Offences Act (POA) 1985, s.20(3); Costs in Criminal Cases (General) Regulations 1986, reg. 16(1). Practice Direction *Crime: Costs in Criminal Proceedings (No. 2)* [1999] 4 All ER 436.
3 *Ibid.*
4 s.25 Legal Aid Act 1988.
5 PACE, Code D, paras. 3.4, 4.4, and 5.8.
6 s.142 MCA 1980.
7 *How to Appeal: A Guide to the Criminal Appeal Process*, available from Justice, 59 Carter Lane, London EC4V 5AQ, £2.50.
8 Leech, M, *The Prisons Handbook*, 4th edition, 1999. Waterside Press.
9 Applications are to the Divisional Court until the relevant provisions of the Access to Justice Act 1999 are brought into force.
10 See generally, *Justice*.
11 Applications are to the Divisional Court until the relevant provisions of the Access to Justice Act 1999 are brought into force.
12 s.13(1)(a) Criminal Appeal Act 1995.
13 *R.* v. *Graham* [1999] Crim LR 677.

Appendices

APPENDIX 1

The European Convention on Human Rights (extracts)

ARTICLE 2: RIGHT TO LIFE

1. Everyone's right to life shall be protected by law. No one shall be deprived of his life intentionally save in the execution of a sentence of a court following his conviction of a crime for which this penalty is provided by law.

2. Deprivation of life shall not be regarded as inflicted in contravention of this Article when it results from the use of force which is no more than absolutely necessary:

   (a) in defence of any person from unlawful violence;
   (b) in order to effect a lawful arrest or to prevent the escape of a person lawfully detained;
   (c) in action lawfully taken for the purpose of quelling a riot or insurrection.

ARTICLE 3: PROHIBITION OF TORTURE

No one shall be subjected to torture or to inhuman or degrading treatment or punishment.

ARTICLE 5: RIGHT TO LIBERTY AND SECURITY

1. Everyone has the right to liberty and security of person. No one shall be deprived of his liberty save in the following cases and in accordance with a procedure prescribed by law:

   (a) the lawful detention of a person after conviction by a competent court;

(b) the lawful arrest or detention of a person for non-compliance with the lawful order of a court or in order to secure the fulfilment of any obligation prescribed by law;

(c) the lawful arrest or detention of a person effected for the purpose of bringing him before the competent legal authority on reasonable suspicion of having committed an offence or when it is reasonably considered necessary to prevent his committing an offence or fleeing after having done so;

(d) the detention of a minor by lawful order for the purpose of educational supervision or his lawful detention for the purpose of bringing him before the competent legal authority;

(e) the lawful detention of persons for the prevention of the spreading of infectious diseases, of persons of unsound mind, alcoholics or drug addicts or vagrants;

(f) the lawful arrest or detention of a person to prevent his effecting an unauthorised entry into the country or of a person against whom action is being taken with a view to deportation or extradition.

2. Everyone who is arrested shall be informed promptly, in a language which he understands, of the reasons for his arrest and of any charge against him.

3. Everyone arrested or detained in accordance with the provisions of paragraph 1(c) of this Article shall be brought promptly before a judge or other officer authorised by law to exercise judicial power and shall be entitled to trial within a reasonable time or to release pending trial. Release may be conditioned by guarantees to appear for trial.

4. Everyone who is deprived of his liberty by arrest or detention shall be entitled to take proceedings by which the lawfulness of his detention shall be decided speedily by a court and his release ordered if the detention is not lawful.

5. Everyone who has been the victim of arrest or detention in contravention of the provisions of this Article shall have an enforceable right to compensation.

ARTICLE 6: RIGHT TO A FAIR TRIAL

1. In the determination of his civil rights and obligations or of any criminal charge against him, everyone is entitled to a fair and public hearing within a reasonable time by an independent and impartial tribunal established by law. Judgment shall be pronounced publicly but the press and public may be excluded from all or part of the trial in

the interest of morals, public order or national security in a democratic society, where the interests of juveniles or the protection of the private life of the parties so require, or to the extent strictly necessary in the opinion of the court in special circumstances where publicity would prejudice the interests of justice.

2. Everyone charged with a criminal offence shall be presumed innocent until proved guilty according to law.

3. Everyone charged with a criminal offence has the following minimum rights:

    (a) to be informed promptly, in a language which he understands and in detail, of the nature and cause of the accusation against him;

    (b) to have adequate time and facilities for the preparation of his defence;

    (c) to defend himself in person or through legal assistance of his own choosing or, if he has not sufficient means to pay for legal assistance, to be given it free when the interests of justice so require;

    (d) to examine or have examined witnesses against him and to obtain the attendance and examination of witnesses on his behalf under the same conditions as witnesses against him;

    (e) to have the free assistance of an interpreter if he cannot understand or speak the language used in court.

ARTICLE 8: RIGHT TO RESPECT FOR PRIVATE AND FAMILY LIFE

1. Everyone has the right to respect for his private and family life, his home and his correspondence.

2. There shall be no interference by a public authority with the exercise of this right except such as is in accordance with the law and is necessary in a democratic society in the interests of national security, public safety or the economic well-being of the country, for the prevention of disorder or crime, for the protection of health or morals, or for the protection of the rights and freedoms of others.

ARTICLE 10: FREEDOM OF EXPRESSION

1. Everyone has the right to freedom of expression. This right shall include freedom to hold opinions and to receive and impart information and ideas without interference by public authority and regardless

of frontiers. This Article shall not prevent States from requiring the licensing of broadcasting, television or cinema enterprises.

2. The exercise of these freedoms, since it carries with it duties and responsibilities, may be subject to such formalities, conditions, restrictions or penalties as are prescribed by law and are necessary in a democratic society, in the interests of national security, territorial integrity or public safety, for the prevention of disorder or crime, for the protection of health or morals, for the protection of the reputation or rights of others, for preventing the disclosure of information received in confidence, or for maintaining the authority and impartiality of the judiciary.

ARTICLE 11: FREEDOM OF ASSEMBLY AND ASSOCIATION

1. Everyone has the right to freedom of peaceful assembly and to freedom of association with others, including the right to form and to join trade unions for the protection of his interests.

2. No restrictions shall be placed on the exercise of these rights other than such as are prescribed by law and are necessary in a democratic society in the interests of national security or public safety, for the prevention of disorder or crime, for the protection of health or morals or for the protection of the rights and freedoms of others. This Article shall not prevent the imposition of lawful restrictions on the exercise of these rights by members of the armed forces, of the police or of the administration of the State.

ARTICLE 14: PROHIBITION OF DISCRIMINATION

The enjoyment of the rights and freedoms set forth in this Convention shall be secured without discrimination on any ground such as sex, race, colour, language, religion, political or other opinion, national or social origin, association with a national minority, property, birth or other status.

Form of undertaking recommended by the Law Society for children's video evidence

UNDERTAKING

Form of undertaking recommended by the Law Society for use by solicitors when receiving recorded evidence of a child witness prepared to be admitted in evidence at criminal trials in accordance with section 54 of the Criminal Justice Act 1991:

I/We acknowledge receipt of the recording marked 'evidence of . . .'.

I/We undertake that whilst the recording is in my/our possession I/we shall:

(a) not make or permit any other person to make a copy of the recording;
(b) not release the recording to [name of the accused];
(c) not make or permit any disclosure of the recording or its contents to any person except when in my/our opinion it is necessary in the course of preparing the prosecution, defence, or appeal against conviction and/or sentence;
(d) ensure that the recording is always kept in a locked, secure container when not in use;
(e) return the recording to you when I am/we are no longer instructed in the matter.

APPENDIX 3

Forms commonly used by solicitors

CONTENTS

3.1

Application for review of refusal of criminal legal aid

APP5

Please write the page numbers of the pages you are submitting in the adjoining box.

Please complete in block capitals

Your details

Title: _____ Initials: _____

Surname: _____

First name: _____

Surname at birth: _____
(if different)

Date of birth: _____ / _____ / _____

National insurance number: |__|__|__|__|__|__|__|__|__|

Sex: ☐ Male   ☐ Female

Marital status: ☐ Single   ☐ Married   ☐ Cohabiting

☐ Separated   ☐ Divorced   ☐ Widowed

Place of birth: _____ Job: _____
(town)

Current address: _____

Town: _____

County: _____ Postcode: _____

Acting solicitor's details

➤ *Please ask your solicitor fo fill in this section.*

Legal aid supplier number: |__|__|__|__|__|__|__| |__|__|__|__|__|__|__|

Name of firm: _____

Phone: _____

Name of acting solicitor: _____

➤ *The acting solicitor must have a valid practising certificate. The Board cannot pay for any work done during any period in which the acting solicitor does not have a practising certificate.*

Solicitor's reference: _____

Contact name for enquiries: _____

APP5   **Page 1**   V. 2 October 1997   (c) Legal Aid Board 1998   Capsoft UK Ltd 01/99

Case details

What are the alleged offence(s)? _____

Date of main offence: _____ / _____ / _____

Are the offence(s) ☐ Triable either way ☐ Indictable only

What is the date of the next hearing? ___ / ___ / ___ Name of Court: _____

What is the purpose of the next hearing?_____

How do you intend to plead? ☐ Not guilty ☐ Guilty ☐ Mixed plea

Reason(s) why you think legal aid should be granted

►*Complete the boxes in this section that apply to you and give brief details or reasons for each in the space provided.*

►*You may need the help of a solicitor to complete this section of the form.*

☐ It is likely that I will lose my liberty because:

I am subject to a: ☐ community service order ☐ deferment of sentence

☐ conditional discharge ☐ supervision order ☐ care order

☐ probation order ☐ suspended or partly suspended prison sentence

Tell us the nature of the offence and when was the order made:

☐ It is likely that I will lose my livelihood because:

☐ It is likely that I will suffer serious damage to my reputation because:

☐ A substantial question of law is involved, namely:

APP5   **Page 2**

Reason(s) why you think legal aid should be granted

☐ I shall be unable to understand the court proceedings or state my own case because:

    ☐ My knowledge of English is inadequate

    ☐ I suffer from mental illness or mental or physical disability
     ➤ *Give details of the disability*

☐ Witnesses have to be traced or interviewed on my behalf;
  ➤*Give details*

☐ The case involves expert cross examination of a prosecution witness because:

☐ It is in someone else's interests that I am represented because:

☐ Any other reason(s):

Enclosures
    ➤ *Only copies should be sent*

☐ Form 1 - Copy of the application for legal aid in criminal proceedings

☐ Form 2 - Copy of notification of refusal to grant legal aid issued by the Magistrates' Court

☐ Other ➤ *Give details*

Declaration to be signed by the applicant

As far as I know all the information I have given is true and I have not withheld any relevant information.
I understand that if I knowingly give false information or withhold relevant information my criminal legal aid may
be stopped or cancelled and criminal proceedings may be taken against me.

Signed: _____ Date: ____/____/____

APP5   **Page 3**   (c) Legal Aid Board 1998
                          V. 2 October 1997

3.2

Application for amendment or prior authority in criminal cases

APP7

Please complete in block capitals

Please write the page numbers of the pages you are submitting in the adjoining box.

Your client's details

Legal aid order number: _____

Title: _____ Initials: _____

Surname: _____

First name: _____

Surname at birth: _____
(if different)

Date of birth: ____ / ____ / ____

National insurance number: | | | | | | | | | | |

Sex: ☐ Male   ☐ Female

Marital status: ☐ Single   ☐ Married   ☐ Cohabiting

☐ Separated   ☐ Divorced   ☐ Widowed

Place of birth: _____ Job: _____
(town)

Current address: _____

Town: _____

County: _____ Postcode: _____

Current acting solicitor's details

Legal aid supplier number: | | | | | | | | || | | | | | |

Name of firm: _____

Phone: _____

Name of acting solicitor: _____

➤ *The acting solicitor must have a valid practising certificate. The Board cannot pay for any work done during any period in which the acting solicitor does not have a practising certificate.*

Solicitor's reference: _____

Contact name for enquiries: _____

APP7   **Page 1**   V.2 October 1997   (c) Legal Aid Board 1998   Capsoft UK Ltd 01/99

Type of application

➤ *The Magistrates' Court notice of refusal must be attached where appropriate*

☐ Prior authority ☐ Change solicitor ☐ To assign counsel

☐ To instruct QC without junior ☐ To withdraw legal aid order

Case details

Main offence: _____ Date of offence: ___ / ___ / _____

Likely plea: ☐ Guilty ☐ Not Guilty ☐ Mixed plea

Date of next hearing: _____ / _____ / _____

Purpose of next hearing: _____

Details of application

➤ *For prior authority applications complete page 3.*

Please give details of and reasons for the application:

APP7 **Page 2**

Prior authority details

Tell us what authority you are seeking and why it is required. If you wish to obtain a medical report, state whether as to fitness to plead and/or plea and/or disposal:

Give a brief summary of the prosecution case. You may attach the copy advance disclosure or extracts:

Give a summary of the defence or mitigation. Attach a copy of your client's statement and details of any previous convictions, if available in either case:

Type of expenditure: *(e.g. medical report)* _____

Name of expert: _____

Company name: _____

Address: _____

Town: _____

County: _____ Postcode: _____

Phone: _____ Type/status: _____

Total authority: £_____ *(before apportionment, if appropriate)*

Preparation: £_____ Preparation-hourly rate: £_____

Cost of travel time: £_____ Travel - hourly rate: £_____

How many alternative quotes have been obtained? _____

What were the amounts quoted? _____

If there are any other defendants who would benefit from the expenditure and with whom there is no conflict of interest, what consideration has been given to a joint instruction?

Name(s) of other defendant(s): _____

APP7 **Page 3**

New acting solicitor's details

➤ *Complete if change of solicitor requested.*

Legal aid supplier number: |___|___|___|___|___|___|___| |___|___|___|___|___|___|___|

Name of firm: _____

Phone: _____

Name of new acting solicitor: _____

➤*The acting solicitor must have a valid practising certificate. The Board cannot pay for any work done during any period in which the acting solicitor does not have a practising certificate.*

Solicitor's reference: _____

Contact name for enquiries: _____

Enclosures

➤ *Only copies should be sent.*

☐ Magistrates' Court notice of refusal

☐ Legal Aid Order and any subsequent amendments

☐ Advance disclosure

☐ Client's statement

☐ Other ➤ *Give details*

Solicitor's certificate

I certify that the information provided is correct.

Signed: _____ Date: ___/___/___

(A Solicitor or a Fellow of the Institute of Legal Executives)

Name: _____

APP7   **Page 4**   (c) Legal Aid Board 1998
V.2 October 1997

243

3.3

STATEMENT OF WITNESS

(Criminal Justice Act 1967, s.9
Magistrates' Courts Act 1980, s.102
Magistrates' Courts Rules 1981, r.70)

STATEMENT OF [*name of witness*]

_____

Age of witness (If over 21, enter over 21)

_____

Address

_____
_____
_____

This statement (consisting of pages each signed by me) is true to the best of my knowledge and belief and I make it knowing that, if it is tendered in evidence, I shall be liable to prosecution if I have wilfully stated in it anything which I know to be false or do not believe to be true.

Dated the   day of   19

Signed: Signature witnessed by:

_____
_____
_____
_____

Signed: Signiture witnessed by

_____

3.4

EXPERTS' INSTRUCTION NOTES

LEGAL AID CASES

It is prudent in this legal aid case to apply for an authority to the Legal Aid Board. A request for authority involves the calculation of the work to be carried out pursuant to the advocate's advice or our letter of instruction.

The Board may grant an authority up to a maximum fee only. When deciding on a maximum fee carefully consider how much time you may spend on this case and build in a margin for error. This firm may only be paid sums up to the maximum fee by the Board; further payments are discretionary and if we do not receive payment, neither will you!

A list of the documents provided by us to enable you to make an assessment is attached, marked Schedule A. When calculating your maximum fee, remember that your assessment should generally include the following:

(a) perusal of all documents listed in Schedule A;

(b) attendance on client if necessary;

(c) viewing prosecution exhibits at source;

(d) perusal of required scientific journals and authorities;

(e) preparation of report.

Your maximum fee should be calculated on Schedule B which we intend to submit to the Board. Please make any further comments for the Board in an accompanying letter.

Please retain the papers referred to in Schedule A until we notify you of the Board's decision. If our application is refused, please return them. If our application is accepted we will tell you the maximum fee allowed, which must not be exceeded.

If you receive formal notification from us to proceed and it is necessary to examine any prosecution exhibits, please contact us and we will ask the CPS to authorise you to make arrangements to do so with the laboratory and police officer in charge of the case.

Please send us three copies of your report including your curriculum vitae and let us have a note of your charges to date.

Please let us also have details of your availability for the next three months. If the case is not concluded within that period, we will request your availability dates at three monthly intervals.

Please remember these terms of service requirements when calculating your maximum fee and contact us if you have any queries about them.

At the end of the case we will require all case papers to be returned to us.

SCHEDULE A: Documents sent to expert

Name of expert:

Name of client:	File no:
CHARGE SHEET	[ ]
ADVANCE DISCLOSURE	[ ]
CUSTODY RECORD	[ ]
TAPE/TRANSCRIPT	[ ]
DEFENDANT'S STATEMENT	[ ]
MEDICAL REPORT	[ ]
PHOTOGRAPHS	[ ]
ADVOCATE'S OPINION	[ ]
WITNESS(ES) STATEMENT(S)	(LIST)
DEPOSITIONS	(LIST)
NOTICE(S) OF ADDITIONAL EVIDENCE	(LIST)

We confirm that the documents indicated have been forwarded to the expert.

Dated: Signed:

SCHEDULE B: Expert calculation of maximum fee

Name of expert:

Qualifications:

Years of experience:

Calculation of fees: Specify under individual heading

Perusal documents: Schedule A

View prosecution exhibits
at source:

Attend client:

Perusal journals
and authorities:

Prepare report:

Maximum fee:

Dated: Signed:

3.5

NOTICE OF APPLICATION RELATING TO BAIL TO BE MADE TO THE CROWN COURT

AT:

UNIQUE CASE REFERENCE NO . . . .

CROWN COURT NUMBER . . . .

[OR]

SERIAL NUMBER AND . . . .

NAME AND LOCATION OF MAGISTRATES' COURT . . . .

. . . .

TAKE NOTICE that an application relating to bail will be made to the Crown Court

at

on   or to be notified

at   or to be notified

on behalf of the defendant

1.   **Defendant:**

Surname . . . . Date of birth . . . .

Forenames . . . .

Home address . . . .

. . . .

2.   **Solicitor for the applicant:**

Name . . . .

Address . . . .

3.   **If defendant is in custody state:**

place of detention . . . .

prison number . . . .

length of time in custody . . . .

date of last remand . . . .

4. **State particulars of proceedings during which the defendant was committed to custody or bailed unconditionally including:**

(a) the stage reached in the proceedings as at the date of this application:

. . . .

. . . .

(b) the offences alleged:

. . . .

. . . .

5. **Give details of next appearance in court of case pending before magistrates:**

Place . . . . Date . . . .

Time . . . .

Give details of any previous applications for bail or variations of conditions of bail:

. . . .

. . . .

6. **Nature and grounds of application:**

(a) State fully the grounds relied on and list previous convictions (if any):

. . . .

. . . .

. . . .

. . . .

. . . .

(b) Give details of any proposed sureties and answer any objections raised previously:

. . . .

. . . .

. . . .

. . . .

. . . .

3.6

MAGISTRATES' COURT

NOTICE OF APPEAL TO CROWN COURT, AGAINST CONVICTION, ORDER OR SENTENCE

TO the Justices' Clerk of the Magistrates' Court sitting at [*place*]

AND TO the Branch Crown Prosecutor, Crown Prosecution Service, [*address*]

TAKE NOTICE THAT I, [*name and address of appellant*]

intend to appeal to the Crown Court at [*address*] against:

* my conviction

* the sentence which was passed upon me [*state sentence*]

* the order made against me [*state order*]

(* delete as appropriate)

on [*date*] by the Magistrates' Court above for the offence(s) set out below

[*state offence(s)*]

Dated [*date*]   Signed [*appellant's signature*]

Unique case reference number

3.7

NOTICE OF APPLICATION TO VARY BAIL CONDITIONS

TO the Clerk to the Justices of the Magistrates' Court sitting at [*place*]

AND TO the Branch Crown Prosecutor, Crown Prosecution Service, [*address*]

Name of defendant:

Address:

Offence(s) alleged:

Next bail date:

Name(s) of co-defendant(s):

TAKE NOTICE THAT I intend to make application to the Court at 10.00 a.m./ 2.00 p.m. on . . . . to vary the defendant's bail conditions as follows:

Reason for application:

Date: _____   Signature of Solicitor . . . .

Unique case reference no:

Note: At least one full working day's notice of application is normally required. The defendant must usually attend the hearing in person.

3.8

NOTICE OF APPLICATION TO VARY BAIL CONDITIONS IMPOSED BY A CUSTODY OFFICER AT A POLICE STATION

TO the Clerk to the Justices of the Magistrates' Court sitting at

AND TO the Custody Officer,

Name of defendant:

Address:

Offence(s) alleged:

Next hearing date:

Conditions of bail imposed by Custody Officer:

Reasons for imposing conditions of bail:

Grounds of application:

Name and address of Surety

Date: . . . .
Signature of Solicitor

Unique case reference no:

3.9

(a) Application to review order for non-disclosure

To [   ]   Court
CPS/R   v
URN/Case Number

CC to CPS

Application to review an order for non-disclosure (rule 5)

We represent the accused in this matter

Please treat this letter as our application to review the order for non-disclosure made by the court on [
   ]

The reason(s) why the accused believes the court should review the question are as follows

(b) Correspondence to obtain third party disclosure

TO
CPS

Re: R/CPS   v.   [   ]
        [   ] Court
        URN/Case Number

We act for the defendant in this case. We understand that relevant evidence is held by [ ]

This evidence is material to the investigation because [   ]

Please bring this letter to the attention of the investigating officer and invite him/her to investigate the evidence under Code 3.4. and provide an amended schedule of non-sensitive material accordingly.

(c) **Application to extend time for service of defence statement (Reg 3(3) and rule 8)**

To [   ] Court

CPS/R v [   ]
URN Case Number
CC to CPS

Application for extension of time under The Criminal Procedure and Investigations Act 1996 (Defence Disclosure Time Limits) Regulations 1997

We act for the accused named above

Please treat this letter as our application for an extension of the period during which the accused may serve the defence statement

> (a)   The accused believes, on reasonable grounds, that it is not possible for him/her to give a defence statement under section 5/6 of the Act during the period of 14 days from (purported) compliance by the prosecution of its obligation under s.3 of the Act [or the period ordered by the court on [   ]

> (b)   The grounds for so believing are
> .
> .
> .

> (c)   The number of days by which the accused wishes the period to be extended is

> (d)   A copy of the notice was served [today] on the prosecutor

(see for procedure Crown Court/Magistrates' Courts (Criminal Procedure and Investigations Act 1996) (disclosure) Rules 1997)

(d) **Witnesses at court**

To

Crown Prosecution Service

Prosecution of   [   ]

[   ] Magistrates' Court

URN

We act for the defendant whose case was committed to the   [   ]
Crown Court on   [   ]

Please treat this letter as notice that all witnesses [except]
should attend to give evidence at the trial unless we notify you
in writing to the contrary.

(e) Application for disclosure

To [   ] Court

CPS/R v
URN/Case Number

cc to CPS

Application for disclosure (rule 7)

We act for the accused in this matter

Please treat this letter as our application for disclosure

(a) The material to which this application relates is

(b) That material has not been disclosed to the accused

(c) The reason(s) why the material might be expected to assist the applicant's defence as disclosed by the defence statement given under section 5 is/are

(d) A copy of this notice was served [today] on the prosecution

(f) Application to use confidential documents

TO [   ] Court

CPS/R   v.
URN/Case Number

cc to CPS

Application for use or disclosure of confidential documents

We act for the accused in this matter

Please treat this letter as our application to use/disclose as set out below

(ai)   The object(s) which the applicant seeks to use or disclose is/are

(aii)   The proceedings for whose purpose he/she was given or allowed to inspect it/them is/are

[(b)   The information recorded in the object specified above is   ]

(c)   The reason(s) why the applicant seeks permission to use or disclose the object or any information specified above is/are

(d)   The proceedings in connection with which the applicant seeks to use or disclose the object or information referred to above are:

(e)   The names and addresses of persons to whom the applicant seeks to disclose the object or information referred to above are:

3.10

The Court of Appeal Criminal Division

Form **NG**
(Forms 2 & 3)

NOTICE and GROUNDS of appeal or application for leave to appeal
(Criminal Appeal Act 1968)　　CAO No.　　　/　　　/

● Please read the notes for guidance overleaf. Write in BLACK INK and USE BLOCK CAPITALS

ON COMPLETION PLEASE SEND THIS FORM TO THE CROWN COURT WHERE TRIED OR SENTENCED

The appellant
give full name

Prison index no.

Surname _____

Forenames _____

If in custody give Prison Index Number and address where detained

Address _____

_____

Post code _____ Date of birth _____

The Court where tried or sentenced

Give details if the case was transferred from another court

The Crown Court at _____

Name of Judge _____

Underline the dates of conviction and sentence

Dates of appearance in the Crown Court _____

Total period of remand in custody prior to sentence _____

The conviction(s) and sentence(s)

The full Crown Court case number(s) must be given, and particulars of ALL counts, offences and sentences included.

Crown Court case number(s)	Count or charge no.	Offence	Sentence

Number of offences taken into consideration

Total sentence

Applications　　SEE NOTE 5
The appellant is applying for: *Please tick as appropriate*

☐ Extension of time in which to apply for leave to appeal against conviction and/or sentence

☐ Leave to appeal against conviction

☐ Leave to appeal against sentence

☐ Legal aid

☐ Bail

☐ Leave to call a witness

Notes for guidance on the completion of this form

1. Everyone who is convicted or sentenced in the Crown Court in circumstances where an appeal would lie to the Court of Appeal Criminal Division should have advice or assistance on appeal. Provision for this is included in a trial legal aid order (section 30(7) Legal Aid Act 1974).

2. Solicitors and counsel are expected to be familiar with 'A Guide to Proceedings in the Court of Appeal Criminal Division' (available from any Crown Court Centre and reproduced at volume 77(1983) Criminal Appeal Reports 138).

3. Separate forms should be submitted for convictions or sentences which do not arise in the same proceedings.

4. This notice will be treated as a notice of appeal where leave to appeal is not required.

5. **Applications**

   ● Extension of time   This form should be sent to the appropriate officer of the Crown Court within 28 days of the conviction, sentence, verdict or finding appealed against. If the appellant is in custody the form should be handed to the prison authority (or other person having custody) for forwarding to the Crown Court, and the date of handing in should be recorded on the form.

   The period of 28 days cannot be extended except by leave of the Court of Appeal Criminal Division and the reasons for the delay will be required.

   NOTE that the time for applying for leave to appeal against conviction runs from the date of **conviction** even where sentence is passed on a later date.

   ● Leave to appeal against conviction

   ● Leave to appeal against sentence   See note 6

   ● Legal aid   A legal aid order made in the Crown Court does not provide for oral argument before the Court of Appeal. If legal aid is sought for this purpose it should be applied for.

   ● Bail   Where bail is applied for **Form B** must also be completed. If Form B accompanies Form NG it should be submitted to the Crown Court but if submitted later should be sent to:— The Registrar, Criminal Appeal Office, Royal Courts of Justice, Strand, London WC2A 2LL.

   ● Leave to call a witness (Conviction applications only)

   Application made on **Form W** which should be included only where leave is sought to call a witness in support of an application for leave to appeal against **conviction**. A separate form is required for each witness. If Form W accompanies Form NG it should be sent to the Crown Court but if submitted later should be sent to:— The Registrar, Criminal Appeal Office, Royal Courts of Justice, Strand, London WC2A 2LL.

6. **Grounds of appeal**

   Where grounds have been settled by counsel they must be signed by counsel, with the name of counsel printed underneath, and attached to this form. There is no obligation to include a copy of counsel's advice although in some cases it may be helpful to do so. Grounds must be settled with sufficient detail to enable matters relied upon to be clearly identified. Wording such as "the conviction is unsafe and unsatisfactory" or "the sentence is in all circumstances too severe" will be ineffective as grounds and an extension of time may have to be applied for (see note 5).

7. Where a certificate that the case is fit for appeal has been granted by the trial judge this should be stated and see generally paragraph 17 of 'A Guide to Proceedings in the Court of Appeal Criminal Division'.

8. Where an appellant has been **granted** leave to appeal he is entitled to be present on the hearing of his appeal. It will be assumed that an appellant in custody is applying for leave to be present at any hearing for which leave to be present is required unless he indicates to the contrary.

Grounds of appeal   see notes 6 and 7

I understand that if I am in custody, and the single judge and/or the court is of the opinion that the appeal is plainly without merit, an order may be made that time spent in custody as an appellant shall not count towards sentence.

I also understand that whether or not I am in custody the court may make an order for payment of costs against me, including the cost of any transcript obtained.

This form should be signed by the appellant but may be signed by his/her legal representative *provided* the WARNING set out above has been explained to him, and he is sent a copy of this form.

Signature of appellant

Date _____

*Delete as appropriate

Details of any person signing *on behalf* of the appellant:

Name _____
Solicitor/Counsel*

Address _____

post code   DX number

Telephone No.   Reference

FOR PRISON USE

This notice was handed to me by the appellant today.

Signed _____
                  Prison Officer

Date _____

Appellant's Index No. _____
EDR. _____
PED. _____

FOR CROWN COURT USE

Notice received:

Signed _____ Date _____

Sent to CAO:

Signed _____ Date _____

This Notice must be sent to the Registrar of Criminal Appeals together with trial documents **forthwith**

FOR CRIMINAL APPEAL OFFICE USE

Received:

Acknowledged (date) ....

FOR CROWN COURT USE

Immediately upon receipt of Form NG the Crown Court must complete and send tear off slips 1-4 overleaf as applicable and record the action taken below:

tick appropriate boxes

Date sent

_____

Signed

_____

Slip 1
(Acknowledgement)
☐ sent to _____

Slip 3
(Monetary penalty/order)
☐ _____ Mags. Ct

Slip 2
(Sentencing remarks)
☐ Messrs _____

Slip 4
(Statements)
☐ CPS _____

**Slip 4   Request for witness statements from prosecution
(to be sent in all cases involving committals for sentence)**

To: Crown Prosecution Service   From: Crown Court at _____

Dear Sir,   Date _____

Rv _____   Crown Court Ref. _____

Would you please forward forthwith witness statements/statement of facts in the above case, enclosing this slip for reference purposes, to:

The Registrar,Criminal Appeal Office   (telephone 01-936-6011/6014   Yours faithfully,
Royal Courts of Justice,   DX: RCJ 44450 Strand
Strand, London WC2A 2LL   FAX: 01-936-6900)

**Slip 3   Notification to Magistrates of appeal in cases involving monetary penalty or
order (to be sent in all cases involving monetary penalty or order)**

To: Clerk to the Justices   From: Chief Clerk

_____ Magistrates   Crown Court at _____

Dear Sir,   Date _____

Rv _____   Crown Court Ref. _____

I write to inform you that in this case in which you are responsible for enforcing the monetary penalty or order the above-named has lodged notice of appeal to the Court of Appeal Criminal Division.

                         Yours faithfully,

**Slip 2   Request for transcript of sentencing observations
(to be sent if application/appeal is against sentence only)**

                                                                  From: Chief Clerk

To Messrs_____ (Shorthand-   Crown Court at _____
Dear Sir,   Writers)   Date _____

Rv _____   Crown Court Ref. _____

Date of sentence _____ Note taker _____

Would you please supply transcript (top and one carbon) of **Judges observations on passing sentence** (including any co-accused), enclosing this slip for reference purposes, to:

The Transcript Section, Criminal Appeal Office   (telephone 01-936-6817   Yours faithfully,
Royal Courts of Justice,   DX:RCJ 44450 Strand
Strand, London WC2A 2LL   FAX: 01-936-6900

Slip 1   Acknowledgement of form NG   From: Chief Clerk
(to be sent in all cases to sender of form NG)   Crown Court at _____

To: _____   Crown Court Ref. _____

                                                                  Date _____

_____ Your ref _____

_____Rv _____

Dear Sir,
I acknowledge receipt of forms NG (B* W*) which have been forwarded to the Registrar of Criminal Appeals for attention. All further communications should be addressed to:

            The Registrar, Criminal Appeal Office   Yours faithfully,
            Royal Courts of Justice, Strand, London WC2A 2LL
            (Tel 01-936-6011/6014; DX: RCJ 44450 Strand; FAX: 01-936-6900)

* Delete as appropriate

3.11

<table>
<tr><td colspan="2">

The Court of Appeal Criminal Division
NOTICE OF APPLICATION FOR BAIL

Criminal Appeal Act 1968

If possible this form should be lodged at the Crown Court at the same time as form N.G. If this application is made at a later stage it should be sent directly to the Registrar of Criminal Appeals, Royal Courts of Justice, Strand, London WC2A 2LL, quoting the Criminal Appeal Office reference No:

Telephone 071-936-6011/6014, DX:RCJ 44450-Strand, Fax No. 071-936-6900

Please read the notes for guidance overleaf. Write in BLACK INK and use BLOCK CAPITALS

</td><td>

FOR CROWN COURT USE   Form **B**

NOTICE RECEIVED   (Form 4)

Signed . . . .

Date . . . .

    SENT TO C.A.O.

Signed . . . .

Date . . . .

</td></tr>
</table>

1. Particulars of Appellant

Forenames   Surname

FOR USE IN CRIMINAL APPEAL OFFICE

Ref No.   /   /

Date received:

Address (Give address where detained)

_____
_____
_____

INDEX NUMBER

Address if granted bail

_____
_____
_____

2. Proposed sureties *(if relevant)*

A) Name _____

Address _____
         _____
         _____

Occupation _____

£ _____

B) Name _____

Address _____
         _____
         _____

Occupation _____

£ _____

3. If bail was granted before trial or sentence state:—   Amount of recognizances

Were the sureties the persons named above?   Yes/No *(Delete as appropriate)*   £ _____

What, if any, special conditions were imposed?   and £ _____

4. The Appellant applies for bail pending appeal on the following ground(s):

Signed   Date   Address and status of person signing on appellant's behalf

Appellant/Legal rep *(Delete as appropriate)*

F1455 (Rev 4/91)

Notes

1. An application for bail will be considered in the light of the grounds of appeal or application for leave to appeal. Accordingly it is usual for the application for bail to be submitted to the Court or Judge together with other applications and the transcript of the proceedings at the trial. This imposes some delay. Generally strong grounds of appeal or application for leave to appeal have to be shown before bail is granted. An application for bail cannot stand alone; it must be supported by Notice of Application for leave to appeal or Notice of Appeal (Form NG).

2. Do not repeat the grounds of appeal or application for leave to appeal as the grounds for bail. Mention any other special grounds which the Judge or Court might consider, e.g. medical grounds.

3. Time spent on bail does not count towards sentence.

4. Notice in writing of intention to make an application relating to bail must be served on the prosecutor at least 24 hours before the application is made, unless the Court or a Judge otherwise directs.

3.12

Court of Appeal Criminal Division
NOTICE OF APPLICATION FOR WITNESS
ORDER and/or LEAVE TO CALL A WITNESS
Criminal Appeal Act 1968

FOR CROWN COURT USE	Form **W**
NOTICE RECEIVED	(Form 6)

Signed . . . .

Date . . . .

SENT TO C.A.O.

Signed . . . .

Date . . . .

If possible this form should be lodged at the Crown Court at the same time as form N.G. If this application is made at a later stage it should be sent directly to the Registrar of Criminal Appeals, Royal Courts of Justice, Strand, London WC2A 2LL, quoting the Criminal Appeal Office reference No:

Telephone 071-936-6011/6014, DX:RCJ 44450-Strand, Fax No. 071-936-6900

Please read the notes for guidance below. Write in BLACK INK and use BLOCK CAPITALS

1.   Particulars of Appellant

FOR USE IN CRIMINAL APPEAL OFFICE
Ref No.   /   /
Date received:

Forenames   Surname

Address (Give address where detained)   Address if granted bail

_____   _____
_____   _____
_____   _____

INDEX NUMBER

2.   Particulars of witness

Forenames   Surname

Do you want a witness order?   Yes/No*
(a witness order is not required if the witness would attend the Court of Appeal voluntarily).

Address

_____

Was the witness called at the trial?   Yes/No*

_____

* Delete as appropriate

The witness can now give the following evidence (which was not given at the trial):—

The evidence was not given at the trial for the following reasons:—

Signed	Date	Address and status of person signing on appellant's behalf
Appellant/Legal rep (Delete as appropriate)		

Notes: 1.   A witness cannot be called without the leave of the Court of Appeal. Before giving leave to call a witness, the court will consider, with other matters, whether the evidence, if received, would afford any grounds for allowing the appeal, whether the evidence is likely to be credible, and whether there is reasonable explanation for failure to adduce the evidence at the trial. Do not set out in the form the evidence which the witness gave at the trial.

   2.   A separate form must be used for each witness.

   3.   Do not apply in respect of a witness in mitigation of sentence only.

F1460 (Rev 4/91)

State of case form

CRIMINAL DEFENCE

STATE OF CASE FORM

File ref:	Nat. ins. no.:	Fee earner:

Client name: | Surname at birth:
 | Place of birth:

Address:

Telephone no.	Occupation:
Date of birth:	Marital status:

Offence(s):

Plea:

Summary/Either way/Indictable only

Guilty/Not guilty

E/W Election: Summary E/W

Bail conditions OR custody address:

Surety details – name and address:

DATE OF OFFENCE: | **DATE OF CHARGE:**

Co-defendant's solicitor details:

Special features: Juvenile/ Expert evidence/Interpreter/Mental health

Legal Aid: Yes/No	Green Form: Yes/No	Full application made: Yes/No
	Extension: Yes/No Hrs:	Granted: Yes/No
Private: Yes/No	Funds on account: Yes/No	Amount: £

Discontinuance: Appropriate: Yes/No Requested: Yes/No

Documentation	Requested	Received
Advance information	Yes/No	Yes/No
Custody rec./Taped interview	Yes/No	Yes/No
Committal bundle	Yes/No	Yes/No
Medical/Psychiatric report	Yes/No	Yes/No
Instructions	Initial: Yes/No	Yes/No
	Full: Yes/No	Yes/No
Client care letter	Approp.: Yes/No Sent on:	
Request unused material	Yes/No	Yes/No

Dates of hearing	Result	Fee earner attending court
1st		
2nd		
3rd		
4th		

Franchising reviews:

Additional information White/Black/Asian/Other Job: Kept/Lost

PTI time guidelines for Crown Court cases

Interval	Relevant Factors	Guideline
Grant of police bail under section 47(3) PACE until return to the police station	(unless protracted investigation or other compelling consideration)	3 weeks
Summons cases: completion of investigation or reporting for process to laying of information	Most cases CPS advice required	3 weeks 5 weeks
Summons cases: laying of information to first listing	Most cases Young Offenders	5 weeks 3 weeks
Summons cases: laying of information to production of summons	All cases	1 week
Charge cases: charge to first appearance	Subject to section 47 PACE as amended by section 46 Crime and Disorder Act	
Charge cases: charge to CPS receipt of file	Local agreement	
First appearance to plea/mode of trial	Bail Custody	4 weeks 2 weeks
Not guilty plea to summary trial	Bail Custody	8 weeks 2 weeks
Prosecution preparation of case	Bail	4 weeks
Adjournment after not guilty plea where full file required	Bail	4 weeks
Not guilty plea to CPS receipt of full files	Bail Custody	3 weeks 1 week

Interval	Relevant Factors	Guideline
Mode of trial to committal	Either-way, bail	8 weeks
	Either-way, custody	6 weeks
	Either-way, young offenders	6 weeks
Mode of trial to CPS receipt of full file	Either-way, bail	4 weeks
	Either-way, custody	3 weeks
	Either-way, young offenders	3 weeks[1]
Receipt of full file to committal papers served	Either-way, bail	2 weeks
	Either-way, custody	10 days
	Either-way, young offenders	10 days[1]
Committal papers served to committal hearing	Either-way, bail	2 weeks
	Either-way, custody	11 days
	Either-way, young offenders	11 days[1]
First appearance to committal	Indictable-only, bail	8 weeks
	Indictable-only, custody	6 weeks
First appearance to CPS receipt of full file	Indictable-only, bail	4 weeks
	Indictable-only, custody	3 weeks
Receipt of full file to committal papers served	Indictable-only, bail	2 weeks
	Indictable-only, custody	10 days
Committal papers served to committal hearing	Indictable-only, bail	2 weeks
	Indictable-only, custody	11 days
Committal to start of trial	Bail	16 weeks
	Custody	8 weeks
Committal to first listing	Bail	6 weeks
	Custody	4 weeks
Conviction to sentence	All cases	4 weeks

[1] Extrapolated from equivalent time guidelines for adult custody cases

APPENDIX 6

Time-limits introduced by ss.43–44 Crime and Disorder Act 1998

Ss. 43–44 CDA 1998 amend s.22 Prosecution of Offences Act 1995 to:

- allow different time-limits for different types of cases – to enable more exacting time-limits for juvenile cases and longer time-limits for serious fraud cases;

- allow the staying of proceedings and the defendant's release as the sanction for breach, rather than the acquittal of the defendant. Re-institution requires the authority of a senior prosecutor and must take place within three months of the date the proceedings were stayed. After that, re-institution will only be allowed with the leave of the court. Where the time-limit for arrest to first listing expires before charge, a juvenile cannot be charged for the same offence unless new evidence comes to light. New time-limits will then operate;

- time-limits are suspended rather than stopped when a defendant absconds. On the person's arrest, the court may add an additional period taking into account the disruption caused to the prosecution.

The time-limit can be extended by the court due to:

- illness/absence of the accused, a necessary witness, a judge or magistrates;*

- a postponement which is occasioned by the ordering by the court of separate trials in the case of two or more accused or two or more offences;*

- some other good and sufficient cause;

and the court is satisfied that the prosecution has acted with all due diligence and expedition.

* These two provisions were brought into force on 1 June, 1999.

271

Ss.43–44 CDA 1998 insert a new s.22A into the 1985 Act to allow for the introduction of statutory time-limits for young offenders for the periods between:

- arrest and first listing;
- conviction and sentence.

Different time-limits can be set for different offenders allowing tighter time-limits for persistent young offenders.

A persistent young offender is a young person aged between 10 and 17 who has been sentenced by any criminal court in England and Wales on three or more separate occasions for one or more recordable offences and within three years of the last sentencing occasion is subsequently arrested or has an information laid against him for a further recordable offence.

Time-limit pilots will run for 18 months from 1 November 1999, in the Narey Pilot areas.

Working with interpreters

REGISTERED PUBLIC SERVICE INTERPRETERS

RPSIs are those who have met the criteria for appearing in the National Register, namely:

- an appropriate level of educational attainment (i.e. a degree or equivalent);
- a high level of fluency in both the written and oral form of English and of the other language;
- a relevant interpreting qualification (such as the Diploma in Public Service Interpreting);
- a body of relevant interpreting experience at the appropriate quality standard;
- relevant references;
- personal suitability.

RPSIs agree to abide by a code of conduct, which sets out the standards which the public services expect of interpreters admitted to the National Register. In order to maintain these standards, public services and clients who are dissatisfied with the performance of an interpreter recruited through the Register are requested to supply details to the Institute of Linguists. Any disciplinary action will be decided upon by the disciplinary panel as described in the Code. The Code of Conduct is registered with the Office of Fair Trading (Registration No. RMS/21 51).

COMPETENCE

RPSIs are expected to:

- have a written and spoken command of both languages, including any specialist terminology, current idioms and dialects;

- understand the relevant procedures of the particular discipline in which they are working;

- maintain and develop their written and spoken command of English and other languages;

- be familiar with the cultural backgrounds of both parties.

PROCEDURE

RPSIs will:

- interpret truly and faithfully what is said, without anything being added, omitted or changed; in exceptional circumstances a summary may be given if requested, and consented to by both parties;

- disclose any difficulties encountered with dialects or technical terms, and if these cannot be satisfactorily remedied, withdraw from the assignment;

- not enter into the discussion, give advice or express opinions or reactions to any of the parties;

- intervene only:

  - to ask for clarification;

  - to point out that a party may not have understood something;

  - to alert the parties to a possible missed cultural inference; or

  - to ask for accommodation for the interpreting process (for instance if someone is speaking too quietly or too fast);

- not delegate work, nor accept delegated work, without the consent of the client;

- be reliable and punctual at all times;

- state (in criminal trial) if they have been involved in interpreting at the police station on the same case.

ETHICAL AND PROFESSIONAL

RPSIs will:

- respect confidentiality at all times and not seek to take advantage of any information disclosed during their work;

- act in an impartial and professional manner;

- not discriminate directly or indirectly, on the grounds of race, colour, ethnic origin, age, nationality, religion, gender or disability;

- disclose information, including any criminal record, which may make them unsuitable in any particular case;

- disclose immediately if the interviewee or immediate family is known or related;

- disclose any business, financial, family or other interest which they might have in the matter being handled;

- not accept any form of reward, whether in cash or otherwise, for interpreting work other than payment by the employer.

FINDING AN INTERPRETER

The Institute of Linguists maintains the National Register of Public Service Interpreters (the National Register). The Council for the Advancement of Communications with Deaf People (CACDP) maintains the National Directory of Sign Language Interpreters (the National Directory). It is proposed that by the end of 2001, all interpreters used in court will be chosen from the National Register or National Directory.

The National Register contains Registered Public Service Interpreters (RPSIs) at one of two levels. Interim level is awarded to interpreters who have work experience but are not yet qualified or who have appropriate qualifications but not yet sufficient experience. Full level interpreters are both appropriately qualified (holding the Diploma in Public Service Interpreting or an equivalent qualification) and can demonstrate evidence of adequate work experience. An entry on the Register specifying that they have taken the legal training option demonstrates an understanding of court procedures. In order to provide interpreters for rare languages, there is a further small category of "non-assessed" interpreters. An assessment has been made of the quantity and quality of their experience as interpreters but not of their qualifications.

Similarly, for Sign Language interpreting, CACDP is the national assessment and awarding body.

REGISTERED QUALIFIED AND TRAINEE SIGN LANGUAGE INTERPRETERS

Registered Qualified Sign Language Interpreters (RQSLIs) are those who have passed the CACDP professional interpreting examination and are required to abide by the code of ethics and complaints procedure. Registered Trainee Sign Language Interpreters (RTSLIs) are those who have passed CACDP stage 3 (advanced) examination in British sign language, are attending a recognised interpreting training programme and are also bound by the code of ethics and complaints procedure. The National Directory contains further details and includes the interpreters' code of ethics and complaints and disciplinary procedure.

The solicitor's preferred choice should be an RPSI or CACDP registered interpreter. Details of RPSIs can be obtained by telephoning the Law Society Library Tel. 020 7320 5946 Fax 020 7831 1687 or subscribing to the National Register. The National Register is usually updated bi-annually and available in hard copy and on computer disk. Further information about registration, professional etiquette and disciplinary procedure is available from the Institute of Linguists, Saxon House, 48 Southwark Street, London SE1 1UN, tel. 020 7940 3100. The National Directory is updated annually. The contact address is CACDP, Pelaw house, The School of Education, University of Durham, School of Education, Durham DH1 1TA, telephone 0191 374 3607.

Geographical considerations alone should not preclude the engagement of an RPSI or Registered Sign Language Interpreter in preference to an unregistered interpreter. If an interpreter from the National Register or National Directory is not available, the solicitor should aim to instruct an interpreter who as far as possible meets the National Register criteria which are set out in this appendix, p. 273.

WORKING WITH AN INTERPRETER

Before the interview

1. Give the interpreter as much advance notice as possible.

2. Provide clear information about the proposed assignment when you first contact the interpreter, including:

- the date and time you need the interpreter;
- clear instructions, with a map if necessary, for reaching the venue;
- transport arrangements: details of available parking space, suitable public transport, or specific arrangements if work is to be carried out during unsociable hours;
- the name and telephone number of the person the interpreter is to contact on arrival or in case of delay;
- the name of the client involved, to ensure that your client is not known personally to the interpreter, placing his impartiality at risk;
- the language and/or dialect you need: if you are unsure, contact an interpreter in the language you think might be right, and ask for advice; if your client is present, it may be helpful to ask the interpreter to cross-check the language match over the telephone;
- an outline of the subject matter, to allow the interpreter to research any terminology or procedures in advance, time permitting; the interpreter should refuse an assignment which is beyond his competence.

3. Consider whether you need the interpreter to translate a letter from you to your client, setting out the time, date and place of the proposed appointment and giving travel instructions.

4. Confirm the above arrangements in writing where possible.

5. You may need to consult your client who, depending on the nature of the case, may wish to speak through an interpreter of the same sex.

6. Make proper accommodation for the interpreter. Arrange the seating so that you and your client face each other. The interpreter should be seated in between and to one side so that he can hear easily, without preventing you from talking directly to your client; the interpreter must not be perceived as being on one 'side' or the other. Provide the interpreter with work space to write notes (e.g. dates, addresses, numbers) if necessary.

7. Provide water for refreshment.

8. Allow for rest breaks.

DURING THE INTERVIEW

Always face your client, using direct speech. The interpreter should not be asked to interview, nor expected to know what information to look for, nor how to process the information received.

1. Introduce yourself to your client. Allow the interpreter to introduce himself to your client, and to explain the interpreter's role: that is, to give an impartial, complete and confidential rendition of everything that is said.

2. Establish how your client's name should be recorded for formal documents and how your client wishes to be addressed.

3. It may be helpful to explain who you are and what your job is. Ensure your client understands the function of any other professionals who may be involved.

4. Explain fully structures and procedures which your client may be unfamiliar with.

5. The interpreter may intervene if required, and explain the reasons for doing so to both parties, such as:

   - to clarify something which has been said before interpreting it;
   - to alert one of the parties that, in spite of accurate interpretation, the other might not have fully understood what has been said;
   - to alert both parties to a missed cultural inference: knowledge of a piece of information may incorrectly have been assumed;
   - to ask for accommodation to the interpreting process – for instance, if someone is speaking too quietly or too fast;

6. Ask your client if you are not sure of relevant attitudes, perceptions or cultural norms. Do not ask the interpreter.

7. Different cultures approach conflict resolution and the exchange and presentation of information in different ways. You may need to alter your interviewing techniques to accommodate differing forms of communication.

8. At the end of every two or three sentences (never in the middle of a sentence) the interpreter needs to interpret.

9. Express yourself clearly and unambiguously.

10. Use appropriate language. For example, jargon or popular language can be difficult to interpret accurately. Avoid using double negatives or using a question as a statement; avoid where possible use of paired, redundant phrases e.g. 'will and testament' or 'freely and voluntarily'.

11. For the communication to be effective, check mutual understanding regularly by asking open questions.

12. At the end of the interview, clearly summarise what has been decided and point out the next steps to be taken.

AFTER THE INTERVIEW

1. Check with your interpreter that working procedures were effective and satisfactory.

2. Complete any necessary forms to ensure payment of the interpreter.

FURTHER INFORMATION

For comprehensive information on working with interpreters see: *Non-English speakers and the English Legal System* by Ann Corsellis, 1994, published by the Institute of Criminology, University of Cambridge. Further information about registration, professional etiquette and disciplinary procedures is available from the Institute of Linguists, Tel: 020 7359 7445.

APPENDIX 8

Record of use of interpreters

Information about Interpreters

Record to be attached to client's file

Name of client:

Name of court:

Unique case reference no:

A. Action to be Taken

Information to be sent to (*enter 'court' or 'interpreter'*)			
For (*type of hearing*)			
On (*date*)			

B. Details of Person for Whom an Interpreter is Required

Use a different form for each defendant/witness

1. Defendant/defence witness (*delete as appropriate*)

2. Country/region of origin:

3. Name:

4. Sex:

5. Age:

6. Best language:

7. Dialect if any:

For deaf/deafened people note whether British or other sign language or lip speaking required.

8. Language of literacy   Fluent/modest/elementary/nil

9. Knowledge of English   Nil/a few words/modest

10. Above checked via interpreter Y/N

---

11. Preferences in selection of an interpreter: _____

(note both information and strength of preference 1–5)

Sex _____

Age _____

Religion _____

Ethnic origin _____

Other _____

C. Briefing of Interpreter Required

12. Date			
Time			
Place of the hearing			

13. **Subject content**
(the interpeter will be helped by having a sight of the copy of the statement made to the solicitor by the person named above, as well as copies of any prosecution witness statements which are likely to be put to him/her in cross-examination)

14. **Technical contect**
(the case may involve technical matters such as medical or forensic evidence, psychiatric reports, or financial transactions)

15. **Procedures**
(where other than common ones may be involved)

16. **Terminology**
(technical, formal or slang terms not commonly understood. It may be useful for a glossary to be compiled in both languages, checked and passed on to maintain consistency during a case)

17. **Contact point at solicitor's firm**

Name: _____

Address: _____

Tel: _____

Fax: _____

18. **Terms of engagement** Legal Aid Board/Central Funds/Private
(the solicitor should make it clear to the interpreter what the terms of engagement are and when s/he is not responsible for the interpreter's fees)

D. Record of Interpreters Involved in the Case to Date

Date (*interpreter used*)			
Agency (*who instructed interpreter*)			
Place (*where interpreter used*)			
Interpreter (*name and NRPSI no.*)			

E. Record of Legal Translators Involved in the Case to Date
(DPSI holders are assessed as being competent to translate straightforward, short texts. A more complex and lengthy text, such as an extradition document, may well have to be referred to a qualified specialist and perhaps a legally qualified one.)

Date			
Agency			
Name and address of translator			

F. Information Given to Non-English Speaker
(enter Y/N against each item, and date of hearing it refers to)

Method
(enter either 'T' if text in own language or 'E' if explanation via interpreter)

i) Date, time and place of hearing:			
ii) Purpose of the hearing:			
iii) The procedures to be used:			

Home Office Circular 24/98: reducing delays: addressing the reasons for non-compliance with the pre-trial issues (PTI) time guidelines (extracts)

PROVISION OF TAPE RECORDINGS OF INTERVIEW

19. Paragraph 4.16 Code E of the Codes of Practice of the Police and Criminal Evidence Act 1984 states that a copy of the interview tape shall be provided to the suspect as soon as practicable if he has been charged or informed that he will be prosecuted.

20. It is recognised that not all forces have fast-copying facilities in stations. However, every effort should be made to ensure that a copy of the tape is forwarded to the defendant or his solicitor as soon as possible after charge or notification of prosecution. In addition, there is nothing to prevent a solicitor from making his or her own audio recording of the interview with the suspect. The police should accommodate any request by the solicitor to make a separate audio recording using their own audio recording equipment. The request may be refused only if there are individual circumstances specific to the case which may prejudice the course of the investigation. This will reduce the number of occasions on which solicitors ask the courts for adjournments to obtain copies of interview tapes before advising their clients on pleas.

CONFIDENTIAL INSTRUCTIONS AT POLICE STATIONS

21. Delays in court may be avoided by ensuring that the conditions are right for a solicitor to take confidential instructions from a detainee at a police station. Paragraph 6.1 Code C of the PACE Codes of Practice states that all people in police detention must be informed that they may at any time consult and communicate privately with a solicitor.

22. Every effort should be made to provide appropriate facilities to enable an interview between a detainee and a solicitor to take place. The essential criteria for such facilities are:

    • privacy: the interview must take place out of earshot;
    • security: the safety of the solicitor must be ensured: there should be a panic strip or button within reach in case of emergency; interview may be monitored by custody staff both for security and safety, provided aural privacy is maintained;
    • suitable facilities: a desk, chairs and adequate heating, lighting and ventilation are the minimum requirements.

23. Wherever possible, a designated room should be made available for the purpose of consultation, as indicated in the model layouts shown in the Home Office Police Buildings Design Guide April 1994. However, it is recognised that such a room may not always be available, either because there is none in the police station or because it is occupied during the time available for the interview.

24. Where a designated room exists but is currently occupied, provided that there are no particular time constraints the custody officer should invite the solicitor to wait until such time as the room becomes free. However, if time does not allow, or if there is no designated room in the police station, other arrangements may prove to be necessary and the custody officer may need to consider other options where the above criteria are not compromised. There may be some other suitable room available, for example an interview room (after it has been demonstrated that the audiotape equipment has been switched off). Only as a last resort should a police cell or a secure visits room be offered. The latter is generally not adapted to confidentiality in view of the screen separating the solicitor from the detainee, although in some custody suites the partition can be moved so that the room can double effectively as a solicitor's facility.

ENQUIRIES

25. Enquiries relating to this circular should be addressed to Louisa Carrad, Procedures and Victims Unit, Home Office, Room 338, Queen Anne's Gate, London SW1H 9AT. Tel: 020 7273 3521.

The cautioning of offenders: Home Office Circular 18/1994

1. The purposes of this Circular are to provide guidance on the cautioning of offenders, and in particular:

    –   to discourage the use of cautions in inappropriate cases, for example for offences which are triable on indictment only;
    –   to seek greater consistency between police force areas; and
    –   to promote the better recording of cautions.

2. This Circular, the terms of which have been discussed with the Association of Chief Police Officers and the Crown Prosecution Service, replaces Circular 59/1990 which is hereby cancelled. Some amendments have been made to the national standards for cautioning established by Circular 59/1990; the revised standards, which should be read in conjunction with this Circular, are attached. The general principles underlying those standards are unchanged: properly used, cautioning continues to be regarded as an effective form of disposal, and one which may in appropriate circumstances be used for offenders of any age.

3. Circular 59/1990 left cautioning decisions to the discretion of the police; there is no intention of reducing this discretion, which in the vast majority of cases is properly used. The decision to caution is in all cases one for the police, and although it is open to them to seek the advice of multi-agency panels, this should not be done as a matter of course. It is important that cautions should be administered quickly, and where such advice is sought it must not lead to unnecessary delay.

4. It is apparent that there is some inconsistency between forces about the circumstances in which they consider it appropriate to administer a caution. It is impossible to lay down hard and fast rules such as that first-time offenders must be cautioned, or that certain minor offences should attract only a caution regardless of the offender's record. Nor does the presumption in favour of diverting juveniles from the courts mean that they should automatically be cautioned, as opposed to prosecuted, simply because they are juveniles. Ultimately the proper

use of discretion is a matter of common sense: the questions to be asked in each case are:

- whether the circumstances are such that the caution is likely to be effective, and
- whether the caution is appropriate to the offence.

Serious offences

5. Previous guidance discouraged the use of cautioning for the most serious offences, especially for those triable only on indictment. Statistics indicate, however, that cautions are administered in such cases – there were 1,735 in 1992. Cautions have been given for crimes as serious as attempted murder and rape: this undermines the credibility of this disposal. Cautions should never be used for the most serious indictable-only offences such as these, and only in exceptional circumstances (one example might be a child taking another's pocket-money by force, which in law is robbery) for other indictable-only offences, regardless of the age or previous record of the offender.

6. Other offences, less grave in themselves, may nevertheless be too serious for a caution to be appropriate. The factors which will be relevant in making this judgement are too varied for it to be practicable to list them, but they include the nature and extent of the harm or loss resulting from the offence, relative to the victim's age and means; whether the offence was racially motivated; whether it involved a breach of trust; and whether the offence was carried out in a systematic and organised way. Comprehensive lists of such 'gravity factors' have been drawn up by several forces, and these can help in assessing the seriousness of an offence.

7. Efforts should be made to find out the victim's view about the offence, which may have a bearing on how serious the offence is judged to be. It should not, however, be regarded as conclusive. Where a caution has been given and the victim requests the offender's name and address in order to institute civil proceedings, the information should be disclosed, unless there is good reason to believe that it might be used for an improper purpose such as retaliation.

The offender's record

8. Research into a sample of offenders who were cautioned in 1991 indicates that 8 per cent had already received two or more cautions. Multiple cautioning brings this disposal into disrepute; cautions

should not be administered to an offender in circumstances where there can be no reasonable expectation that this will curb his offending. It is only in the following circumstances that more than one caution should be considered:

– where the subsequent offence is trivial;

or

– where there has been a sufficient lapse of time since the first caution to suggest that it had some effect.

Consistency

9. There are significant variations between forces – and indeed between stations within forces – in the number of offenders who are cautioned as a proportion of those who are either cautioned or convicted. In 1992 this figure for indictable offences varied, as between forces, from 27 per cent to 57 per cent. This discrepancy may result from differing perceptions of the boundary between informal warnings and formal cautions (see below), or of that between formal cautions and prosecutions. Either way, this degree of variation is undesirable. Accordingly, forces which caution a disproportionately high or low number of offenders should ensure that their force guidelines on cautioning are sound and are being interpreted sensibly.

10. Where there is doubt about whether a prosecution should be brought or a caution given in a particular case, it will often be useful to seek the opinion of the Crown Prosecution Service at an early stage in order to avoid disagreement (and in particular the undesirable outcome of an offender escaping without censure of any kind through being considered to be suitable neither for a caution nor for prosecution). If it is the offender's history, rather than the nature of the offence, which renders the case in the view of the police unsuitable for a caution, the Crown Prosecution Service's attention should be drawn to the fact.

Recording

11. The accurate recording of cautions is essential in order both to avoid multiple cautioning and to achieve greater consistency. This will be made easier when computerised national criminal records are introduced, which will permit a brief description of the offence to be recorded. In the meantime, existing recording systems should be improved, where possible, particularly so as to provide a central force record where this does not already exist. It is essential that records

should be checked before a caution is given. When an offender is cautioned on the same occasion for more than one offence, he should be counted as having received one caution only.

12. If a person who is initially suspected of a serious offence is found to have committed a less serious one for which he is then cautioned, it is important that the caution should be recorded as having been given for the lesser offence.

'Informal cautions'

13. There is no intention of inhibiting the practice of taking action short of a formal caution by giving an oral warning, but this should not be recorded as a caution in the criminal statistics nor (unlike a caution) may it be cited in subsequent court proceedings. The expression 'informal caution' used in Circular 59/1990 is confusing and is not recommended.

Supporting cautions

14. Circular 59/1990 made it clear that police officers should not become involved in negotiating reparation or compensation, although these were features which might properly support the use of a caution. In several areas 'caution plus' schemes incorporating voluntary arrangements of this kind have been developed, apparently to the satisfaction of victims. Since caution plus needs further evaluation before a decision can be made on its future, it would be helpful if forces participating in such schemes would monitor the results.

15. In the case of juvenile offenders, it will often be desirable for the police to liaise with local statutory and voluntary agencies about the ways in which assistance might be offered to the juveniles and their families to prevent re-offending. Such support can be especially valuable if a young person is cautioned for a sexual offence.

16. Any enquiries about this Circular should be addressed to Richard Chown, C1 Division, Home Office, Queen Anne's Gate SW1A 9AT. Tel: 020 7273 2535.

Richard Stoate

Head of C1 Division

NATIONAL STANDARDS FOR CAUTIONING (REVISED)

Aims

1. The purposes of a formal caution are:

   - to deal quickly and simply with less serious offenders;
   - to divert them from unnecessary appearance in the criminal courts; and
   - to reduce the chances of their re-offending.

Note 1A. A caution is not a form of sentence. It may not be made conditional upon the satisfactory completion of a specific task such as reparation or the payment of compensation to the victim. Only the courts may impose such requirements.

Decision to caution

2. A formal caution is a serious matter. It is recorded by the police; it should influence them in their decision whether or not to institute proceedings if the person should offend again; and it may be cited in any subsequent court proceedings. In order to safeguard the offender's interests, the following conditions must be met before a caution can be administered:

   - there must be evidence of the offender's guilt sufficient to give a realistic prospect of conviction;
   - the offender must admit the offence;
   - the offender (or, in the case of a juvenile, his parents or guardian) must understand the significance of a caution and give informed consent to being cautioned.

Note 2A. Where the evidence does not meet the required standard, a caution cannot be administered.

Note 2B. A caution will not be appropriate where a person does not make a clear and reliable admission of the offence (for example if intent is denied or there are doubts about his mental health or intellectual capacity).

Note 2C. If an offence is committed by a juvenile under the age of 14, it is necessary to establish that he knew that what he did was seriously wrong.

Note 2D. In practice consent to the caution should not be sought until it has been decided that cautioning is the correct course. The significance of the caution must be explained: that is, that a record will be kept of the caution, that the fact of a previous caution may influence the decision whether or not to prosecute if the person should offend again, and that it may be cited if the person should subsequently be found guilty of an offence by a court. In the case of a juvenile this explanation must be given to the offender in the presence of his parents or guardian, or other appropriate adult. The special needs of other vulnerable groups should also be catered for, in accordance with the Code of Practice for the Detention, Treatment and Questioning of Persons by Police Officers.

Public interest considerations

3.   If the first two of the above requirements are met, consideration should be given to whether a caution is in the public interest. The police should take into account the public interest principles described in the Code for Crown Prosecutors.

Note 3A. There should be a presumption in favour of not prosecuting certain categories of offender, such as elderly people or those who suffer from some sort of mental illness or impairment, or a severe physical illness. Membership of these groups does not, however, afford absolute protection against prosecution, which may be justified by the seriousness of the offence.

Note 3B. Two factors should be considered in relation to the offender's attitude towards his offence: the wilfulness with which it was committed and his subsequent attitude. A practical demonstration of regret, such as apologising to the victim and/or offering to put matters right as far as he is able, may support the use of a caution.

Note 3C. The experience and circumstances of offenders involved in group offences can vary greatly, as can their degree of involvement. Although consistency and equity are important considerations in the decision whether to charge or caution, each offender should be considered separately. Different disposals may be justified.

Views of the victim

4.   Before a caution can be administered it is desirable that the victim should normally be contacted to establish:

   −   his or her view about the offence;
   −   the nature and extent of any harm or loss, and their significance relative to the victim's circumstances;
   −   whether the offender has made any form of reparation or paid compensation.

Note 4A. If a caution is being, or likely to be, considered its significance should be explained to the victim.

Note 4B. In some cases where cautioning might otherwise be appropriate, prosecution may be required in order to protect the victim from further attention from the offender.

Note 4C. If the offender has made some form of reparation or paid compensation, and the victim is satisfied, it may no longer be necessary to prosecute in cases where the possibility of the court's awarding compensation would otherwise have been a major determining factor. Under no circumstances should police officers become involved in negotiating or awarding reparation or compensation.

Administration of a caution

5. A formal caution should be administered in person by a police officer, and wherever practicable at a police station. A juvenile must always be cautioned in the presence of a parent, guardian or other appropriate adult. Members of other vulnerable groups must be treated in accordance with Code of Practice C.

Note 5A. The officer administering the caution should be in uniform and normally of the rank of inspector or above. In some cases, however, a Community Liaison Officer or Community Constable might be more appropriate, or in the inspector's absence the use of a sergeant might be justified. Chief Officers may therefore wish to consider nominating suitable 'cautioning officers'.

Note 5B. Where the person is elderly, infirm or otherwise vulnerable, a caution may be administered less formally, perhaps at the offender's home and in the presence of a friend or relative or other appropriate adult.

Recording cautions

6. All formal cautions should be recorded and records kept as directed by the Secretary of State. The use of cautioning should also be monitored on a force-wide basis.

Note 6A. Formal cautions should be cited in court if they are relevant to the offence under consideration. In presenting antecedents, care should be taken to distinguish between cautions and convictions, which should usually be listed on separate sheets of paper.

Note 6B. Chief officers may also wish to keep records of cases in which action short of a formal caution has been taken, and the reasons for it. But care should be taken not to record anything about an individual which implies that he is guilty of an offence when the evidence is in any doubt. Offences dealt with by action short of a formal caution may not be cited in court.

APPENDIX 11

Available sentences

Age (last birthday)	10–11	12–13	14	15	16	17	18	19	20	21 or over
Discharge (G)	*	*	*	*	*	*	*	*	*	*
Fine	*	*	*	*	*	*	*	*	*	*
Driving disqualification E	E	E	E	E	E	E	E	E	E	E
Compensation Order	*	*	*	*	*	*	*	*	*	*
Deprivation of Property	*	*	*	*	*	*	*	*	*	*
Probation					*	*	*	*	*	*
Drugs Treatment and Testing					E	E	E	E	E	E
Community Service					*	*	*	*	*	*
Combination Order					*	*	*	*	*	*
Curfew Order	E	E	E	E	*	*	*	*	*	*
Supervision Order	*	*	*	*	*	*				
Reparation Order	E	E	E	E	E	E				
Attendance Centre Order	*	*	*	*	*	*	*	*	*	
Action Plan order	E	E	E	E	E	E				
Secure Training Order		F	F							
Detention Order CYPA 1933 s.53	A	A	B	B	B	B				
Detention in a Young Offender Inst					C F	C F	C F	D	D	D
Detention and Training Order	E	E	E	E	E	E				
Custody for Life							*	*	*	
Imprisonment (including susp term and life)										*
Detention in default or for contempt							*	*	*	
Parenting Order	E	E	E	E	E	E				

Notes:
* = the order is available
A = sentence available when offence carries 14 years or more and for indecent assault on a women or a man.
B = A + SS1 and 3 RTA 88
C = minimum term is two months, maximum is twenty four months
D = minimum term is twenty one days, maximum term is maximum term of imprisonment (Other than life) for offence concerned.
E = Available upon order made under C(S) A97 or CL and DA 98 on area by area basis
F = Ceases on operation of C and DA 98 order
G = Excluded for antisocial behaviour Order, Sex Offender Order and, save in exceptional circumstances, for conviction for offence within two years of warning.

293

Early release dates

(a) prisoner serving under 12 months

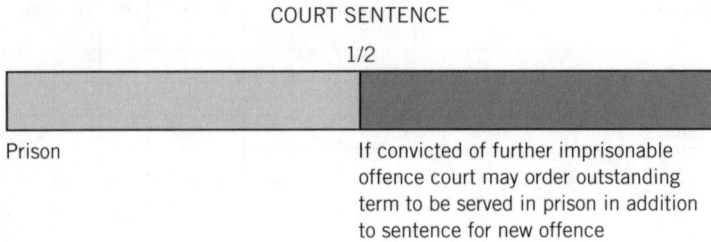

COURT SENTENCE

1/2

Prison

If convicted of further imprisonable
offence court may order outstanding
term to be served in prison in addition
to sentence for new offence

(b) new automatic conditional release (ACR) scheme for prisoners serving from 12
months to less than four years

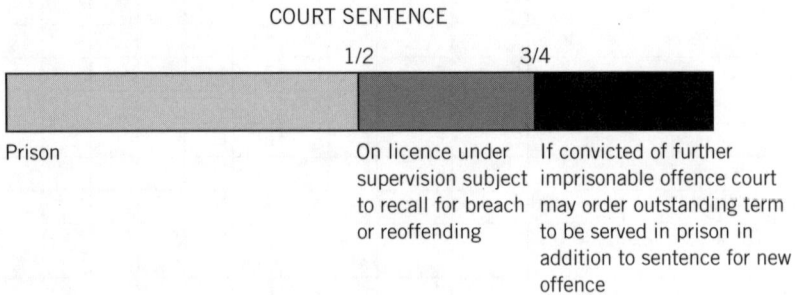

COURT SENTENCE

1/2   3/4

Prison

On licence under   If convicted of further
supervision subject   imprisonable offence court
to recall for breach   may order outstanding term
or reoffending   to be served in prison in
                       addition to sentence for new
                       offence

(c) new discretionary conditional release (DCR/parole) scheme for prisoners
serving four years and over

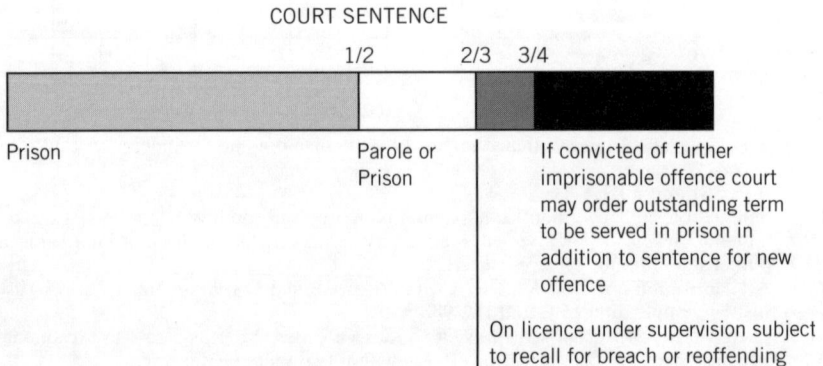

COURT SENTENCE

1/2   2/3   3/4

Prison

Parole or   If convicted of further
Prison   imprisonable offence court
                may order outstanding term
                to be served in prison in
                addition to sentence for new
                offence

                On licence under supervision subject
                to recall for breach or reoffending

Guidance on the interests of justice test for the grant of legal aid issued jointly by the Lord Chancellor's Department, Legal Aid Board and Justices' Clerks' Society (May 1994)

1. INTRODUCTION

This guidance is issued jointly by the Lord Chancellor's Department, Legal Aid Board and Justices' Clerks' Society, and is recommended for use by justices' clerks and their staff, Area Committees of the Legal Aid Board, the Crown Court and practising lawyers when considering and completing applications for legal aid in criminal proceedings.

It supersedes previous guidance, *Legal Aid in Criminal Proceedings* and *Guide-lines for the Consideration of Legal Aid Applications*, issued by the Justices' Clerks' Society in 1990 and 1991 respectively. This new guidance is issued following a recent research report, commissioned by the Legal Aid Board, into why grant rates for criminal legal aid vary from court to court,[1] the implementation of the Criminal Justice Acts 1991 and 1993 and case-law thereunder, and the Magistrates' Association Sentencing Guidelines 1993.

2. CRITICISMS OF THE PRESENT SYSTEM

Uncertainty over whether legal aid in criminal cases was being granted in the magistrates' courts in accordance with the requirements of the Legal Aid Act 1988 and regulations thereunder resulted in the Comptroller and Auditor-General being unable to approve the Lord Chancellor's Department's Legal Aid Account in 1990/91, 1991/92 and 1992/93. That uncertainty has increased following the findings of the research report referred to at paragraph 1 above.

The report was commissioned by the Legal Aid Board. Its findings were:

- differences between courts in granting legal aid are attributable to the approaches of individual clerks;

- grants are more likely to be made according to court clerks' perception of the seriousness of the case, rather than according to the statutory criteria;

- applications for legal aid are often of poor quality, and the information provided to courts is frequently inadequate.

Consequently, the Lord Chancellor has directed that guidance be issued to remind justices' clerks of the requirements of the Legal Aid Act 1988 and to promote greater consistency of approach to the consideration of criminal legal aid applications generally.

3. THE LAW

(a) Justices' clerks and other granting authorities are reminded that there is no authority to grant legal aid other than in accordance with the Legal Aid Act 1988. They are further reminded that the discretion granted to them under that Act should be exercised reasonably; that is, in a way which takes into account the relevant factors and does not take into account any that are irrelevant. Relevant factors here include, but are not limited to, the 'interests of justice criteria' discussed from paragraph 7 onwards (see p. 107). The Lord Chancellor will shortly lay before Parliament regulations directing granting authorities to record the specific reasons why they consider that particular applications do or do not meet the criteria under which they have been made. This will apply to applications determined by magistrates, by justices' clerks or by Area Committees of the Legal Aid Board.

(b) Section 21(5) of the Legal Aid Act 1988 provides that legal aid shall not be granted unless the applicant's financial resources are such as to require assistance in meeting the costs of legal representation. Section 21(2) provides that, subject to means, representation may be granted where it is desirable in the interests of justice. Regulation 11(3) of the Legal Aid in Criminal and Care Proceedings (General) Regulations 1989 requires that a Legal Aid Order shall not be made until the court or the justices' clerk has considered the applicant's statement of means, unless the applicant is incapable of furnishing such a statement on account of his physical or mental condition. Guidance on the financial test is contained in the Justices' Clerks Accounting Manual, and in the

Circular issued every March to those courts with responsibility for the grant of legal aid. Copies of that Circular are available from the Lord Chancellor's Department on request.

(c) The factors set out in section 22(2) have no application in those instances where statute provides that legal aid shall be granted to a person whose means are such that he cannot meet the likely cost of representation. These provisions are:

(3) Subject to subsection (5) below, representation must be granted:

(a) where a person is committed for trial on a charge of murder, for his trial;

(b) where the prosecutor appeals or applies for leave to appeal to the House of Lords, for the proceedings on the appeal;

(c) where a person charged with an offence before a magistrates' court –

(i) is brought before the court in pursuance of a remand in custody when he may be again remanded or committed in custody, and

(ii) is not, but wishes to be, legally represented before the court (not having been legally represented when he was so remanded),

for so much of the proceedings as relates to the grant of bail, and

(d) where a person:

(i) is to be sentenced or otherwise dealt with for an offence by a magistrates' court or the Crown Court, and

(ii) is to be kept in custody to enable enquiries or a report to be made to assist the court, for the proceedings on sentencing or otherwise dealing with him.

(d) Moreover, there are statutory restrictions on a court passing certain sentences on a person who is not legally represented, unless either he applies for legal aid and the application is refused on the ground that it does not appear his means are such that he requires assistance; or he refuses or fails to apply for legal aid. Accordingly, an applicant whose means are insufficient to meet the cost of legal representation shall be granted legal aid before the court passes or makes any of the following sentences or orders:

(i) A sentence of imprisonment on a person who has not been previously sentenced to imprisonment by a court in any part of the UK (Powers of Criminal Courts Act 1973, s.21(1));

(ii) A sentence of detention in a young offender institution under the Criminal Justice Act 1982, s.1A (Criminal Justice Act 1982, s.3);

(iii) A sentence of custody for life under the Criminal Justice Act 1982, s.8(2) (Criminal Justice Act 1982, s.3);

(iv) An order for detention under the Children and Young Persons Act 1933, s.53(2) (Criminal Justice Act 1982, s.3).

4. EXERCISE OF DISCRETION

(a) This guidance is intended to assist those determining applications for the grant of criminal legal aid in the interpretation of the limits of their discretion. It is issued for guidance only. It does not affect the right and responsibility of granting authorities to exercise their discretion in every case in deciding whether the interests of justice test (including the criteria in section 22 of the Legal Aid Act 1988) has been met.

(b) Section 21(7) of the Legal Aid Act 1988 provides that 'where a doubt arises whether representation under this Part should be granted to any person, the doubt shall be resolved in that person's favour'.

5. INSUFFICIENT INFORMATION

(a) If it is not possible to make a proper determination because insufficient information has been provided on the application form, or some detail needs clarification, it is suggested that this does not constitute a 'doubt' for the purposes of section 21(7). In such circumstances, further detail should be requested from the applicant or the applicant's solicitor. Section 21(7) should only come into play if, once all the appropriate information has been provided, a genuine doubt remains as to whether a grant of legal aid should be made.

(b) The granting authority is entitled to sufficient information to enable it to reach a properly informed decision on the grant of legal aid, and is entitled to ask for, and receive, such information. If an application does not contain sufficient information, further details should be sought. When seeking further information, the granting authority may declare to the applicant that the application will not be considered for grant until such time as the information is received and that it would be prudent for him to await a final decision before incurring any further costs.

6. LEGAL AID APPLICATIONS – GENERAL CONSIDERATIONS

(a) Every application for legal aid must be considered on its merits and must be determined in accordance with the provisions of Part V of the Legal Aid Act 1988.

(b) The specific criterion or other interests of justice consideration which is relied upon must be identified clearly in the application form.

(c) The decision must always be based on the information contained in the form of application for legal aid, together with any other oral or written information provided by or on behalf of the applicant, particulars of the offence(s) alleged as set out in the information(s) before the court, and any other relevant particulars which may be properly taken into account as a result of statements made in open court during the course of the proceedings against the applicant. If the decision to grant or refuse legal aid is influenced by information provided orally, then the relevant information provided should be clearly recorded on the application.

(d) In respect of offences triable either-way, the approach to the grant of legal aid should be the same whether the offence is to be tried in the Crown Court or the magistrates' court; accordingly, for example, an accused charged with an offence triable either-way, who does not merit legal aid for summary trial, should not automatically be granted legal aid simply because he elects to be tried at the Crown Court.

(e) It is suggested that the need for a Newton hearing (i.e. a dispute on the facts following a plea of guilty) may justify a grant of legal aid if, for example, witnesses need to be traced by a legal representative or expert cross-examination is necessary. This may also apply for other disputes of fact and/or law arising after a guilty plea.

7. THE INTERESTS OF JUSTICE CRITERIA – DETAILED CONSIDERATIONS

(a) The factors set out in section 22 of the Legal Aid Act 1988 apply to proceedings by way of a trial by or before a magistrates' court or the Crown Court or on an appeal to the Crown Court against conviction.

(b) Section 22(2) specifies five factors which must be taken into account when a competent authority is determining whether it is in the interests of justice that representation be granted.

(c) In some cases the interaction of two or more of the factors may dictate that legal aid should be granted when neither by itself would have sufficed. For example, whereas a minor question of law could normally be dealt with under the Green Form Scheme, or a person's knowledge of English may be adequate rather than good, those two factors in combination could merit a grant of legal aid. Where such interaction is used this should clearly be noted on the application form.

(d) The five factors (considered below) are not exhaustive:

Section 22(2) states that 'The factors to be taken into account . . . shall include the following . . .'. In R. v. *Liverpool City Magistrates, ex parte*

McGhee it was stated that '. . . these magistrates were plainly wrong in regarding the factors statutorily identified [in section 22(2) (a)–(e)] as being exhaustive and there may be, according to the circumstances of a particular case, other than the identified factors which have to be taken into consideration in deciding whether or not the justice of the case requires that legal aid should be granted.'

(e) While some applications may rely on all or several of the factors, an application which relies on only one must be given equal consideration. It also follows from *McGhee* that reliance on none of the statutory factors is not necessarily fatal. When a non-statutory factor is held to have founded or supported the grant of legal aid this should be clearly specified on the application form.

(f) For example, where the behaviour of a defendant is so disruptive as to distract the court from the exercise of its judicial function, that alone could justify a grant of legal aid if the presence of a lawyer would mitigate the distraction – if only, as a last resort, enabling the court to continue the hearing in the absence of the defendant but in the presence of his legal representative. It is further suggested that behaviour which affects the court's administrative performance is outside the scope of section 22 and cannot, therefore, be the basis for a grant of legal aid.

8. SECTION 22(2)(A) – THE OFFENCE IS SUCH THAT IF PROVED IT IS LIKELY THAT THE COURT WOULD IMPOSE A SENTENCE WHICH WOULD DEPRIVE THE ACCUSED OF HIS LIBERTY OR LEAD TO LOSS OF HIS LIVELIHOOD OR SERIOUS DAMAGE TO HIS REPUTATION

(a) Likelihood of deprivation of liberty

(i) The person considering the application must be provided with sufficient information to enable him to be satisfied that, in the event of a conviction, the accused's liberty would be at risk. Accordingly, information about the seriousness and circumstances of the offence alleged should be taken into account, including details of any aggravating circumstances which, in the event of the accused being convicted, might expose him to a more severe sentence than would normally be the case. Details relating to previous convictions should also be supplied for the purposes of determining seriousness. Regard should also be had to the gravity of the offence. Where any aggravating factors influence the decision on the grant of legal aid, these should be clearly recorded.

(ii)   It is recommended that reference in appropriate cases be made to *The Magistrates' Association Sentencing Guidelines* issued on 20 September 1993, which provide examples of 'seriousness indicators' (aggravating factors and mitigating factors) for various types of offence.

(iii) The onus is on the applicant to state why such a sentence is likely.

(iv)   Legal aid should normally be granted where there is a real and practical (as opposed to theoretical) risk of imprisonment or other form of deprivation of liberty. For example, an offender of previous good character, charged with possessing a small quantity of cannabis, would have difficulty in establishing that he was likely to lose his liberty because, although the offence is punishable with three months' imprisonment on summary conviction, it would be most unusual for any court to pass a custodial sentence for such an offence.

(v)   For the purpose of determining whether the accused is likely to lose his liberty, etc., regard should be had to the sentencing approaches of courts generally and, in particular, to the sentencing approach of the court before which the accused is appearing.

(vi)   The likelihood of conviction should not be taken into account; the grant of legal aid should not be based on the merits of the defence; conviction should always be assumed.

(vii) 'Deprivation of liberty' includes any sentence of imprisonment, whether immediate or suspended; detention in a young offender institution; custody for life; detention under section 53(2) of the Children and Young Persons Act 1933; hospital and guardianship orders.

(viii) As noted above, section 22(2)(a) refers specifically to the likelihood of deprivation of liberty and it has been a matter of some debate whether community sentences are capable of falling within that category. This debate has now been settled by the judgement in *R.* v. *Liverpool City Magistrates, ex parte McGhee.* In giving judgment, Rose LJ said that '. . . I am not persuaded . . . that the risk of a community service order amount[s] to a risk of deprivation of liberty within the meaning of that section' [section 22(2)(a)]. In concurring, Waller J said '. . . I am also clear that the words in section 22(2)(a) "The offence is such that if proved it is likely that the court would impose a sentence which would deprive the accused of his liberty", do not include a community service order'. The judgment went on to state that the possibility of a community service order being made might be a factor to be considered when considering whether or not to grant legal aid, and Rose LJ made plain that this should not be taken to imply that legal aid should be granted if community service was likely. It was, however, a factor other than the listed factors which could be taken into account in particular cases.

(ix)   Legal aid should normally be granted:

(a) upon a committal to the Crown Court for sentence (*R. v. Serghiou* [1966] 3 All ER 637);

(b) where the court is considering making a recommendation for deportation (*R. v. Edgehill* [1963] 1 All ER 181);

(c) where the court is considering making a hospital order (*R. v. King's Lynn Justices, ex parte Fysh* [1964] Crim LR 143).

(x)   A grant of legal aid for mitigation only might be appropriate, for example, when the court's assessment of the gravity of the case is substantially altered by factors which come to light after conviction. Courts should also bear in mind the statutory restrictions on imposing certain sentences as referred to at paragraph 3(d) of these notes (see p. 297).

(b) Loss of livelihood

(i)   It follows from the provisions of the Act that the granting authority should consider how likely it is that loss of livelihood will result from a sentence imposed by the court on conviction. It is suggested that legal aid should only be granted where there is a real risk of loss of livelihood.

(ii)   The applicant must explain why he believes that it is likely that he will lose his livelihood. In some cases this will be obvious, e.g. a bank clerk accused of an offence of dishonesty; in others it may be obscure, e.g. a teacher convicted of indecency with a child is likely to lose his livelihood, but a coach driver convicted of a similar offence might not appear so vulnerable until he explains to the court that he drives school buses. The likely loss of livelihood should be a direct consequence of the conviction or the sentence.

(iii) It is suggested that loss of livelihood would normally refer to current livelihood. Therefore, someone who is not currently employed would be less likely to meet this criterion, although other criteria under section 22 may be met, such as 'serious damage to reputation' (e.g. see paragraph 8(c)(v), p. 303).

(iv)   Assertions that disqualification from driving will result in a loss of livelihood should be examined critically. There can seldom be justification to grant legal aid to resist a mandatory driving disqualification alone arising from a drink/driving charge unless a cogent argument as to special reasons can be put forward. Though a grant could be justified in exceptional circumstances (e.g. if the applicant could show that the disqualification would result in a real risk of dismissal), legal aid would not usually be justified where the accused sought to avoid a 'totting-up' disqualification, having acquired twelve or more penalty points.

(c) Serious damage to reputation

(i) In many cases, conviction will damage the accused's reputation. However, section 22 refers to serious damage. It is considered that this would relate to those cases in which the offence, or the offender's circumstances, are such that the disgrace of conviction, or consequent damage to the applicant's standing, would greatly exceed the direct effect of the penalty which might be imposed. 'Reputation' for these purposes is a question of good character, including honesty and trustworthiness. Social class and position should not be taken into account. The loss of reputation consequent of a conviction for dishonesty is absolute and not relevant to the amount.

(ii) As a general rule, offences of varying degrees of seriousness attract different levels of damage to reputation. The Act refers to serious damage as justifying the grant of legal aid.

(iii) An effective plea in mitigation for any charge may lessen the severity of the sentence and thereby lessen the seriousness of the damage to reputation. An applicant who either has a previous conviction for a like offence or a conviction for a more serious offence can be assumed to have lost reputation and the criterion will not apply. However, the fact that a person has previous convictions should not preclude consideration of Legal Aid under this head. For example, it may be that someone with a previous conviction for a minor assault might still suffer serious damage to reputation if convicted of an offence of dishonesty or a sexual offence.

(iv) In deciding upon the seriousness of the damage to reputation, it is suggested that special factors about the accused, for example religious background, might aggravate the damage to reputation caused by a conviction which may not have the same effect on another person. This could also apply, for example, to someone engaged in voluntary work such as drug use prevention, where a conviction for possession of a drug could particularly undermine their integrity.

(v) Consideration should be given to whether an accused who is undertaking vocational or professional training might suffer damage to reputation so serious that there is a risk that future livelihood might be lost.

9. SECTION 22(2)(B) – THE DETERMINATION OF THE CASE MAY INVOLVE CONSIDERATION OF A SUBSTANTIAL QUESTION OF LAW

(i) Legal aid should only be granted under this criterion if a question of law is raised which the applicant cannot be expected to deal with unaided and is a substantial question and is relevant to the applicant's case. It should be noted that this criterion may also apply when legal aid is being considered for an appeal against conviction.

If the applicant intends to plead guilty, the likelihood of substantial questions of law arising must generally be remote, though there may be exceptions, such as some 'special reasons' (such as laced drinks) in drink/driving cases. There may also be some instances in which sentencing considerations could give rise to a substantial question of law.

(ii) The defence solicitor should specify the point of law on the application form. Quite often issues coming before the courts involve mixed questions of fact and law but again, in such circumstances, to justify grant of legal aid the question of law must be a substantial one.

(iii) Except in circumstances where the applicant faces serious or complex charges, legal aid should not generally be granted solely for the purpose of obtaining advice as to the appropriate plea, since this can rarely be described as a substantial question of law. Preliminary advice as to plea can usually be provided satisfactorily by advice from the duty solicitor or from any solicitor under the Green Form Scheme.

10. SECTION 22(2) (C) – THE ACCUSED MAY BE UNABLE TO UNDERSTAND THE PROCEEDINGS OR TO STATE HIS OWN CASE BECAUSE OF HIS INADEQUATE KNOWLEDGE OF ENGLISH, MENTAL ILLNESS OR OTHER MENTAL OR PHYSICAL DISABILITY

(a) Inadequate knowledge of English.

(i) Legal aid should not be granted unless the applicant's knowledge is sufficiently poor to prevent him from following the proceedings or conducting his case. It is suggested that the fact that the services of an interpreter are available is not a sufficient ground for refusing legal aid under this criterion.

(ii) The accused's difficulties of comprehension may differ with the complexity of the case; he may be able to manage in a very straightforward case but may be unable to do so in a more complex one. Courts should, therefore, consider carefully whether the stated impediment to understanding is likely to be operative in the particular case.

(iii) Generally, it is the ability to understand spoken English which is important. It should be borne in mind that, while the language of the courts is often technical, it is the responsibility of those working in the courts to use plain English. A lack of fluent literacy will not, in most cases, impair the accused's ability to prepare and present his case. Relevant factors could include the degree of literacy, the complexity of the case and the extent of reading required.

(b) Mental or physical disability

(i) Legal aid should be granted if the applicant is unable to follow the proceedings or properly conduct his case by reason of substantial physical disability, for example deafness or blindness, or by reason of mental disorder, mental impairment or subnormality.

(ii) Courts may think it appropriate to request a medical report or certificate, especially in cases where it is claimed that the applicant is suffering from a form of mental illness that is likely to worsen significantly due to a court hearing and, as a consequence, is unlikely to be able to represent himself properly.

11.

(a) Trace and interview witnesses.

(i) Details of the witnesses, and why there is a necessity for representation to trace and/or interview them, should be included in the application. If details of witnesses are not included, consideration of the legal aid application should be deferred until the applicant has provided the court with sufficient information to make a determination.

(b) Expert cross-examination of a prosecution witness.

(i) In cases where the applicant requires legal aid for the benefit of expert cross-examination of prosecution witnesses, he should be expected to explain why this is necessary.

(ii) It should be noted that section 22(2)(d) refers to expert cross-examination of a witness and not only to cross-examination of an expert witness. Giving judgment in *R.* v. *Liverpool City Magistrates, ex parte McGhee*, Rose LJ said 'These justices . . . were clearly under the misapprehension ... that because expert witnesses were not to be called, the factor identified in part of section 22(2)(d) was not satisfied. That, in itself, as it seems to me, is sufficient to flaw the approach of these justices'.

Thus, legal aid should be granted under this heading when there is a need for professional cross-examination of a witness. This may very likely be the case when the evidence is provided by an expert, since an accused person would rarely be capable, for example, of cross-examining a medical or handwriting expert. It may also apply in other cases, such as those where shades of emphasis in the evidence can make an action appear more sinister than it was in fact. But in considering applications under this heading, the emphasis should be clearly on the nature of the evidence, rather than on the status of the person providing the evidence.

12. SECTION 22(2)(E) – IT IS IN THE INTERESTS OF SOMEONE OTHER THAN THE ACCUSED THAT THE ACCUSED BE REPRESENTED

(i)   It should be borne in mind when considering legal aid under this heading that section 34A of the Criminal Justice Act 1988 provides that a defendant charged with certain offences specified in section 32(2) of that Act shall not cross-examine in person any child witness who is an alleged victim or alleged witness to the commission of the offence.

(ii) It is suggested that legal aid should also be considered when, for example, the accused is charged with a sexual offence where it is desirable that the complainant should be spared the great strain of being cross-examined by a person whom they believe has committed a sexual offence against them.

(iii) This principle may also apply where the alleged victim or witness of, for example, an offence against the person or a burglary is very young or elderly, when cross-examination by the accused might put them under undue strain.

THE LAW SOCIETY'S COMMENTS ON THE GUIDELINES

The Law Society's Criminal Law Committee has made the following comments on this guidance to the Lord Chancellor's Department, the Justices' Clerks' Society and the Legal Aid Board:

1. The case of *R.* v. *Liverpool City Magistrates, ex p. McGhee* [1993] CLR 609 is limited to deciding that a community service order did not amount to a deprivation of liberty under section 22(2) of the Legal Aid Act 1988. Other community penalties may still amount to a deprivation of liberty, such as a curfew order.

2. Paragraph 11(b)(2) of the guidance incorrectly states the position in relation to the need for legal aid in order to conduct expert cross-examination of a witness for the prosecution. The guidance states that 'the emphasis should be clearly on the nature of the evidence, rather than on the status of the person providing the evidence'. There is no basis for this assertion and defendants should not be expected to conduct a cross-examination of a police witness themselves.

3. The guidance given in paragraph 12(iii) is inappropriate, as it suggests that a burglary where the victim is a very young or elderly person may, otherwise, not attract legal aid.

4. The guidance is inaccurate in its reference to the law in paragraph 3(d), which lists the circumstances in which legal aid shall be granted to a person whose means are such that he cannot meet the likely cost of representation, in that it excludes the reference in section 21(11) of the Legal Aid Act 1988 to 'a person who has not attained the age of 18 who is committed under section 23 of the Children and Young Persons Act 1969 to the care of a local authority or a remand centre'.

5. The guidance is also incorrect in its reference in paragraph 10(b)(i), where it has substituted 'is unable to follow the proceedings or properly conduct his case' for the words used in section 22(ii)(c) of the Legal Aid Act 1988, '*may* be unable'.

End note

1 R Young, T Moloney and A Sanders, 'In the Interests of Justice? The Determination of Criminal Legal Aid Applications by Magistrates' Courts in England and Wales'. Legal Aid Board; September 1992.

The Code for Crown Prosecutors (June 1994)

1. INTRODUCTION

1.1 The decision to prosecute an individual is a serious step. Fair and effective prosecution is essential to the maintenance of law and order. But even in a small case, a prosecution has serious implications for all involved – the victim, a witness and a defendant. The Crown Prosecution Service applies the *Code for Crown Prosecutors* so that it can make fair and consistent decisions about prosecutions.

1.2 The Code contains information that is important to police officers, to others who work in the criminal justice system and to the general public. It helps the Crown Prosecution Service to play its part in making sure that justice is done.

2. GENERAL PRINCIPLES

2.1 Each case is unique and must be considered on its own, but there are general principles that apply in all cases.

2.2 The duty of the Crown Prosecution Service is to make sure that the right person is prosecuted for the right offence and that all relevant facts are given to the court.

2.3 Crown Prosecutors must be fair, independent and objective. They must not let their personal views of the ethnic or national origin, sex, religious beliefs, political views or sexual preference of the offender, victim or witness influence their decisions. They must also not be affected by improper or undue pressure from any source.

3. REVIEW

3.1 Proceedings are usually started by the police. Sometimes they may consult the Crown Prosecution Service before charging a defendant. Each case that the police send to the Crown Prosecution Service is reviewed by a Crown Prosecutor to make sure that it meets the tests set out in this Code. Crown Prosecutors may decide to continue with the original charges, to change the charges or sometimes to stop the proceedings.

3.2 Review, however, is a continuing process so that Crown Prosecutors can take into account any change in circumstances. Wherever possible, they talk to the police first if they are thinking about changing the charges or stopping the proceeedings. This gives the police the chance to provide more information that may affect the decision. The Crown Prosecution Service and the police work closely together to reach the right decision, but the final responsibility for the decision rests with the Crown Prosecution Service.

4. THE CODE TESTS

4.1 There are two stages in the decision to prosecute. The first stage is the evidential test. If the case does not pass the evidential test, it must not go ahead, no matter how important or serious it may be. If the case does pass the evidential test, Crown Prosecutors must decide if a prosecution is needed in the public interest.

4.2 This second stage is the public interest test. The Crown Prosecution Service will only start or continue a prosecution when the case has passed both tests. The evidential test is explained in section 5 and the public interest test is explained in section 6.

5. THE EVIDENTIAL TEST

5.1 Crown Prosecutors must be satisfied that there is enough evidence to provide a 'realistic prospect of conviction' against each defendant on each charge. They must consider what the defence case may be and how that is likely to affect the prosecution case.

5.2 A realistic prospect of conviction is an objective test. It means that a jury or bench of magistrates, properly directed in accordance with the law, is more likely than not to convict the defendant of the charge alleged.

5.3 When deciding whether there is enough evidence to prosecute, Crown Prosecutors must consider whether the evidence can be used and is reliable. There will be many cases in which the evidence does not give any cause for concern. But there will also be cases in which the evidence may not be as strong as it first appears. Crown Prosecutors must ask themselves the following questions:

Can the evidence be used in court?

(a) Is it likely that the evidence will be excluded by the court? There are certain legal rules which might mean that evidence which seems relevant cannot be given at a trial. For example, is it likely that the evidence will be excluded because of the way in which it was gathered or because of the rule against using hearsay as evidence? If so, is there enough other evidence for a realistic prospect of conviction?

Is the evidence reliable?

(b) Is it likely that a confession is unreliable, for example, because of the defendant's age, intelligence or lack of understanding?
(c) Is the witness's background likely to weaken the prosecution case? For example, does the witness have any dubious motive that may affect his or her attitude to the case or a relevant previous conviction?
(d) If the identity of the defendant is likely to be questioned, is the evidence about this strong enough?

5.4 Crown Prosecutors should not ignore evidence because they are not sure that it can be used or is reliable. But they should look closely at it when deciding if there is a realistic prospect of conviction.

6. THE PUBLIC INTEREST TEST

6.1 In 1951, Lord Shawcross, who was Attorney-General, made the classic statement on public interest, which has been supported by Attorneys-General ever since: 'It has never been the rule in this country – I hope it never will be – that suspected criminal offences must automatically be the subject of prosecution'. (House of Commons Debates, volume 483, column 681, 29 January 1951.)

6.2 The public interest must be considered in each case where there is enough evidence to provide a realistic prospect of conviction. In cases of any seriousness, a prosecution will usually take place unless there are public interest factors tending against prosecution which clearly outweigh those tending in favour. Although there may be public interest factors against prosecution in a particular case, often the prosecution should go ahead and those factors should be put to the court for consideration when sentence is being passed.

6.3 Crown Prosecutors must balance factors for and against prosecution carefully and fairly. Public interest factors that can affect the decision to prosecute usually depend on the seriousness of the offence or the circumstances of the offender. Some factors may increase the need to prosecute but others may suggest that another course of action would be better.

The following lists of some common public interest factors, both for and against prosecution, are not exhaustive. The factors that apply will depend on the facts in each case.

Some common public interest factors in favour of prosecution

6.4 The more serious the offence, the more likely it is that a prosecution will be needed in the public interest. A prosecution is likely to be needed if:

(a) a conviction is likely to result in a significant sentence;
(b) a weapon was used or violence was threatened during the commission of the offence;
(c) the offence was committed against a person serving the public (for example, a police or prison officer, or a nurse);
(d) the defendant was in a position of authority or trust;
(e) the evidence shows that the defendant was a ringleader or an organiser of the offence;
(f) there is evidence that the offence was premeditated;
(g) there is evidence that the offence was carried out by a group;
(h) the victim of the offence was vulnerable, has been put in considerable fear, or suffered personal attack, damage or disturbance;
(i) the offence was motivated by any form of discrimination against the victim's ethnic or national origin, sex, religious beliefs, political views or sexual preference;
(j) there is a marked difference between the actual or mental ages of the defendant and the victim, or if there is any element of corruption;
(k) the defendant's previous convictions or cautions are relevant to the present offence;
(l) the defendant is alleged to have committed the offence whilst under an order of the court;

(m) there are grounds for believing that the offence is likely to be continued or repeated, for example, by a history of recurring conduct; or

(n) the offence, although not serious in itself, is widespread in the area where it was committed.

Some common public interest factors against prosecution

6.5 A prosecution is less likely to be needed if:

(a) the court is likely to impose a very small or nominal penalty;

(b) the offence was committed as a result of a genuine mistake or misunderstanding (these factors must be balanced against the seriousness of the offence);

(c) the loss or harm can be described as minor and was the result of a single incident, particularly if it was caused by a misjudgement;

(d) there has been a long delay between the offence taking place and the date of the trial, unless:

 – the offence is serious;
 – the delay has been caused in part by the defendant;
 – the offence has only recently come to light; or
 – the complexity of the offence has meant that there has been a long investigation;

(e) a prosecution is likely to have a very bad effect on the victim's physical or mental health, always bearing in mind the seriousness of the offence;

(f) the defendant is elderly or is, or was at the time of the offence, suffering from significant mental or physical ill health, unless the offence is serious or there is a real possibility that it may be repeated. The Crown Prosecution Service, where necessary, applies Home Office guidelines about how to deal with mentally disordered offenders. Crown Prosecutors must balance the desirability of diverting a defendant who is suffering from significant mental or physical ill health with the need to safeguard the general public;

(g) the defendant has put right the loss or harm that was caused (but defendants must not avoid prosecution simply because they can pay compensation); or

(h) details may be made public that could harm sources of information, international relations or national security.

6.6 Deciding on the public interest is not simply a matter of adding up the number of factors on each side. Crown Prosecutors must decide how important each factor is in the circumstances of each case and go on to make an overall assessment.

The relationship between the victim and the public interest

6.7 The Crown Prosecution Service acts in the public interest, not just in the interests of any one individual. But Crown Prosecutors must always think very carefully about the interests of the victim, which are an important factor, when deciding where the public interest lies.

Youth offenders

6.8 Crown Prosecutors must consider the interests of a youth when deciding whether it is in the public interest to prosecute. The stigma of a conviction can cause very serious harm to the prospects of a youth offender or a young adult. Young offenders can sometimes be dealt with without going to court. But Crown Prosecutors should not avoid prosecuting simply because of the defendant's age. The seriousness of the offence or the offender's past behaviour may make prosecution necessary.

Police cautions

6.9 The police make the decision to caution an offender in accordance with Home Office guidelines. If the defendant admits the offence, cautioning is the most common alternative to a court appearance. Crown Prosecutors, where necessary, apply the same guidelines and should look at the alternatives to prosecution when they consider the public interest. Crown Prosecutors should tell the police if they think that a caution would be more suitable than a prosecution.

7. CHARGES

7.1 Crown Prosecutors should select charges which:

(a) reflect the seriousness of the offending;
(b) give the court adequate sentencing powers; and
(c) enable the case to be presented in a clear and simple way.

This means that Crown Prosecutors may not always continue with the most serious charge where there is a choice. Further, Crown Prosecutors should not continue with more changes than are necessary.

7.2 Crown Prosecutors should never go ahead with more charges than are necessary just to encourage a defendant to plead guilty to a few. In the same way, they should never go ahead with a more serious charge just to encourage a defendant to plead guilty to a less serious one.

7.3 Crown Prosecutors should not change the charge simply because of the decision made by the court or the defendant about where the case will be heard.

8. MODE OF TRIAL

8.1 The Crown Prosecution Service applies the current guidelines for magistrates who have to decide whether cases should be tried in the Crown Court when the offence gives the option. (See the *National Mode of Trial Guidelines* issued by the Lord Chief Justice; see Appendix 17, p. 337.) Crown Prosecutors should recommend Crown Court trial when they are satisfied that the guidelines require them to do so.

8.2 Speed must never be the only reason for asking for a case to stay in the magistrates' courts. But Crown Prosecutors should consider the effect of any likely delay if they send a case to the Crown Court, and any possible stress on victims and witnesses if the case is delayed.

9. ACCEPTING GUILTY PLEAS

9.1 Defendants may want to plead guilty to some, but not all, of the charges. Or they may want to plead guilty to a different, possibly less serious, charge because they are admitting only part of the crime. Crown Prosecutors should only accept the defendant's plea if they think the court is able to pass a sentence that matches the seriousness of the offending. Crown Prosecutors must never accept a guilty plea just because it is convenient.

10. RE-STARTING A PROSECUTION

10.1 People should be able to rely on decisions taken by the Crown Prosecution Service. Normally, if the Crown Prosecution Service tells a suspect or defendant that there will not be a prosecution, or that the prosecution has been stopped, that is the end of the matter and the case will not start again. But occasionally there are special reasons why the Crown Prosecution Service will re-start the prosecution, particularly if the case is serious.

10.2 These reasons include:

(a) rare cases where a new look at the original decision shows that it was clearly wrong and should not be allowed to stand;
(b) cases which are stopped so that more evidence which is likely to become available in the fairly near future can be collected and prepared. In these cases, the Crown Prosecutors will tell the defendant that the prosecution may well start again;
(c) cases which are stopped because of a lack of evidence but where more significant evidence is discovered later.

11. CONCLUSION

11.1 The Crown Prosecution Service is a public service headed by the Director of Public Prosecutions. It is answerable to Parliament through the Attorney-General. The *Code for Crown Prosecutors* is issued under section 10 of the Prosecution of Offences Act 1985 and is a public document. This is the third edition and it replaces all earlier versions. Changes to the Code are made from time to time and these are also published.

11.2 The Code is designed to make sure that everyone knows the principles that the Crown Prosecution Service applies when carrying out its work. Police officers should take account of the principles of the Code when they are deciding whether to charge a defendant with an offence. By applying the same principles, everyone involved in the criminal justice system is helping the system to treat victims fairly, and to prosecute defendants fairly but effectively.

11.3 The Code is available from:

Crown Prosecution Service
Information Branch
50 Ludgate Hill
London
EC4M 7EX

Tel: 020 7273 8078
Fax: 020 7329 8377

Part 2, Criminal legal aid: a guide to eligibility

6. Legal Representation

6. Legal Representation:

_____Note_____

a) If you do not give the name and address of a solicitor the court will select a solicitor for you.

b) You must tell the solicitor that you have named him, unless he has helped you complete this form.

c) If you have been charged together with another person or persons, the court may assign a solicitor other than the solicitor of your choice.

a) The solicitor I wish to act for me is

b) Give the firm's name and address (if known)

In the magistrates' courts representation will generally provide for a solicitor only. Representation by both solicitor and counsel may be made where the offence is indictable, including an either way offence, and the court thinks it desirable because the offence is exceptionally grave, difficult or complex (reg 48(2)). However an order cannot provide for representation by counsel on a bail application in the magistrates' court (reg 44(2)).

The applicant will normally be assigned the solicitor of his own choice unless there is another legally aided defendant in the same case and the cases are to be heard together. In this situation the same solicitor may be assigned to two or more defendants unless the interests of justice require separate representation. Separate representation may be justified where there is a conflict of interest between the accused. This could arise where in his defence one of the accused is blaming another accused.

Further guidance on the assignment of legal representation under a criminal legal aid order in multi-defendant cases (and in relation to the location of a solicitor in terms of the cost of travel and to change of representation) is given in LCD Circular JC93(1) issued in March 1993. A copy of the circular is at Annex G.

PART 2   **THE APPLICATION FORM**

7. Reasons for wanting Legal Aid

7. Reasons for wanting Legal Aid:

- To avoid the possibility of your application being delayed or legal aid being refused because the court does not have enough information about the case, you must complete the rest of the form.
- When deciding whether to grant legal aid, the court will need to know the reasons why it is in the interest of justice for you to be represented.
- If you need help in completing this form, and especially if you have previous convictions, you should see a solicitor. He may be able to advise you free of charge or at a reduced rate.

> Note: If you plead NOT GUILTY neither the information in this form nor that in your statement of means will be made available to the members of the court trying your case unless you are convicted or you consent. If you are acquitted, only the financial information you have given in your statement of means will be given to the court.

Tick any boxes which apply and give brief details or reasons in the space provided

The applicant should have ticked one or more of the boxes in section 7 and completed the details section of the form.

In considering the application you should note in the space provided by each factor whether or not the reasons given justify the grant of legal aid. For example, factor 7(a) (It is likely that I will lose my liberty), might be noted "This court is unlikely to impose a custodial sentence for possession of a small quantity of cannabis", or "Custodial sentence likely in this court for breach of probation order".

If the information justifying the decision is already on the form, then cross reference may be made to this to avoid duplication. For example, the applicant may have ticked box 7(a) (It is likely that I will lose my liberty) and written "nature of offence" in the details box having already described the offence fully in section 2 of the form. In this case, provided local sentencing policy is not a factor, simply write "No" or "Not for this offence" or "Agreed" in the reasons box. The less detail there is elsewhere on the form the more detail there will need to be in the reasons box. Other grounds may be less susceptible to this approach. For example, if an applicant offering no defence to a charge of driving with excess alcohol has ticked box 7(c) (It is likely that I will lose my livelihood) and written "Effect of disqualification" in the details box, then the entry in the reasons box might be "No - disqualification mandatory penalty for this offence".

If one factor justifies the grant of legal aid there is no need to go on to consider the other factors relied on by the applicant. Where none of the factors put forward justify grant, go on to consider any other interests of justice factors that may be relevant to the application. These may include factors that are not listed on the application form or in the Act. Any such factors considered should be noted in the appropriate box on Form 1.

Where all the relevant factors have been considered and none on its own justifies grant then consider the application as a whole. If two or more factors taken together justify grant then this must be reflected in the record of decision on the interests of justice test.

PART 2   **THE APPLICATION FORM**

	Details	Reasons for grant or refusal *for court use only*
a) It is likely that I will lose my liberty ☐ *You should consider seeing a solicitor before answering this question*		

b) I am subject to a: suspended or partly suspended prison sentence ☐ conditional discharge ☐ probation order ☐ supervision order ☐ deferment of sentence ☐ community service order ☐ care order ☐ combination order ☐ *Give details as far as you are able including the nature of the offence and when the order was made.*		

7(a) and 7(b) likelihood of deprivation of liberty

The application must include sufficient information to enable you to be satisfied that, in the event of a conviction, the accused's liberty would be at risk.

The onus is on the applicant to state why such a sentence is likely. Information about the seriousness and circumstances of the offence alleged should be taken into account, including details of any aggravating circumstances which might expose him to a more severe sentence than would normally be the case. Details relating to previous convictions should also be supplied for the purposes of determining seriousness. Regard should also be had to the gravity of the offence.

Where any aggravating factors influence the decision on the grant of legal aid, these should be recorded.

The Magistrates' Association Sentencing Guidelines or local guidelines may provide examples of "seriousness indicators" (aggravating factors and mitigating factors) for various types of offence.

Legal aid should normally be granted where there is a real and practical risk of imprisonment or other form of deprivation of liberty. For example, an offender of previous good character, charged with possessing a small quantity of cannabis, would have difficulty in establishing that he was likely to lose his liberty. Although the offence is punishable with three months' imprisonment on summary conviction, it would be most unusual for any court to pass a custodial sentence for such an offence.

Take account of the sentencing approaches both of courts generally and of your court when deciding whether the accused is likely to lose his liberty.

The likelihood of conviction should not be taken into account; the grant of legal aid should not be based on the merits of the defence; conviction should always be assumed.

Deprivation of liberty includes any sentence of imprisonment, whether immediate or suspended; detention in a young offender institution; custody for life; detention under section 53(2) of the Children and Young Persons Act 1933; hospital and guardianship orders. In this context a community service order does not amount to deprivation of liberty within the meaning of the Act. (R v Liverpool City Magistrates ex parte McGhee).

Legal aid should normally be granted:

- upon a committal to the Crown Court for sentence (R v Serghiou [1966] 3 All ER 637);

- where the court is considering making a recommendation for deportation (R v Edgehill [1963] 1 All ER 181);

- where the court is considering making a hospital order (R v King's Lynn Justices ex parte Fysh (1964) Crim.LR.143).

A grant of legal aid for mitigation only might be appropriate, for example, when the court's assessment of the gravity of the case is substantially altered by factors which come to light after conviction. Courts should also bear in mind the statutory restrictions on imposing certain sentences (see 3 above).

c) It is likely that I will lose my livelihood ☐		

7(c) loss of livelihood

The applicant must explain why he believes that it is likely that he will lose his livelihood. In some cases this will be obvious, eg. a bank clerk accused of an offence of dishonesty; in others it may be obscure, eg. a teacher convicted of indecency with a child is likely to lose his livelihood, but a coach driver convicted of a similar offence might not appear so vulnerable until he explains to the court that he drives school buses. The likely loss of livelihood should be a direct consequence of the conviction or the sentence.

Consider how likely it is that loss of livelihood will result from a sentence imposed by the court on conviction. Legal aid should be granted only where there is a real risk of loss of livelihood.

Loss of livelihood would normally refer to current livelihood. Someone who is not currently employed would be less likely to meet this criterion, although other criteria under the Act may be met, such as "serious damage to reputation". An exception might be where someone is genuinely unemployed for a very short period between jobs when loss of livelihood could be treated as a relevant factor.

Assertions that disqualification from driving will result in a loss of livelihood should be examined critically. There can seldom be justification to grant legal aid to resist a mandatory driving disqualification alone arising from a drink/driving charge unless a cogent argument as to special reasons can be put forward. Though a grant could be justified in exceptional circumstances (eg. if the applicant could show that the disqualification would result in a real risk of dismissal), legal aid would not usually be justified where the accused sought to avoid a "totting-up" disqualification, having acquired twelve or more penalty points.

PART 2   **THE APPLICATION FORM**

d) It is likely that I will suffer serious damage to my reputation ☐

7(d) Serious damage to reputation

In many cases, conviction will damage the accused's reputation. However, the Act refers to <u>serious</u> damage. This will usually relate to those cases in which the offence, or the offender's circumstances, are such that the disgrace of conviction, or consequent damage to the applicant's standing, would greatly exceed the direct effect of the penalty which might be imposed. "Reputation" for these purposes is a question of good character, including honesty and trustworthiness. Social class and position should not be taken into account. The loss of reputation consequent on a conviction for dishonesty is absolute and not relevant to the amount.

As a general rule, offences of varying degrees of seriousness attract different levels of damage to reputation. The Act refers to <u>serious</u> damage as justifying the grant of legal aid.

An effective plea in mitigation for any charge may lessen the severity of the sentence and thereby lessen the seriousness of the damage to reputation. An applicant who either has a previous conviction for a <u>like</u> offence or a conviction for a more serious offence can be assumed to have lost reputation and the criterion will not apply. However, the fact that a person has previous convictions should not preclude consideration of legal aid under this head. For example, it may be that someone with a previous conviction for a minor assault might still suffer serious damage to reputation if convicted of an offence of dishonesty or a sexual offence.

In deciding on the seriousness of the damage to reputation, special factors about the accused, for example religious or cultural background, might aggravate the damage to reputation caused by a conviction which may not have the same effect on another person. This could also apply, for example, to someone engaged in voluntary work such as drug use prevention, where a conviction for possession of a drug could particularly undermine their integrity.

Consideration should be given to whether an accused who is undertaking vocational or professional training might suffer damage to reputation so serious that there is a risk that future livelihood might be lost.

e) A substantial question of
    law is involved ☐
    *(You will need the help of a
    solicitor to answer this
    question)*

(Please give authorities to be quoted with law reports references)

7(e) A substantial question of law is involved

Legal aid should only be granted under this criterion if a question of law is raised which the applicant cannot be expected to deal with unaided and is a substantial question and is relevant to the applicant's case. This criterion may also apply when legal aid is being considered for an appeal against conviction.

If the applicant intends to plead guilty, the likelihood of substantial questions of law arising must generally be remote, though there may be exceptions, such as some "special reasons" (eg laced drinks) in drink/driving cases. There may also be some instances in which sentencing considerations could give rise to a substantial question of law.

The defence solicitor should specify the point of law on the application form. Quite often issues coming before the courts involve mixed questions of fact and law but again, in such circumstances, to justify grant of legal aid the question of law must be a substantial one.

Unless the applicant faces serious or complex charges, legal aid should not generally be granted solely for the purpose of obtaining advice as to the appropriate plea, since this can rarely be described as a substantial question of law. Preliminary advice as to plea can usually be provided satisfactorily by advice from the duty solicitor or from any solicitor under the Green Form Scheme.

PART 2   **THE APPLICATION FORM**

f) I shall be unable to understand the court proceedings or state my own case because: i) My understanding of English is inadequate ☐ ii) I suffer from a disability *(Give full details)* ☐	**Details**	**Reasons for grant or refusal** *(for court use only)*

7(f)(i) inadequate knowledge of English

Legal aid should not be granted unless the applicant's knowledge is sufficiently poor to prevent him from following the proceedings or conducting his case. The fact that the services of an interpreter are available is not a sufficient ground for refusing legal aid under this criterion.

The level of understanding may differ with the complexity of the case; the applicant may be able to manage in a very straightforward case but may be unable to do so in a more complex one. Courts should, therefore, consider carefully whether the stated impediment to understanding is likely to be operative in the particular case.

Generally, it is the ability to understand spoken English which is important. It should be borne in mind that, while the language of the courts is often technical, it is the responsibility of those working in the courts to use plain English. A lack of fluent literacy will not, in most cases, impair the accused's ability to prepare and present his case. Relevant factors could include the degree of literacy, the complexity of the case and the extent of reading required.

7(f)(ii) mental or physical disability

Legal aid should be granted if the applicant is unable to follow the proceedings or properly conduct his case by reason of substantial physical disability, for example deafness or blindness or a speech impediment, or by reason of mental disorder, mental impairment or subnormality.

Courts may request a medical report or certificate, especially in cases where it is claimed that the applicant is suffering from a form of mental illness that is likely to worsen significantly due to a court hearing. As a consequence, the applicant is unlikely to be able to represent himself properly.

g) Witnesses have to be traced and/or interviewed on my behalf *(State circumstances)* ☐		

7(g) trace and interview witnesses

The application should include details of the witnesses, and state why representation is necessary to trace and/or interview them. If details of witnesses are not included, consideration of the application should be deferred until the applicant has provided sufficient information to make a determination.

h) The case involves expert cross examination of a prosecution witness *(Give brief details)* ☐		

7(h) expert cross-examination of a prosecution witness

The applicant should explain why he needs legal aid for the benefit of expert cross-examination of prosecution witnesses. The Act refers to expert cross-examination of a witness and <u>not</u> only to cross-examination of an expert witness. The fact that expert witnesses are not to be called does not mean that this criterion cannot apply (<u>R v Liverpool City Magistrates ex Parte McGhee</u>).

Legal aid should be granted under this heading when there is a need for professional cross-examination of a witness. This is likely to be the case when the evidence is provided by an expert, since an accused person would rarely be capable, for example, of cross-examining a medical or handwriting expert. It may also apply in other cases, such as those where shades of emphasis in the evidence can make an action appear more sinister than it was in fact. But in considering applications under this heading, the emphasis should be clearly on the nature of the evidence, rather than on the status of the person providing the evidence.

PART 2   **THE APPLICATION FORM**

i) It is in someone else's interest that I am represented ☐		

7(i) Someone else's interest that the accused is represented

It should be borne in mind when considering legal aid under this heading that section 34A of the Criminal Justice Act 1988 provides that a defendant charged with certain offences specified in section 32(2) of that Act shall not cross-examine in person any child witness who is an alleged victim or alleged witness to the commission of the offence.

Legal aid should also be considered when, for example, the accused is charged with a sexual offence where it is desirable that the complainant should be spared the great strain of being cross-examined by a person whom they believe has committed a sexual offence against them.

This principle may also apply where the alleged victim or witness of, for example, an offence against the person or a burglary is very young or elderly, when cross-examination by the accused might put them under undue strain.

PART2 **THE APPLICATION FORM**

j) Any other reasons (Give full particulars) ☐		

7(j) Other reasons

The Act specifies five factors that must be taken into account when determining whether it is in the interests of justice that representation be granted but the five factors are not exhaustive. When a non-statutory factor is held to have founded or supported the grant of legal aid this should be clearly specified on the application form.

An example of a non-statutory factor could be where the behaviour of a defendant is so disruptive as to distract the court from the exercise of its judicial function. That alone could justify a grant of legal aid if the presence of a lawyer would mitigate the distraction and allow the court to continue the hearing in the absence of the defendant but in the presence of his legal representative. Behaviour that affects the court's **administrative** performance is unlikely to bear on the interests of justice and so could not be the basis for a grant of legal aid.

PART 2   **THE APPLICATION FORM**

For Court use only

Any additional factors considered when determining the application, including any information given orally.

Decision on the interests of justice test

I have considered all available details of all the charges and it is / is not* in the interests of justice that representation be granted because:

Signed _____   Proper Officer

Date _____

*Cross out whichever does not apply

Decision on the interests of justice test

In most cases it will not be necessary to write a lengthy statement of reasons for grant or refusal in the box at the end of the form. Usually a note on the lines of "...see (a) above" will suffice.

In some cases a more detailed statement of reasons will be needed. Where the decision is based on information given orally, then a statement of reasons will be necessary. A statement will also be needed where a number of factors taken together are the reason for grant. The statement might take the form "...while the question of law involved is not a substantial one, and the defendant's knowledge of English is adequate although not fluent, I consider that the combination of these two factors justifies the grant of legal aid". Where doubt about whether representation should be granted has, in accordance with the Act, been resolved in the applicant's favour then a statement of reasons should be given.

The statement of reasons must include enough detail so that anyone inspecting the records can see clearly that legal aid has been granted or refused in accordance with the Act and the regulations. It must be clear from the record why the grant of legal aid was or was not considered to be in the interests of justice.

Magistrates' Association Sentencing Guidelines: aggravating/mitigating factors

Offence	Aggravating factors	Mitigating factors
Abstracting electricity	Offence committed on bail High usage Prolonged period Special equipment Previous convictions and failures to respond to previous sentences, if relevant	Short period
Affray	Offence committed on bail Busy public place Group action People put in fear Vulnerable victim(s) Previous convictions and failures to respond to previous sentences, if relevant	Single offender
Aggravated vehicle-taking	Offence committed on bail Avoiding detection or apprehension Competitive driving: racing, showing off Disregard of warnings, e.g. from passengers or others in vicinity Excessive speed Evidence of alcohol or drugs Group action Pre-meditated	Keys left in car No alcohol or drugs involved Minor damage Single incident Speed not excessive

Offence	Aggravating factors	Mitigating factors
	Serious injury/damage Serious risk Previous convictions and failures to respond to previous sentences, if relevant	
Assault – actual bodily harm	Offence committed on bail Deliberate kicking Extensive injuries Group action Offender in position of authority Premeditated Victim particularly vulnerable Victim serving public Weapon Previous convictions and failures to respond to previous sentences, if relevant	Impulsive action Minor injury Provocation
Assault on a police officer	Offence committed on bail Any injuries caused Gross disregard for police authority Group action Premeditated Previous convictions and failures to respond to previous sentences, if relevant	Impulsive action Unaware that person was a police officer
Burglary (dwelling)	Offence committed on bail Deliberately frightening occupants Group offence Night time Professional operation Soiling, ransacking, damage Previous convictions and failures to respond to previous sentences, if relevant	Day time Low value No damage or disturbance No forcible entry

Offence	Aggravating factors	Mitigating factors
Burglary (non-dwelling)	Offence committed on bail Deliberately frightening occupants Group offence Night time Professional operation Ram raiding Soiling, ransacking, damage Previous convictions and failures to respond to previous sentences, if relevant	Day time Low value No damage or disturbance No forcible entry
Common assault	Offence committed on bail Group action Offender in position of authority Premeditated Victim particularly vulnerable Victim public servant Previous convictions and failures to respond to previous sentences, if relevant	Impulsive action Provocation Trivial nature of action
Criminal damage	Offence committed on bail Deliberate Fire raising Group offence Serious damage Previous convictions and failures to respond to previous sentences, if relevant	Impulsive action Minor damage Provocation
Careless driving	Excessive speed High degree of carelessness Serious risk Offence committed on bail Previous convictions and failures to respond to previous sentences, if relevant	Difficult weather conditions Minor risk Momentary lapse Negligible/parking damage

Offence	Aggravating factors	Mitigating factors
Dangerous driving	Offence committed on bail Avoiding detection or apprehension Competitive driving, racing, showing off Disregard of warnings, e.g. from passengers or others in vicinity Evidence of alcohol or drugs Excessive speed Prolonged, persistent, deliberate bad driving Serious risk Previous convictions and failures to respond to previous sentences, if relevant	Momentary risk not fully appreciated No alcohol or drugs involved Single incident Speed not excessive
Driving – no insurance	Deliberate driving without insurance LGV, HGV, PCV, or minicabs No reference to insurance ever having been held Offence committed on bail Previous convictions and failures to respond to previous sentences, if relevant	Accidental oversight Genuine mistake Insurance held but clearly not covering the driver or use Recently expired insurance – weeks? – months? Responsibility for providing insurance resting with another – the parent/owner/lender/hirer Smaller vehicle, e.g. moped
Driving while disqualified by Court Order	Offence committed on bail Efforts to avoid detection Long distance drive Planned, long-term evasion Recent disqualification Previous convictions and failures to respond to previous sentences, if relevant	Emergency established Short distance driven

Offence	Aggravating factors	Mitigating factors
Class A drugs – production, supply, possession with intent to supply	COMMIT FOR TRIAL These offences are not usually dealt with in magistrates' courts and should normally be committed to the Crown Court for trial	
Class A drugs – possession	Offence committed on bail An amount other than a very small quantity Previous convictions and failures to respond to previous sentences, if relevant	Very small quantity
Class B drugs – supply: possession with intent to supply	Offence committed on bail Commercial production Large amount Previous convictions and failures to respond to previous sentences, if relevant	Small amount
Class B drugs – possession	Offence committed on bail Large amount Previous convictions and failures to respond to previous sentences, if relevant	Small amount
Cultivation of cannabis	Offence committed on bail Commercial cultivation Large quantity Previous convictions and failures to respond to previous sentences, if relevant	Small scale cultivation for personal use
Drunk and disorderly	Offence committed on bail Busy public place Offensive language or behaviour With group	Account should be taken of any time spent in custody

Offence	Aggravating factors	Mitigating factors
	Previous convictions and failures to respond to previous sentences, if relevant	
Failing to stop Failing to report	Offence committed on bail Evidence of drinking Serious injury and failure to stop or remain at scene Serious injury and/or serious damage Previous convictions and failures to respond to previous sentences, if relevant	Failed to stop but reported Negligible damage No one at scene but failed to report Stayed at scene but failed to give full particulars Stayed at scene but left before giving full particulars
Fear or provocation of violence	Offence committed on bail Busy public place Group action People put in fear Vulnerable victims Previous convictions and failures to respond to previous sentences, if relevant	Single offender
Handling stolen goods	Offence committed on bail Adult involving children High value Organiser or distributor Stolen to order Previous convictions and failures to respond to previous sentences, if relevant	Impulsive action Low value Single item for personal use
Harassment, alarm or distress	Offence committed on bail Group action Vulnerable victim Previous convictions and failures to respond to previous sentences, if relevant	Single offender

Offence	Aggravating factors	Mitigating factors
Making off without payment	Offence committed on bail Deliberate plan Large sum Two or more involved Victim particularly vulnerable Previous convictions and failures to respond to previous sentences, if relevant	Impulsive action
Obstructing a police officer	Offence committed on bail Gross disregard for police authority Group action Premeditated Previous convictions and failures to respond to previous sentences, if relevant	Genuine misjudgement Impulsive action Minor obstruction Unaware that person was a police officer
Obtaining by deception	Offence committed on bail Committed over lengthy period Large sums or valuable goods Two or more involved Victim particularly vulnerable Previous convictions and failures to respond to previous sentences, if relevant	Impulsive action Short period Small sum
Social security – false representation to obtain benefit	Offence committed on bail Fraudulent claims over a long period Large amount Organised group offence Planned deception Previous convictions and failures to respond to previous sentences, if relevant	Ignorance of regulations Offence of omission

Offence	Aggravating factors	Mitigating factors
Taking vehicle without consent	Offence committed on bail Group action Premeditated Related damage Vulnerable victim Previous convictions and failures to respond to previous sentences, if relevant	Keys left in car Misunderstanding with owner
Theft (general)	Offence committed on bail Large amount Planned Sophisticated Vulnerable victim Previous convictions and failures to respond to previous sentences, if relevant	Impulsive action Small amount Voluntary restitution
Theft from a shop	Offence committed on bail Adult involving children High value Organised teams Planned Previous convictions and failures to respond to previous sentences, if relevant	Impulsive action Low value
Theft from vehicle	Offence committed on bail High value Organised team Planned Related damage Previous convictions and failures to respond to previous sentences, if relevant	Car unlocked Impulsive action
Theft in breach of trust	Offence committed on bail Casting suspicion on others Committed over a period Large amount	Impulsive action Newly employed junior Single item Small amount

Offence	Aggravating factors	Mitigating factors
	Planned Senior employee Sophisticated Vulnerable victim Previous convictions and failures to respond to previous sentences, if relevant	
TV licence evasion	Offence committed on bail Deliberate evasion Lengthy unlicensed use Previous convictions and failures to respond to previous sentences, if relevant	Accidental oversight Confusion of responsibility Very short unlicensed use
Violent disorder	Offence committed on bail Busy public place Large group People put in fear Vulnerable victims Previous convictions and failures to respond to previous sentences, if relevant	
Wounding – grievous bodily harm	Offence committed on bail Deliberate kicking Extensive injuries Group action Offender in position of authority Premeditated Victim particularly vulnerable Victim serving public Weapon Previous convictions and failures to respond to previous sentences, if relevant	Impulsive action Provocation

National Mode of Trial Guidelines 1995

The purpose of these guidelines is to help magistrates decide whether or not to commit 'either-way' offences for trial in the Crown Court. Their object is to provide guidance not direction. They are not intended to impinge upon a magistrate's duty to consider each case individually and on its own particular facts.

These guidelines apply to all defendants aged 18 and above.

GENERAL MODE OF TRIAL CONSIDERATIONS

Section 19 of the Magistrates' Courts Act 1980 requires magistrates to have regard to the following matters in deciding whether an offence is more suitable for summary trial or trial on indictment:

(1) the nature of the case;
(2) whether the circumstances make the offence one of a serious character;
(3) whether the punishment which a magistrates' court would have power to inflict for it would be adequate;
(4) any other circumstances which appear to the court to make it more suitable for the offence to be tried in one way rather than the other;
(5) any representations made by the prosecution or the defence.

CERTAIN GENERAL OBSERVATIONS CAN BE MADE:

(a) The court should never make its decision on the grounds of convenience or expedition.
(b) The court should assume for the purpose of deciding mode of trial that the prosecution version of the facts is correct.
(c) The fact that the offences are alleged to be specimens is a relevant

consideration; the fact that the defendant will be asking for other offences to be taken into consideration, if convicted, is not.

(d) Where cases involve complex questions of fact or difficult questions of law, including difficult issues of disclosure of sensitive material, the court should consider committal for trial.

(e) Where two or more defendants are jointly charged with an offence each has an individual right to elect his mode of trial. (This follows the decision in *R. v. Brentwood Justices ex parte Nicholls.*)

(f) In general, except where otherwise stated, either-way offences should be tried summarily unless the court considers that the particular case has one or more of the features set out in the following pages and that its sentencing powers are insufficient.

(g) The court should also consider its power to commit an offender for sentence, under section 38 of the Magistrates' Courts Act 1980, as amended by section 25 of the Criminal Justice Act 1991, if information emerges during the course of the hearing which leads them to conclude that the offence is so serious, or the offender such a risk to the public, that their powers to sentence him are inadequate. This amendment means that committal for sentence is no longer determined by reference to the character or antecedents of the defendant.

FEATURES RELEVANT TO THE INDIVIDUAL OFFENCES

Note: Where reference is made in these guidelines to property or damage of 'high value' it means a figure equal to at least twice the amount of the limit (currently £5,000) imposed by statute on a magistrates' court when making a Compensation Order.

BURGLARY

Cases should be tried summarily unless the court considers that one or more of the following features is present in the case and that its sentencing powers are insufficient.

Magistrates should take account of their powers under section 25 of the Criminal Justice Act 1991 to commit for sentence.

Note: See above paragraph (g).

1. Dwelling house

(1) Entry in the daytime when the occupier (or another) is present.
(2) Entry at night of a house which is normally occupied, whether or not the occupier (or another) is present.
(3) The offence is alleged to be one of a series of similar offences.
(4) When soiling, ransacking, damage or vandalism occurs.
(5) The offence has professional hallmarks.
(6) The unrecovered property is of high value (see page 338 for definition of high value).

Note: Attention is drawn to para. 28(c) of Schedule 1 to the Magistrates' Courts Act 1980, by which offences of burglary in a dwelling cannot be tried summarily if any person in the dwelling was subjected to violence or the threat of violence.

2. Non-dwellings

(1) Entry of a pharmacy or doctor's surgery.
(2) Fear is caused or violence is done to anyone lawfully on the premises (e.g. nightwatchman; security guard).
(3) The offence has professional hallmarks.
(4) Vandalism on a substantial scale.
(5) The unrecovered property is of high value (see page 338 for definition of high value).

THEFT AND FRAUD

Cases should be tried summarily unless the court considers that one or more of the following features is present in the case and that its sentencing powers are insufficient.

Magistrates should take account of their powers under section 25 of the Criminal Justice Act 1991 to commit for sentence.

Note: See paragraph (g) on page 338.

(1) Breach of trust by a person in a position of substantial authority, or in whom a high degree of trust is placed.
(2) Theft or fraud which has been committed or disguised in a sophisticated manner.
(3) Theft or fraud committed by an organised gang.

(4) The victim is particularly vulnerable to theft or fraud, e.g. the elderly or infirm.
(5) The unrecovered property is of high value (see page 338 for definition of high value).

HANDLING

Cases should be tried summarily unless the court considers that one or more of the following features is present in the case and that its sentencing powers are insufficient.

Magistrates should take account of their powers under section 25 of the Criminal Justice Act 1991 to commit for sentence.

Note: See paragraph (g) on page 338.

(1) Dishonest handling of stolen property by a receiver who has commissioned the theft.
(2) The offence has professional hallmarks.
(3) The property is of high value (see page 338 for definition of high value).

SOCIAL SECURITY FRAUDS

Cases should be tried summarily unless the court considers that one or more of the following features is present in the case and that its sentencing powers are insufficient.

Magistrates should take account of their powers under section 25 of the Criminal Justice Act 1991 to commit for sentence.

Note: See paragraph (g) on page 338.

(1) Organised fraud on a large scale.
(2) The frauds are substantial and carried out over a long period of time.

VIOLENCE (SECTIONS 20 AND 47 OF THE OFFENCES AGAINST THE PERSON ACT 1861)

Cases should be tried summarily unless the court considers that one or more of the following features is present in the case and that its sentencing powers are insufficient.

Magistrates should take account of their powers under section 25 of the Criminal Justice Act 1991 to commit for sentence.

Note: See paragraph (g) on page 338.

(1) The use of a weapon of a kind likely to cause serious injury.
(2) A weapon is used and serious injury is caused.
(3) More than minor injury is caused by kicking, head-butting or similar forms of assault.
(4) Serious violence is caused to those whose work has to be done in contact with the public or who are likely to face violence in the course of their work.
(5) Violence to vulnerable people, e.g. the elderly and infirm.
(6) The offence has clear racial motivation.

Note: The same considerations apply to cases of domestic violence.

PUBLIC ORDER ACT OFFENCES

Cases should be tried summarily unless the court considers that one or more of the following features is present in the case and that its sentencing powers are insufficient.

Magistrates should take account of their powers under section 25 of the Criminal Justice Act 1991 to commit for sentence.

Note: See paragraph (g) on page 338.

1. Cases of violent disorder should generally be committed for trial.

2. Affray

   (1) Organised violence or use of weapons.
   (2) Significant injury or substantial damage.
   (3) The offence has a clear racial motivation.
   (4) An attack upon police officers, prison officers, ambulance men, firemen and the like.

VIOLENCE TO AND NEGLECT OF CHILDREN

Cases should be tried summarily unless the court considers that one or more of the following features is present in the case and that its sentencing powers are insufficient.

Magistrates should take account of their powers under section 25 of the Criminal Justice Act 1991 to commit for sentence.

Note: See paragraph (g) on page 338.

(1) Substantial injury.
(2) Repeated violence or serious neglect, even if the physical harm is slight.
(3) Sadistic violence, e.g. deliberate burning or scalding.

INDECENT ASSAULT

Cases should be tried summarily unless the court considers that one or more of the following features is present in the case and that its sentencing powers are insufficient.

Magistrates should take account of their powers under section 25 of the Criminal Justice Act 1991 to commit for sentence.

Note: See paragraph (g) on page 338.

(1) Substantial disparity in age between victim and defendant, and the assault is more than trivial.
(2) Violence or threats of violence.
(3) Relationship of trust or responsibility between defendant and victim.
(4) Several similar offences, and the assaults are more than trivial.
(5) The victim is particularly vulnerable.
(6) Serious nature of the assault.

UNLAWFUL SEXUAL INTERCOURSE

Cases should be tried summarily unless the court considers that one or more of the following features is present in the case and that its sentencing powers are insufficient.

Magistrates should take account of their powers under section 25 of the Criminal Justice Act 1991 to commit for sentence.

Note: See paragraph (g) on page 338.

(1) Wide disparity of age.
(2) Breach of position of trust.
(3) The victim is particularly vulnerable.

Note: Unlawful sexual intercourse with a girl under 13 is triable only on indictment.

DRUGS

1. Class A

    (a) Supply; possession with intent to supply. These cases should be committed for trial.
    (b) Possession.

    Should be committed for trial unless the amount is consistent only with personal use.

2. Class B

    (a) Supply; possession with intent to supply. Should be committed for trial unless there is only small scale supply for no payment.

    (b) Possession.

    Should be committed for trial when the quantity is substantial and not consistent only with personal use.

DANGEROUS DRIVING

Cases should be tried summarily unless the court considers that one or more of the following features is present in the case and that its sentencing powers are insufficient.

Magistrates should take account of their powers under section 25 of the Criminal Justice Act 1991 to commit for sentence.

Note: See paragraph (g) on page 338.

(1) Alcohol or drugs contributing to dangerousness.
(2) Grossly excessive speed.
(3) Racing.

(4) Prolonged course of dangerous driving.
(5) Other related offences.

CRIMINAL DAMAGE

Cases should be tried summarily unless the court considers that one or more of the following features is present in the case and that its sentencing powers are insufficient.

Magistrates should take account of their powers under section 25 of the Criminal Justice Act 1991 to commit for sentence.

Note: See paragraph (g) on page 338.

(1) Deliberate fire-raising.
(2) Committed by a group.
(3) Damage of a high value.
(4) The offence has clear racial motivation.

Note: Offences set out in Schedule 2 to the Magistrates' Courts Act 1980 (which includes offences of criminal damage which do not amount to arson) must be tried summarily if the value of the property damaged or destroyed is £5,000 or less.

APPENDIX 18

List of police file contents

Up-date October 1999

Form No.	Description	Remand	File type Expedited	Full
MG1	File front sheet	◉	◉	◉
MG4	Charge(s)	◉	◉	◉
MG4A	Police grant of conditional bail	•	•	•
MG4B	Variation of police conditional bail	•	•	•
MG4C	Police conditional bail surety/security	•	•	•
MG5	Case summary	◉		
MG6	Confidential information	•	•	•
MG6B	Police officer's disciplinary record			•
MG6C	Police schedule of non-sensitive unused material			•
MG6D	Police schedule of sensitive material			•
MG6E	Disclosure officer's report			•
MG7	Remand application form	◉		
MG8	Breach of court bail conditions form	•		
MG9	Witness list			◉
MG10	Witness non-availability			◉
MG11	Copies of statements from witnesses			
	Key witnesses	◉	◉	
	All witnesses			◉
MG12	Exhibit list			◉
MG14	Written statement under caution		•	•
MG15	Record of taped interview	•		•
	Short descriptive note		◉	
MG16	Previous convictions defendant	•	•	•
MG16A	Previous convictions witnesses			•
MG17	Previous cautions defendant	•	•	•
MG18	TIC forms		•	•
MG19	Compensation form		•	•
MG20	Further evidence/information report			
MG21	Custody remand update			
MG21A	Bail enquiry form			

Legend: ◉ Core documents which must be included in the file.
  • Documents which should be included where available and applicable.

345

MG6 series of police files

Form MG 6

NOT TO BE DISCLOSED

CONFIDENTIAL INFORMATION

Page No............

Name of Defendant: ....
(Surname first)

See following notes when completing this form.

Continuation sheet: Yes ☐   No ☐

Form MG 6

CONFIDENTIAL INFORMATION

For more detailed guidance on completing this form, see the Manual of Guidance.

In addition to any other confidential information to be supplied, details of any of the following issues should be recorded:

1. Others arrested and interviewed and not charged.

2. Other offender(s) being sought.

3. Others charged whose details do not appear on this file.

4. Others cautioned out of the same incident (include names, offences and reasons).

5. Witnesses who have refused to make statements (include names and evidence they could give).

6. Witnesses who could be classed as accomplices (include names and involvement).

7. Strengths or weaknesses of evidence and/or witnesses.

8. Previous conviction/allegations against defendant with similar MO.

9. Matters of local interest.

10. Praiseworthy conduct which should be brought to the attention of the court.

Victim's Charter and Witness Care

11. Views of the victim(s) concerning bail/the decision to prosecute.

12. Vulnerable witness and/or any special requirements (include unwillingness to attend).

13. Child witnesses/child abuse cases.

14. Professional and expert witnesses.

15. Intimidation/victimisation.

Abbreviated file cases

16. Information to be withheld.

17. Relevant previous convictions of witnesses if known.

18. Material which undermines the prosecution case.

19. If no MG 19 on file and compensation is an issue, enter victim's name and address.

Full file cases

20. Material held by third parties to be revealed/disclosed.

Form MG 6B

NOT TO BE DISCLOSED

CONFIDENTIAL INFORMATION

POLICE OFFICER'S DISCIPLINARY RECORD
(see following notes when completing this form)

Name: .... Rank: ....

Warrant No: .... Station: ....

1. I have a disciplinary finding of guilt as indicated below ☐

2. I have a criminal conviction/criminal caution *(see note 2)* ☐

3. I have been charged with a disciplinary offence indicated below but the case has not yet been concluded ☐

4. I have been charged with a criminal offence indicated below but the case has not yet been concluded ☐

(Please tick as appropriate)

Date of finding/charge	Nature of offence/allegation	Punishment	Date of expunction

This information is true to the best of my knowledge and belief and I am aware that I have a continuing obligation to provide update information should circumstances change.

Signature: .... Date: ....

Form MG 6B

1. Please print details.

2. Criminal convictions and criminal cautions to be revealed are for those offences recordable at the National Identification Bureau. Convictions in Scotland or foreign countries also should be revealed. Officers should include bind overs. A completed record of previous convictions and/or cautions should be submitted by the officer with form MG 6B. Bind overs should be shown on the list of cautions.

3. Disciplinary findings of guilt to be revealed are those which arise from an appearance at a FORMAL DISCIPLINARY HEARING before the Chief Constable or a tribunal and have not be expunged.

4. Findings of guilt for 'Neglect of Health', 'Improper Dress or Untidiness' and 'Entering Licensed Premises' are exempt from disclosure unless specifically requested by the prosecutor.

5. Disciplinary findings of guilt where the punishment was a caution are also exempt from disclosure, as they are not recorded on the Police Officer's personal record.

6. Disciplinary findings of guilt resulting in a fine or a reprimand shall be expunged after three years; any other punishment shall be expunged after five years provided that, in either case, the relevant period is free of any further punishment other than a caution (Reg. 17 Police (Discipline) Regulations 1985).

7. There will be occasions when the finding of guilt would have been expunged by the time the Officer's evidence is to be heard at any trial. It is essential that the Officer concerned draws this fact to the attention of the prosecutor.

8. Officers subject of a conviction, or a finding of guilt, are advised to liaise with the Crown Prosecution Service in order to establish an understanding between them as to what is likely to occur should the matter be raised in court.

SCHEDULE 1. POLICE (DISCIPLINE) REGULATIONS 1985

1. Discreditable conduct
2. Misconduct towards a member of a Police Force
3. Disobedience to orders
4. Neglect of duty
5. Falsehood or prevarication
6. Improper disclosure of information
7. Corrupt or improper practice
8. Abuse of authority
9. Racially discriminatory behaviour
12. Damage to police property
13. Drunkenness
14. Drinking on duty or soliciting drink
16. Criminal conduct
17. Being an accessory to disciplinary offences as set out above

NOTE.   Offences under paragraphs 10 (Neglect of health), 11 (Improper dress or untidiness) and 15 (Entering licensed premises), have been deliberately omitted.

Continuation Sheet   Form MG 6C(CONT)

POLICE SCHEDULE OF NON-SENSITIVE
UNUSED MATERIAL

Page No................

R v ....

The Disclosure Officer believes that the following material which does not form part of the prosecution case is NOT SENSITIVE.

			FOR CPS USE	
Item No.	DESCRIPTION	LOCATION	☐	COMMENT

Continuation sheet:
Yes ☐   No ☐

☐ Enter:
D = Disclose to defence
I = Defence may inspect

Form MG 6C

POLICE SCHEDULE OF NON-SENSITIVE
UNUSED MATERIAL

Page No................

R v ....

The Disclosure Officer believes that the following material which does not form part of the prosecution case is NOT SENSITIVE.

Item No.	DESCRIPTION	LOCATION		FOR CPS USE	
			□	COMMENT	

Date:	Continuation sheet: Yes ☐ No ☐	Reviewing lawyer:

□ Enter:
  D = Disclose to defence
  I = Defence may inspect

Form MG 6D

Page No.............

NOT TO BE DISCLOSED

CONFIDENTIAL INFORMATION

POLICE SCHEDULE OF SENSITIVE MATERIAL

R v ....

The Disclosure Officer believes that the following material which does not form part of the prosecution case is SENSITIVE.

☐ *Tick if copy supplied to CPS*

FOR CPS USE

Item No.	Description	Reason for sensitivity	☐	Agree sensitive Yes/No	Court application Yes/No	CPS views

Date:		Continuation sheet: Yes ☐ No ☐	Reviewing lawyer:

Continuation Sheet

Form MG 6D(CONT)

NOT TO BE DISCLOSED

Page No. ....

CONFIDENTIAL INFORMATION

POLICE SCHEDULE OF SENSITIVE MATERIAL

R v ....

The Disclosure Officer believes that the following material which does not form part of the prosecution cases is SENSITIVE.

☐ Tick if copy supplied to CPS

FOR CPS USE

Item No.	Description	Reason for sensitivity	☐	Agree sensitive Yes/No	Court application Yes/No	CPS views

Continuation sheet:

Yes ☐   No ☐

Form MG 6E

Page No. ....

NOT TO BE DISCLOSED

CONFIDENTIAL INFORMATION

DISCLOSURE OFFICER'S REPORT

R v ....

The following items are listed on the schedule(s) for this case and may:
* undermine the prosecution case (primary disclosure) /* assist the defence (secondary disclosure) /* or are required to be supplied under Section 7.3 of the Code (* *delete as applicable*).

Did the investigation of this case commence before 1 April 1997?   Yes ☐   No ☐

☐ *Enter C or D to denote schedule MG6C or 6D and enter item no. from schedule.*

☐ Schedule	Item no.	Reason	Tick if attached

I certify that, to the best of my knowledge and belief, all material which has been retained and made available to me has been revealed to the prosecutor in accordance with the Criminal Procedure and Investigations Act 1996 Code of Practice.

Signature of Disclosure Officer: ....   Date: ....

Name of Disclosure Officer: ....

Continuation sheet: Yes ☐   No ☐

Continuation Sheet

Form MG 6E(CONT)

NOT TO BE DISCLOSED

Page No. ....

| CONFIDENTIAL INFORMATION |

DISCLOSURE OFFICER'S REPORT

R v ....

☐ Enter C or D to denote schedule MG6C or 6D and enter item no. from schedule.

☐ Schedule	Item no.	Reason	Tick if attached

Continuation sheet: Yes ☐   No ☐

Guidance to the police, the CPS and the courts from the TIG on obtaining medical reports in assault occasioning actual bodily harm cases

1. INTRODUCTION

1.1 In some cases of assault occasioning actual bodily harm (ABH), medical reports are obtained or ordered when they are not necessary for any criminal justice activity.

1.2 A recent Trials Issues Group (TIG) time-limits survey concluded that the obtaining of medical reports added significantly to the delay (and thus the cost) of casework through the system.

1.3 Nevertheless, medical reports are regularly required in order to decide on the correct charge or charges; to determine whether there is sufficient evidence to substantiate a charge or to assist the court with issues of compensation and sentencing.

1.4 With a view to implementing Government policy to speed up the progress of cases through the criminal justice system, the TIG have agreed to issue the following guidance to the police, the CPS and the Courts to assist with the issue of whether a medical report needs to be obtained.

1.5 Members of the judiciary have been consulted and support this guidance. Additionally, it has been drawn to the notice of the Law Society and the Bar Council.

2. GUIDANCE AS TO WHETHER A MEDICAL REPORT SHOULD BE OBTAINED IN CASES OF ABH

2.1 There is no rule of law that requires proof of every injury to be substantiated by a medical report.

2.2 The following factors may indicate that a medical report is unnecessary in a case involving ABH:

- by any common sense judgement, the injury is on the minor side, is apparently uncomplicated, and the effects are likely to be temporary, and

- the injury has been adequately described by the victim in a statement, illustrated in a quality coloured photograph (wherever possible), and supported by a police officer's statement wherever practicable.

2.3 Cases of uncommon assault are even less likely to require a medical report since, under *the Offences Against the Persons Charging Standard*, the degree of harm envisaged is likely to be of a more minor nature.

3. ACTION IN THE EVENT OF SOME DOUBT AS TO WHETHER A REPORT SHOULD BE OBTAINED

3.1 In the event of doubt, the plea, or likely plea of the defendant should be considered. A full admission, or likely admission, may aid the decision not to obtain a report.

3.2 If it is decided to obtain a medical report, one should be ordered at the *earliest opportunity*.

3.3 Certain cases, such as those involving fractures, damaged teeth, psychiatric injury, internal injuries and those requiring private medical examination to avoid embarrassment will always require a medical report. Where there is a dispute as to the extent or cause, a medical report may be a central feature of the case.

4. LIMITATIONS OF THIS GUIDANCE

4.1 This guidance is an attempt at sensible advice to avoid unnecessary delay and cost in the criminal justice system in a limited number of cases involving ABH. No attempt should be made, in any circumstances, to discourage victims of crime from obtaining a proper medical examination. This guidance is solely concerned with the issue of whether a medical report is necessary for the criminal prosecution process.

4.2 It must, however, always be remembered that each case must be judged on its individual circumstances as it appears to the relevant decision-maker at the time.

APPENDIX 21

Bar Council's guidance on drafting defence statements

GENERAL COUNCIL OF THE BAR

PROFESSIONAL CONDUCT AND COMPLAINTS COMMITTEE

THE PREPARATION OF DEFENCE CASE STATEMENTS PURSUANT TO THE CRIMINAL PROCEDURE AND INVESTIGATIONS ACT 1996

GUIDANCE OF THE DUTIES OF COUNSEL

(As approved by the PCCC on 24th September 1997)

1. It is becoming increasingly common for solicitors to instruct counsel to draft or settle defence case statements, required under section 5 of the Criminal Procedure and Investigations Act 1996. Often these instructions are given to counsel with no or little previous involvement in the case shortly before the expiry of the time limit.

2. The relevant legislation is set out at para 12-82 *et seq.* of the 1997 edition of Archbold. In summary, however:

    (i)   The time limit for compliance is short – 14 days from service of prosecution material or a statement that there is none. The permitted grounds for an extension of time are limited;[1]

    (ii) The contents of the defence case statement are obviously of great importance to the defendant. An inaccurate or inadequate statement of the defence could have serious repercussions for the Defendant, if the trial judge permits 'appropriate' comment;

    (iii) Whilst it will be the natural instinct of most defence counsel to keep the defence case statement short, a short and anodyne statement may be insufficient to trigger any obligation on the prosecution to give secondary disclosure of prosecution material.

3. Normally it will be more appropriate for instructing solicitors to draw

---

1 See the Defence Disclosure Time Limit Regulations 1997 made pursuant to the Act: Archbold Supplement para 12–93.

the defence case statement, since typically counsel will have had little involvement at this stage.

4. However, there is nothing unprofessional about counsel drafting or settling a defence case statement, although it must be appreciated that there is no provision in the current regulations for graduated fees allowing for counsel to be paid a separate fee for this work. This most unsatisfactory situation (which has arisen, as a result of the 1996 Act, since the graduated fees regulations were negotiated) is being addressed urgently by the Fees and Legal Aid Committee. A barrister has no obligation to accept work for which he will not be paid. The absence of a fee will justify refusal of the instructions by counsel who are not to be retained for the trial and are simply asked to do no more than draft or settle the defence case statement. Where counsel is retained for the trial, Rule 502(b) of the Code of Conduct deems instructions in a legally aided matter to be at a proper fee and counsel would not be justified in refusing to draft or settle a defence case statement on the sole ground that there is no separate fee payable for this work.

5. Many members of the bar will nevertheless feel that, in the interests of their lay client and/or of good relations with instructing solicitors, they cannot refuse the work, even where they would otherwise be entitled to do so. Those who do so need to recognise the crucial importance of:

    (i)   Obtaining all prosecution statements and documentary exhibits;
    (ii) Getting instructions from the lay client, from a properly signed proof and preferably a conference. Those instructions need to explain the general nature of the defence, to indicate the matters on which issue is taken with the prosecution and to give an explanation of the reason for taking issue. They must also give details of any alibi defence, sufficient to give the information required by Section 5(7) of the 1996 Act;
    (iii) Getting statements from other material witnesses;
    (iv) Ensuring that the client realises the importance of the defence case statement and the potential adverse consequences of an inaccurate or inadequate statement;
    (v)   Getting proper *informed* approval for the draft from the client. This is particularly important, given the risks of professional embarrassment if the client seeks to disown the statement during the course of the trial, perhaps when the trial is not going well or when under severe pressure in cross-examination. Counsel ought to insist on getting written acknowledgement from the lay client that:

          (a) he understands the importance of the accuracy and adequacy of the defence case statement for his case;

(b) he has had the opportunity of considering the contents of the statement carefully and approves it.

This may often mean having a conference with the lay client to explain the defence case statement and to get informed approval, although in straightforward cases where counsel has confidence in the instructing solicitor, this could be left to the solicitor. Where this latter course is taken, a short written advice (which can be in a standard form) as to the importance of obtaining the written acknowledgement *before* service of the statement should accompany the draft defence case statement. A careful record should be kept of work done and advice given.

(vi) If there is inadequate time, counsel should ask the instructing solicitor to apply for an extension of time. This needs to be considered at a very early stage, since the application must be made *before* the expiry of the time limit.

6. It follows that counsel ought not to accept any instructions to draft or settle a defence case statement unless given the opportunity and adequate time to gain proper familiarity with the case and to comply with the fundamental requirements set out above. In short, there is no halfway house. If instructions are accepted, then the professional obligations on counsel are considerable.

Memorandum of good practice re early release of bodies in cases of suspicious death

ALL AGENCIES

1. Steps to secure the early release of the body in any suspicious death, including murder, manslaughter, infanticide and causing death by dangerous driving, will be treated as a priority by all agencies involved, subject to the interests of the criminal justice system. All agencies concerned will recognise that early release is essential to assist the victim's family in coping with their grief.

2. No national or local investigative or procedural changes should be introduced without considering the effect on the early release of bodies and ways to minimise any delays.

THE POLICE

3. The Senior Investigating Officer (SIO) should clearly designate in the Policy Book an officer to be the liaison officer with the Coroner, Defence team(s) and Pathologist(s). This officer, who may be a coroner's officer, should also be responsible for production of the necessary file relating to identification, which will allow the opening of an inquest.

4. The SIO should be proactive in pursuing early resolution of all post mortem examinations in cases where a suspect has been arrested or charged. This officer should ensure all necessary action is taken to satisfy the Coroner that all examinations are completed and the body can be released. This should include liaison with whichever agency is conducting forensic examinations associated with the post mortem to ensure early results are obtained. The SIO should have contact with the Coroner and Pathologist when the post mortem report is likely to be delayed (see under Pathologist below).

5. The SIO should co-operate with the Coroner in meeting requests from the defence for early disclosure if this will assist in the early release of the body.

6. In all instances the SIO should ensure the victim's family are kept aware of developments, are provided with the Home Office Victims Family Pack and given appropriate support.

THE CORONER

7. In all cases, a coroner will exercise his discretion judicially and with due regard to the interests of justice. A coroner is not bound to observe the procedures in this memorandum, but is recommended to do so unless he is satisfied that there is good and proper cause to do otherwise.

8. When a death is reported, the coroner will observe the provisions of the Coroners' Rules 1984 (i.e. Rules 5, 6 and 7) so far as the arrangements for the post mortem examination are concerned. In arranging a post mortem examination, the coroner will make clear to the pathologist the circumstances of the death and the need for his report to be supplied without delay and in any event within 14 days (see paragraph 20 below). Where the examination is complete, the Coroner will immediately provide copies of the report, when received, to all those having a proper interest including the Chief Officer of Police, and any person who has been charged in connection with the death (and to their legal advisers). Any photographic or video recording taken at such examination shall also be supplied. (These will be made available by the police.) The next of kin to the deceased should also be advised that the report is available.

9. The Coroner will not, within the fourteen days immediately following the post mortem examination, release the body to those entitled to possession unless he has received written confirmation from all such interested persons that they know no reason why such release should not take place.

10. Where the Coroner is informed by the Chief Officer of Police that a person may be charged with the murder, manslaughter or infanticide of the deceased but no person has been so charged by that date and it appears to the Chief Officer unlikely that any person will be so charged within 28 days from the date of the discovery of the homicide, he or she shall inform the Coroner who shall arrange for a further examination, to be conducted by a suitably qualified forensic pathologist. Such a

pathologist must be independent from the pathologist who performed the initial post mortem (i.e. normally from a different establishment), although that is not to say that they should not discuss their respective findings.

11. It will be a matter for the Coroner to decide whether to provide the police with a copy of the report from any such post mortem examination, but it will normally be proper to do so. The second report will be retained by the coroner, and, in the event that an arrest in connection with the death is subsequently made, he or she will provide a copy of the second report to the defendant or his legal representatives.

12. In the event that significant discrepancies arise between the first and second post mortem reports, the Coroner will, without delay, consider whether to commission a third examination. It will not normally be appropriate to provide the third pathologist with either of the previous reports or to seek to reconcile the differences between the earlier reports. The third pathologist should again be independent of the first two pathologists (i.e. from a different establishment). As soon as the Coroner has decided that no further examination is necessary, the body will be released for disposal by the family/executors.

13. If the Coroner is advised by the Chief Officer of Police that it is likely that a person will be arrested in connection with any of the offences given in paragraph 10 within of 28 days from the date of discovery of the homicide, he or she shall not release the body until a person is charged, or until the expiration of that period, whichever is the shorter. If a person is so charged, the coroner will serve on him a copy of the report of the initial examination and records in accordance with paragraph 8 above. If no charges are made, the procedures set out in paragraph 10 will apply.

14. Unless the Coroner receives written confirmation from all those having a proper interest (other than from those to whom he is proposing to release the body) that they have no objection to the body being released, the Coroner shall, not less than 5 days before the proposed release of the body, notify his intention to do in writing to all those persons who have not confirmed that they have no objection to the release of the body.

15. The Coroner will not normally raise any objection to a further post mortem examination being conducted for or on behalf of any person who may have a proper interest provided that such further examination is conducted without undue delay and after proper notice has been given to the Coroner. Any such examinations will be arranged at the expense of the person concerned, save in the cases of examinations

undertaken pursuant to paragraph 4. However, the Coroner should question the necessity of a second or subsequent post mortems in all cases where it may be unnecessary (e.g. death by dangerous driving cases), if it is likely to delay the release of the body, or where a single post mortem on behalf of all joint defendants would appear to suffice. Care should be taken to ensure that any decision to refuse permission for a further examination and to release the body is not likely to prejudice the interests of justice.

16. The above procedures are not applicable in cases where the identity of the body has not been established. In these circumstances, the imperative will be to ascertain the identity of the body and to contact the next of kin. Once relatives have been contacted, any outstanding enquiries and actions should proceed in accordance with the principles set out in this memorandum.

17. Coroners should ensure that the laboratories to which they or their pathologists entrust histological, toxicological or other analyses in homicide cases understand that the work should be treated as a top priority and not be allowed to unnecessarily delay the release of the body.

THE PATHOLOGIST

18. The time taken for the Pathologist to produce his report is a key factor in the early release of the body. Until this report is produced, important decisions (such as the need for a second post mortem) cannot be taken. The aim will be for the examination to take place within 24 hours, and for the report to be made available to the coroner and the police as soon as possible and in any event within 14 days of the examination, even if histological or toxicological analyses are not then ready (although the reports should be qualified accordingly). Full consultation should take place with the Senior Investigating Officer and Coroner if the report is delayed because of these or for any other reasons.

19. Where further tests need to be carried out by third parties, pathologists should have regard to the approach set out in paragraph 18 above.

THE LAW SOCIETY

20. In most cases where a solicitor is instructed on behalf of a client charged with murder, manslaughter, infanticide (and in some cases of offences under s.1 and 3 (a) Road Traffic Act 1988), it will be necessary to confirm the exact cause of death or to forensically examine the nature and origins of the wounds sustained by the deceased. Such investigations necessarily cause delay in the burial or cremation of the deceased and inevitably prolong the distress to relatives and friends.

21. Advice given by the criminal Law Committee of the Law Society is designed to ameliorate the situation although in no way detracting from or undermining the solicitor's primary duty and obligation to his/her client to procure and acquire evidence in support of the client's case.

PHD judge's questionnaire

Plea and Directions Hearing	The Crown Court at
	Case No. T
Judge's Questionnaire	PTI URN
(In accordance with the practice rules issued by the Lord Chief Justice)	R v
	Date of PDH
A copy of this questionnaire, completed as far as possible with the agreement of both advocates, is to be handed in to the court prior to the commencement of the Plea and Directions Hearing.	Name of Prosecution Advocate at PDH
	Name of Defence Advocate at PDH

1	a	Are the actual/proposed not guilty pleas definitely to be maintained through to a jury trial?	Yes ☐ No ☐
	b	Has the defence advocate advised his client of section 48 of CJPOA 1994? *(Reductions in sentence for guilty pleas)*	Yes ☐ No ☐
	c	Will the prosecution accept part guilty or alternative pleas?	Yes ☐ No ☐
2		How long is the trial likely to take?	
3		What are the issues in the case?	
4		Issues as to the mental or medical condition of any defendant or witness.	
5		Prosecution witnesses whose evidence will be given. Can any statement be read instead of calling the witnesses?	To be read (number) ☐ To be called (number) ☐ Names:

6	a	Number of Defence witnesses whose evidence will be placed before the Court.	Defendant +
	b	Any whose statements have been served which can be agreed and accepted in writing.	

7	Is the prosecution intending to serve any further evidence?	Yes ⏐ No
	If **Yes**, what area(s) will it cover?	
	What are the witnesses' names?	

8	Facts which are admitted and can be reduced into writing. (s10(2)(b) CJA 1967)	

9	Exhibits and schedules which are to be admitted.	

10	Is the order and pagination of the prosecution papers agreed?	

11	Any alibi which should have been disclosed in accordance with CJA 1967?	Yes No

12	a	Any points of law likely to arise at trial?
	b	Any questions of admissibility of evidence together with any authorities it is intended to rely upon.

13	a	Has the defence notified the prosecution of any issue arising out of the record of interview? (*Practice Direction Crime: Tape Recording of police interview 26 May 1989*)	Yes No
	b	What efforts have been made to agree verbatim records or summaries and have they been successful?

Form 5122   *Plea and Directions Hearings in the Crown Court Practice Rules 1995*   2

14	Any applications granted / pending for:	
	(i) evidence to be given through live television links?	Yes [ ] No [ ]
	(ii) evidence to be given by pre-recorded video interviews with children?	Yes [ ] No [ ]
	(iii) screens?	Yes [ ] No [ ]
	(iv) the use of video equipment during the trial?	Yes [ ] No [ ]
	(v) use of tape playback equipment?	Yes [ ] No [ ]
15	Any other significant matter which might affect the proper and convenient trial of the case? (e.g. expert witnesses or other cases outstanding against the defendant)	
16	Any other work which needs to be done. Orders of the Court with time limits should be noted on page 4.	Prosecution Defence
17 a	Witness availability and approximate length of witness evidence.	Prosecution Defence
b	Can any witness attendance be staggered?	Yes No
c	If **Yes**, have any arrangements been agreed?	Yes No
18	Advocates' availability?	Prosecution Defence

Form 5122 *Plea and Directions Hearings in the Crown Court Practice Rules 1995*   3

Case listing arrangements

Name of Trial Judge:

Custody Cases *Fix or warned list within 16 weeks of committal*

Fixed for trial on

Place in warned list for trial   for week beginning

Further directions fixed for

Not fixed or put in warned list
within 16 weeks because:

Bail Cases

Further directions fixed for

Fixed for trial on

Fixed as a floater / backer on

Place in a reserve/warned list for trial for week beginning

List officer to allocate   within   days / weeks

before

Sentence

Adjourned for sentence on

(to follow trial of R v

Other directions, orders, comments

Signed: *Judge*   Date:

Form 5122 *Plea and Directions Hearings in the Crown Court* 4 *Printed on behalf of The Court Service*
(8.95) *Practice Rules 1995*

PDH: supplementary pre-trial checklist for cases involving child witnesses

GUIDANCE NOTES

The following Guidance reflects the advice contained in the Young Witness Pack Handbook *Preparing Young Witnesses for Court* agreed by the Home Office, Lord Chancellor's Department, Crown Prosecution Service, Department of Health, ChildLine, and the NSPCC, the Law Society and the Criminal Bar Association.

This Guidance is not intended to constrain those local schemes which have already been agreed, but go further than the minimum standard set here.

1. PREPARATION FOR THE PLEA AND DIRECTIONS HEARING

It is vital that advocates come to the Plea and Directions Hearing with full instructions including all relevant information from and about the child witness, so that the judge will be in a position to complete the supplementary pre-trial checklist.

2. VIDEO EVIDENCE

The advocates and the judge need to have seen the video in advance of the Plea and Directions Hearing so that decisions can be made about the admissibility of the videotape and so that any technical difficulties can be identified in sufficient time to allow other steps to be taken.

3. MEMORY REFRESHING

Witnesses are entitled to be shown a copy of their statement before being called to give evidence. The videotape is commonly used to refresh the child's memory before the trial – the equivalent of reading the statement beforehand. Viewing the video ahead of time in more informal surroundings helps children "get over" seeing themselves on the screen and makes it more likely that they will concentrate on the contents. It is not satisfactory to show the video for the purpose of refreshing on the day of the trial, before the child watches it again with the jury as most children find it difficult to concentrate through two viewings on the same day.

Crown Prosecution Service policy states that video taped interviews may be shown to the child before the trial unless the video has been ruled inadmissible. There is a need for further guidance as to how the memory of each child should be refreshed if such a ruling is made.

4. CHILD'S PREPARATION FOR COURT

The Bar Code of Conduct states that 'it is a responsibility of a barrister, especially when the witness is nervous, vulnerable or apparently the victim of criminal or similar conduct, to ensure that those facing unfamiliar court procedures are put as much at ease as possible'. The Code supports the view that it is of benefit to child witnesses to meet both prosecuting and defence advocates before trial providing there is no discussion of the evidence. There is also a standard in the Victim's Charter saying 'while you are waiting to give evidence, a representative of the Crown Prosecution Service will introduce himself or herself to you (wherever possible) to tell you what to expect'. This standard is mirrored in the national standards of witness care produced by the Trials Issues Group at 18.2. Such meetings with advocates go some way to demystifying the court process for the child. Experience suggests that meeting the judge before the case starts can also have this effect. Putting young witnesses more at ease assists them to give best evidence.

5. BREAKS FOR CHILD WITNESSES

Although judges and lawyers should invite children to tell the court when they need a break, children's ability to identify when this is necessary should not be relied on. The prosecution should provide information at the PDH from home or school about the child's attention span, bearing in mind that it is likely to be shorter in the stressful atmosphere of the court. This will enable the judge and advocates to plan breaks in the child's testimony. Planned breaks are less likely to occur at a time that would favour one side over another.

> '*We should work on the basis that after half an hour of giving evidence, the child will be tired whether or not there are any obvious manifestations of it*'*
>
> Lord Justice Judge

6. CASE MANAGEMENT

Cases need to be managed robustly to ensure that the case is ready for trial. The commitment to give high priority to child abuse cases is contained in many policy documents, including the 1996 Victim's Charter.

- Section 53 of the Criminal Justice Act 1991 gives the prosecution discretion to avoid delay by transferring certain child witness cases directly from the magistrates' court to the Crown Court.

- The Lord Chancellor's Department Guidelines for Crown Court Listing states that child witness cases are to be given the earliest available fixed date and that trial dates must only be changed in exceptional circumstances.

- The Charter for Court Users emphasises the need to assign the earliest possible date for a trial involving a child witness.

7. DEFENCE WITNESSES

Although most witnesses give evidence on behalf of the prosecution, arrangements for preparation and pre-trial court visits should also be made available on request to young witnesses called by the defence.

---

* A Case for Balance

Index